American Immigrants in Israel

Kevin Avruch

American Immigrants in Israel
Social Identities and Change

The University of Chicago Press
Chicago & London

KEVIN AVRUCH is assistant professor of anthropology
at George Mason University.

The University of Chicago Press, Chicago 60637
The University of Chicago Press, Ltd., London

Library of Congress Cataloging in Publication Data

Avruch, Kevin.
  American immigrants in Israel.

  Bibliography: p.
  Includes index.
  1. Jews, American—Israel.   2. Israel—Emigration
and immigration.   I. Title.
DS113.8.A4A9   305.8'924'05694   81-1291
ISBN 0-226-03241-8   AACR2

To my parents

Contents

Acknowledgments

This book is based upon research in Israel supported by a National Institute of Mental Health predoctoral training grant (MH-12776). Earlier drafts were written with the support of a State of California Dissertation Fellowship, and a grant from the Jerusalem Center for Anthropological Studies. My thanks go to Dr. Edgard E. Siskin of the Jerusalem Center for facilitating its support.

Many people in Israel contributed of themselves and made the research possible. To Murray and Sheila Baumgarten and to Dan Cooper I owe a debt of inestimable dimensions; my hope is that, in years to come, I can repay part of it. Herbert Lewis provided critical support on two continents. Aaron Antonovsky kindly allowed me to read his and David Katz's (then) unpublished manuscript on American immigrants, which provided me a great deal of background material. To Moshe Ben Ari, Gerald Berman, Sue Berrin, Victor Friedman, Eric Gardner, Gordon Raskin, Steven Ross, and Danny Wachs I offer thanks for their friendship, support, and, in some cases, *proteksia*.

Before, during, and after fieldwork I was fortunate to be part of a remarkable assemblage of scholars, colleagues, and friends, in the Department of Anthropology at the University of California, San Diego. Properly, these acknowledgments would comprise a long roster of almost all the faculty, students, and staff in the department between 1972 and 1979; but these individuals were the most centrally connected to the work: F. G. Bailey, David Lipset, Michael Meeker, Michael Smith, Melford Spiro, and Marc Swartz. To David Jordan go special thanks as chairman of my doctoral committee. Elsewhere in the university, Aaron Cicourel and Sanford Lakoff offered guidance and perspective.

ix

Professor Cicourel performed this task at a critical period in the inception of fieldwork, as well. In Raymond Fogelson I acknowledge an early, important, and continuing influence.

To the many immigrants—Israelis of North American background—who gave me their time and spoke so freely of their experiences and feelings in the U.S. and Israel I owe crucial thanks. I offer them with gratitude and respect.

To my wife, Sheila, I owe more than acknowledgments can convey.

Israel
Immigration and Settlement

Introduction

This is a study of American Jews who have immigrated ("made *aliya*") to Israel. Since the founding of the State of Israel in 1948, more than 45,000 Americans have made aliya, with the great majority—about 80 percent—coming in the years following the Six-Day War (1967).

Immigration (*aliya*—literally "ascent") to Israel may be viewed from two perspectives. Broadly, it is one aspect of a complex historical relationship between Diaspora Jewry and Israel. This relationship, so far as American Jews are concerned, has found its most striking expression in the financial, political, and emotional support that the American Jewish community has extended to the Israeli state and to those efforts that preceded the establishment of the state. As an expression of this relationship, the immigration to Israel of American Jews has played a very minor role—at least in terms of number. On the contrary, it is the very lack of centrality of aliya in American Jewish conceptions of support for Israel, the absence of commitment on the part of American Jewry towards its own aliya, that has served to shape the contours of the relationship in very important ways.

More narrowly, then, and in sharp relief to the broad view, aliya may be seen as an option chosen by persons who constitute a distinct minority (less than 1 percent) of American Jews. For the bulk of this study, my perspective on aliya is the narrow one. I am interested in the factors that make immigration to Israel a compelling option to these American Jews: in what motivates their decision to immigrate, and in aspects of their subsequent adjustment to (or "absorption" into) Israeli culture and society.

If we consider American aliya as an instance in the class "international migrations," it is clear that these individuals are not fleeing pestilence, famine, or war; nor are they seeking a haven from institutionalized religious or ethnic persecution. Even more important is the fact that economic or pecuniary concerns are among the least important factors in motivating a decision to immigrate. While an economic model cannot adequately account for American aliya, I shall argue that these immigrants do indeed make "investments," although these are not investments in opportunity structures or in human capital strictly defined. These immigrants are individuals who, while yet in America, invested heavily in their ethnic identity, in their Jewishness. They invested, that is, in a particular conception of self.

Here I must underline two points, the first about ethnic identity in general, the second about Jewishness in particular. Ethnic identity is here conceived to be one component of a total and integrated social identity. Social identity is culturally constituted; in contemporary America other component identities include (but are not limited to) sex or gender, family status, social class, occupation, and political affiliation. Ethnic identity is itself complex, having in any given case national, religious, or linguistic identifications. The important point is that significant differential investment by a person in one component identity over others will affect the total, or integrated, configuration of social identity and, since personal identity is anchored in social identity (Erikson 1963:279), this differential investment has psychodynamic correlates. There is a fashion among some social scientists to treat ethnic identity in purely instrumental terms, as something that is manipulated by actors who are engaged in transactions. Ethnic identity becomes, in Daniel Bell's words, a "strategic site" used by individuals for political and economic gains (1975:169). Without denying the instrumental potentials of ethnic-identity manipulation, I concentrate in this book on the expressive transformations of social identity that are entailed in ethnic-identity manipulation.

The specific identity that is the subject of the study is Jewishness. Although I shall spend some time discussing Jewishness in terms of such attributes as religious, nationalist, or "culturalist" identifications, I want at the outset to invoke Heine's law as a methodological guide. Seymour Lipset writes:

Heinrich Heine suggested over a century ago that the only way one could understand the variations in the behavior of Jews in

different countries was by seeing these differences as adapta-
tions to the dominant behavior patterns within the Gentile
community. (1970:141–42)

In short, this study of American immigrants to Israel is half
about "Jewishness" in contemporary America, and half about
"Americanness" in contemporary Israel. It is about the vicissitudes of both identities in both places.

Of Jewishness in America, of course, this study is a limiting
case, since other American Jews may invest heavily in their
Jewishness and the immigrants constitute less than 1 percent of
American Jewry. I can indicate the chief features of this limiting
case by sketching the main points along the way to a decision for
aliya. First, there is an intense investment in ethnic-Jewish
identification, whether defined primarily by religious, nationalist,
or culturalist attributes. This investment is to the point where
ethnic identity overrides, or subordinates, other component
identities. Social identity is in a sense primordialized towards an
ethnic definition of ideal self. At the same time—and this is crucial—there is increasing disengagement from American society,
and a critique of this society is formulated in terms of a critique of
modernity. The immigrant, thus, is making two sorts of investment: first, in a conception of ideal (ethnic) self, and, second, in a
conception of a community of others where that self is part of a
consensus—an ideal society. And as they reject, in American
society, an image of modernity, they embrace in Israeli society an
image of its opposite. The attributes of a primordial identity are
projected to constitute an image of a primordial society. Israeli
society may then be conceived (while the immigrants are yet in
America) as a gemeinschaft. It is society conceived, in Durkheim's sense, as a single moral community. It is, in fact, an
idealized image of the "traditional society" that the immigrants
cleave to: a society in which a traditionalized social identity
would find consonance in a community of like-minded others.

All of these points, put rather programmatically here, will be
discussed in greater detail in coming chapters. I trust the sketch
has illuminated the limits of the case. As Glazer and Moynihan
have pointed out (1963, 1975), many Americans continue to rely
on ethnic identity to constitute meaningful self-images, and this is
true for many American Jews. Indeed, Glazer and Moynihan
refer in their later collaboration to the contemporary reverses

suffered by—as Milton Gordon put it—the "liberal expectancy" that "primordial...differences between groups would be expected to become of lesser significance" (1975:6–7). But my case represents more than the reversal of this expectancy; it is not merely the intensity of their investment in ethnicity that differentiates these immigrants from other American Jews (or American ethnics). Rather, it is the fact that ethnic identity comes to constitute the image of and for an ideal self and an ideal society. I call this "traditionalization," and this book is a case study of it.

To use a term like traditionalization is to enter an arena characterized by controversy and polemic. Terms such as modernity, modernization, and tradition carry with them much baggage. For both of these reasons I should say a few words now about why I chose to write of certain social identity dynamics using such terms as traditionalization. The details of this use, of course, must await later chapters.

In the first place, the phenomenon I call traditionalization has been noted and commented on by others, who use terms scarcely more "accurate" or less controversial. For example, Glazer and Moynihan, in the work cited above, refer to what Ralf Dahrendorf calls the "refeudalization" of society. "It may be," they add, that "ethnicity is merely part of this larger development" (1975:16). In the same volume Harold Isaacs takes note of "a massive retribalization running sharply counter to all globalizing effects of modern technology and communications" (1975:30). Even if we are all in touch with different parts of the same elephant, it is not clear to me that "refeudalization" or "retribalization" offer more accuracy or less baggage and controversy. Both terms are more evocative than is "traditionalization," but here the effect is not felicitous.

Of course, to argue the virtues of one's own terms by pointing out the defects of others is to make a poor argument. My use of "traditionalization," however, has a specific and germane source. I adopted it originally not in consideration of the immigrants' lives in the United States but in consideration of the dynamics of their "absorption" into Israeli society. Like the United States, Israel is a nation of immigrants, but to an extent far greater than is the case in the U.S. sociology and social anthropology in Israel have concerned themselves with the dynamics (and evaluation) of immigrant acculturation and social integration. Under the influence of S. N. Eisenstadt, a model of immigrant absorption was formulated to take special account of the problems faced by immigrants of Afro-Asian ("Oriental") provenience. They were thought of as traditional individuals coming from traditional societies to modern Israel. Quite logically, then, their acculturation or integration was seen to entail their modernization. As "traditionals" became "moderns," the reasoning went, so would these immigrants become Israelis. Immediately it should be apparent that the case of immigrants from the United States would offer a new perspective on the absorption-cum-modernization model, and it was with this in mind that I developed the notion of traditionalization. Only later in my analysis of the material did I see the relevance of the idea for making sense of the immigrants' lives in, and their emigration from, the United States.

There is a final reason for my reliance on the ideas contained in terms like traditionalization and modernization. This is that the immigrants themselves make use of similar ideas in trying to understand and explain their immigration and adjustment to Israel. To deny or suppress the ideas, therefore, in the interest of avoiding the controversies surrounding them, would be to do violence to the sense of the immigrants' own testimonies. Some of the implications of this problem I address in the work's final chapter; for now I might do well to admit that if there is a drawback in using such terms as tradition and modernity (and their cognate processes) in this book, it lies in their conflation of object and subject—analysand and analyst—as they are typically conceived in the anthropological enterprise. As anthropologist, I was often faced with the reverse of the skeptic's jibe, "Yes, but would the 'natives' express it like that?"

The first part of the book provides the background for the study. In Chapter 2 I begin with a brief history of Zionism, underlining the tensions that existed between the modern and premodern elements of the movement and its ideologies. In the later sections of this chapter I concentrate on the role played by aliya in Zionist ideology and the formation of the State of Israel and, finally, on the role American Jewry has played with respect to these same concerns.

In the third chapter I present a demographic picture of American aliya, bringing together Israeli census and survey work, the results of my own survey based in Jerusalem, and the few demographic studies extant (notably Goldscheider 1974). Those factors that are selective of American immigration are sketched, and where relevant the Americans are compared to three other groups: the American Jewish population, contemporaneously arriving immigrants, and the Israeli Jewish population.

Klita is the Hebrew word meaning "absorption." In Chapter 4, I offer an account of how the potential immigrant gets from New York or Los Angeles to Jerusalem or Tel Aviv. There are services, rights, and subventions to which the new immigrant is entitled, and these are outlined. The nature of these supports involves the new immigrant, immediately, in dealings with the Israeli bureaucracy, and much of what I shall have to say later about the Americans' absorption will center on these bureaucratic encounters. Finally, in this chapter I touch briefly on the politicization of immigrant absorption and on some of the effects of this.

With the historic, demographic, and institutional backgrounds established, I turn in Chapter 5 to the central concerns of the study: motivations for immigration and aspects of subsequent adjustment, acculturation, and integration. The fifth chapter is concerned with questions of motivation, Chapters 6 and 7 with aspects of absorption. In these chapters I develop my ideas on the relationship between identities—social and ethnic—of both the modernizing and traditionalizing kind.

In the final chapter I close with a brief review of some of these models of social change, in the context of a methodological note on doing fieldwork among an "overly complex" people.

This study is based upon fieldwork conducted in Israel between December 1975 and March 1977. My data come predominantly from immigrants (*olim*) of the period following the Six-Day War (1967). I interviewed (wth varying degrees of formality) about 150 individuals: immigrants and aliya emissaries (*shlihim*), and officials of the Jewish Agency and of the Ministry of Immigrant Absorption. Most of the material from government or agency officials is incorporated in Chapter 4. The core of the research consisted of intensive interviews with nineteen immigrant families. Sixteen lived in Jerusalem, three in the Tel Aviv area. Fifteen of the families were interviewed over three separate sessions, two over two sessions, and two families were interviewed once. Husband and wife were interviewed together in at least one session; where children were present, I tried to encourage them to sit in. The total time spent with each family ranged from three to twelve hours. Except for the initial hour of first contact, all the discourse was tape-recorded, and complete transcripts were made. Although I solicited basic demographic information in the first half-hour, roughly the first half of the total interview time was spent in nondirected discourse: "I'm interested in how you came to make aliya, and in your life here is Israel." In the final session with a family, typically, I directed the interview to specific issues that had arisen in earlier sessions.

Based upon these intensive interviews, a schedule for more directed interviews was constructed. It took the form of a questionnaire which was administered to a respondent. The individual was encouraged to amplify his responses, provide illustrations, and so on, and notes were taken as marginalia, to be written up later. In this way one hundred immigrants in the Jerusalem area were interviewed. The questionnaire allowed me to test certain hypotheses raised by the earlier, more intensive interviews (e.g., on the relationship between entrepreneurship and religiousness), and to obtain a broader base from which to make assertions concerning American attitudes towards bureaucracy, the use of personal influence (*proteksia*), the Gush Emunim movement, and so on. The questionnaire also functioned as a rough demographic survey for Jerusalem residents and allowed me to gauge how these residents differed from the American Israeli average (they are more likely to be religiously observant, for example).

Some archival work was done, mainly in the offices of the Association of Americans and Canadians in Israel (AACI), and with the *Jerusalem Post*. As the major English-language newspaper in Israel, the *Post* was valuable on a daily basis: it published many articles of interest to Anglophone immigrants and many letters of condemnation or praise from them.

Participant observation, in the classic sense, was not a major method of research, although as an American Jew (and, on my arrival, a nonspeaker of Hebrew) I found it difficult to avoid sharing the perspective (and it would have been foolish to try to avoid sharing it) of the new immigrant. I attended an *ulpan* (intensive language-school) in Jerusalem for several months, and my compatriots there were new immigrants from a variety of countries. Often, at eight o'clock in the morning, I would hear firsthand the stories—of merchants, bureaucrats, schnorrers, and loves—of the day before. Since most contacts with Americans or Israelis in Israel would end with my being asked of my own plans for aliya, the distinction between participant and observer was blurred, and sometimes challenged, in the eyes of my informants as well as for myself.

I should say a word about the problem of closure. At times it became increasingly difficult to fathom how many ethnographies (or social psychologies) I had involved myself in. There was Israeli society to be considered, but also American society, American Jewish society, and the small "societies" of American Jews who would make aliya—as these existed both in the U.S. and in Israel. Even for the last group—the one that is the focus of this study—I concerned myself with those immigrants who had come to Israel and remained to live there (at least until my final interview with them). But as I note in Chapter 3, some significant proportion of Americans leave Israel. At the very least, some sort of closure for this research awaits work with those individuals.

In Chapter 2 I discuss Zionism and aliya. An understanding of Zionism is important because, by some definitions, all of these immigrants are Zionists. In many cases the Zionist identification is proclaimed by the immigrants themselves; in a few cases immigrants deny emphatically that they are Zionists. But in the past, certain Israelis (among others) have attempted to define "Zionist" by reference to a single set—that comprising immigrants to Israel. By extension, no one can claim to be a Zionist unless he or she is living, or has imminent plans to live, in Israel. As will become evident, this sort of definition excludes many Americans who consider themselves Zionist, and it points to a tension between self-identity (as Zionist or, more broadly, as Jew) in America and Israel that the immigrants feel greatly. Moreover, I will try to place Zionism in the historical and cultural contexts of the breakdown of traditional European Jewish society, to outline its role in a dialectic of the traditional and the modern. In doing this I will suggest another (less nominal) way in which these immigrants are Zionists.

2

Zionism, the State of Israel, and Aliya

The whole plan is essentially quite simple, as it must necessarily be if it is to be comprehensible to all. Let sovereignty be granted us over a portion of the globe adequate to meet our rightful national requirements; we will attend to the rest.

Theodor Herzl, *Der Judenstaat* (1896)

Zionism: Between Tradition and Modernity

The State of Israel arose in fulfillment of the Zionist idea. Zionism is, on one level, a modern nationalism bearing a European stamp: a movement that is heir to the ideas and ideals of the Enlightenment and French Revolution, to the counterrevolution of romanticism, in Western Europe, and to the slow but inexorable decay of post-Enlightenment feudalism in Eastern Europe, in the Russian empire. To be sure, even as a European nationalism, Zionism faced a wider range of problems than most nationalisms; for the Jews lived dispersed, without national land or national language. Both had to be recreated alongside the claim for political sovereignty. On another level, however, Zionism is a movement heir to a set of ideas very different from those of the European Enlightenment or of romanticism. On this level one speaks not of the dispersion of the Jews but of their exile; not of *Volksgeist* but of *am nivhar* (the "Chosen People"); not of national liberation or renaissance but of the End of Days and the coming of the Messiah. Here the lines go back to Mesopotamia, not the eighteenth-century salon or to the Bastille. The proto-Zionist was the composer of Psalm 137.

The yearning for Zion has been a part of Jewish consciousness since the destruction of Jerusalem and the Second Exile, and through the centuries pious individuals or groups made the dangerous journey to settle in one of the four holy cities of Palestine (Jerusalem, Safed, Tiberius, and Hebron). They lived in

11

prayer and study, supported with funds (*halukkah*) given to special emissaries by Jews living in the Diaspora. Sometimes they came because they believed the advent of the Messiah was imminent; occasionally because they believed that by coming they might hasten it. But behind all these beliefs lay the certainty that with the Messiah's coming all the children of Israel surely would be gathered once again about the walls of Jerusalem.

These immigrants were not Zionists, and their messianism was not Zionism. Yet Zionism, at all points of its development up to the present, has had to come to terms with this messianism. It has had to subordinate the messianic element, or be subordinated by it. Zionism began, in the modern era, with the attempts of certain individuals to effect the former. They operated in a transformed European Jewish society and by their efforts transformed this society yet further. Jacob Katz put it this way:

> Jewish society achieved its nationalist transformation with the appearance of a modern idea, later called Zionism, which purged, so to speak, Jewish messianic belief of its miraculous eschatological elements and retained only its political, social, and some of its spiritual objectives. (1973:3)

The Jews of Western Europe entered modernity as the theories of civic, political, and religious reform, propagated during the Enlightenment, culminated in the praxis of the French Revolution. In 1791 the National Assembly recognized Jews as citizens of the Republic, removing all legal restrictions and granting them full equality.

With Emancipation, the status of the Jew, as it was defined in medieval times and as it endured throughout the ancien régime, changed. The secularization of Gentile society, the anticipation of the victory of science and reason over religion and superstition, undermined the old Christian conception of the Jew as wandering, degraded in his exile, until Christ's second coming. In the past the social position of Jews was based on religious differences, but religion itself was such a pervasive and potent force that it was able to structure an ethos that made this difference both legitimate and ultimately meaningful. Merely to apprehend an individual as, religiously, "a Jew" was sufficient to explain his placement in terms ranging from cosmological to occupational.

By 1794, however, the cult of reason had become the religion of the Revolution, and a fierce movement of "dechristianization" (together with spoliation of churches and a massive transfer of wealth) could produce a proclamation such as this:

> Religion is nothing but a mass of stupidities and absurdity. . . . A true republican cannot be superstitious; he bends the knee before no idols; he worships liberty alone; he knows no other cult than that of loving his country and its laws. The cross has become, in the eyes of the humanist thinker, a counterrevolutionary emblem. (In Hampson 1966:205)

The deterioration of religion, as *explanans*, made the status of Jews, as *explanandum*, an anomaly in both the logical and revolutionary senses. Emancipation changed the status of the Jew simply by making him a citizen and by giving him equal rights with other citizens. The problem, however, now became: would the rational and egalitarian heritage of the Enlightenment (and the radical antireligious fervor of the Revolution) prove to be as convincing an *explanans* for the new, elevated status of the Jew, as medieval Christianity had proved to be for the older status? If the answer was to be affirmative, then anti-Semitism ought to disappear, or at least to be limited to deranged or reactionary individuals. If, however, anti-Semitism remained an institutional fact of European life, then its basis had to be sought in the failure of Enlightened universalism to act as *explanans*. And finally, if it was not to be the recrudescence of the medieval Christian world-view that accounted for the failure, then the rationale (for both Gentiles and Jews) for the continued existence of institutionalized anti-Semitism had to lie elsewhere. In the next century, the Emancipated Jewry of Western Europe moved out into Gentile society to test these very hypotheses.

These tests took several forms. Late in the eighteenth century a specifically Jewish Enlightenment, the *Haskalah,* produced works in Hebrew and in European languages that aimed to demonstrate the consonance between modern enlightened European culture and a revivified Hebraic one. Earlier in the century, Reform Judaism began to crystallize in Germany. Judaism was reinterpreted as an "ethical creed"; it was purged by Reform of its messianic components, in liturgy and belief. In civic terms the

implications of Reform were clear: Jews could be loyal German
(or French, or English) "citizens of the Mosaic sect" because, in
all respects save the sectarian, they *were* Germans, Frenchmen,
Englishmen, and so on. In reaction to Reform, traditional
Judaism began to cast itself as Orthodoxy.[1]

In Western Europe, Emancipation allowed the Jews a much
wider field of social and economic intercourse with Gentiles, and
this served to weaken the ties that had insulated and held together
most Jewish communities. In some cases it weakened particular
individuals' self-identification as Jews. In Eastern Europe the
situation was different. While a small and elite group of Eastern
European Jews subscribed to the values of the Haskalah, the
failure of a general Enlightenment to take hold in the larger Gentile society, and indeed the failure of Emancipation itself to occur
(after 1887 Jews were again barred from Russian high schools and
universities) made any program claiming to produce, for example,
"loyal Russian citizens of the Mosaic persuasion" appear ridicu-
lous. In the East it was Jewish secularism, and not the sec-
tarianism of Reform versus Orthodoxy, "which began to chal-
lenge the traditional acceptance of the Jewish unity" (Halpern
1961:16). The response of this Eastern group, against the traditional acceptance of the Jewish plight as a divine decree
(*gezerah*), was not, therefore, religious reform but social reform,
in the guise of nationalism or radicalism. These responses
sharpened as the decay of the Tsarist autocracy continued. Vio-
lent persecution of Jews increased, reaching a climax in the years
of bloody pogroms following the assassination of Alexander II in
1881 and the accession of Alexander III.

Before the pogroms of the East and the Dreyfus affair in re-
publican France (in 1896), adherents of Reform were able to provide a rational explanation for the persistence of institutional
anti-Semitism, namely, the failure on the part of all Jews to embrace the modernized Judaism that Reform represented, on the
one hand, and truly to internalize (or assimilate) the values of
citizenship, on the other. Another version of this theory of persistence went a long way to explain the wretched conditions
under which the Jews of Eastern Europe still lived. Simply put,
the East had yet to experience Enlightenment in a significant way;
the experience, however, was inevitable (one pointed to Tolstoy
and, before 1863—the year of the Polish revolt—to the liberal
policies of Alexander II). When it finally occurred, the Jews of

the East would enjoy the same rights—and duties—as their Western brethren. In the East, meanwhile, the elite group that had broken away from the traditional Judaism of the masses and expounded the values of Haskalah (but not of Reform, per se), accepted implicitly this explanation. They found themselves waiting for deliverance not by the Messiah of Isaiah but by Reason.

So long as the universalism of the Enlightenment held the Western European field, this theory of the persistence of anti-Semitism made sense. The gore of the pogroms and the humiliation of Dreyfus at the Ecole Militaire rendered the theory nonsensical. For the nineteenth century also had seen the rise and articulation of the powerful reaction to rational, enlightened universalism in the form of romanticism (in art) and of nationalism (in politics). As the theories of Rousseau gave way to those of Gobineau there emerged, finally, an *explanans* of the status of the Jew potent enough to replace the discarded image of medieval Christianity: Jews must remain separate, and despised, not for religious reasons but for national ones. They constitute not a separate "church" (or sect) but a separate nation. And it was on the basis of such a calculus that the Jew could be differentiated, once again and in "meaningful" terms, from his fellow citizens. Opponents of Jewish integration and emancipation no longer needed to argue their case in medieval Christian terms which—in the West, at least—were discomfiting. Henceforth the exclusion of Jews (and the explanation of their still degraded status) could be rationalized for the most "modern" of reasons: the *raison d'état*.

Nationalistic fervor was, of course, a double-edged sword, and soon the Jews too were arguing their case with reference to the nationalistic aspirations of Greeks, Poles, Italians, and Hungarians. Such writers as Alkalai, Kalischer, Hess, and Pinsker all preceded Herzl in arguing for a Jewish nation in a Jewish homeland, Zion. Herzl, even while appealing to the communities of the traditional East, formulated his case for Jewish nationalism from thoroughly modern sources. In particular, he drew on the legacy of the Enlightenment (a belief in reason coupled with a belief in rational action) and wedded this to the new canons of nationalistic self-interest. Herzl argued for no less than the "historical inevitability" of a Jewish state. The *Judennot*, the Jewish plight, was not a religious or social problem, as in medieval times, but a national problem. The Jews, "one people," were an unassimilable mass in the bodies politic of Europe, East and West. Their very presence engendered tensions within nations because they, too, were a nation, lacking only a physical homeland in which they might develop. Gentile states, therefore, owed it to their stability and integration to aid and abet the Jews in their nationalistic program.

Zionism developed in large measure according to a European theme, though in a general history of Europe its development may be merely a coda. As a social and political movement it can then be understood as an adaptation to the process of modernization as it was going on in Europe—taking into account the processual variation that differentiated Eastern Europe from Western. It is from this source that one may trace the modern symbols of Zionist nationalism (class, party, state, etc.) or, indeed, begin to speak, in Mannheim's sense, of a "Zionist ideology."

But Zionism did not arise de novo from European history. Like all movements of its kind, Zionist nationalism was culturally constituted (in the broadest sense of the term), and traditional Jewish culture provided its own symbols, as it had for millennia, for an explanation of Jewish suffering. This is to say that if one wants to understand Zionism as a consequence of a process of European modernization, then it is still necessary to specify the tradition against which such modernization may be principally counterposed. The tradition was Jewish: the conditions of the counterposing specified, uniquely, the Jewish condition. Yet in the opposition between modernism and traditionalism, Zionism, paradoxically, occupied neither position but partook—symbolically—of both. Against tradition it denied the meaning of Jewish history as a *gezerah* about which men were powerless to act. Against modernism it opposed absolutely the promise and rewards of Jewish de-ethnicization, which was spoken of derisively as "assimilation." And as for the keystone of Jewish traditionalism, ideas of exile and messianism, Zionism succeeded in synthesizing these traditional elements with other, modern, ideas to emerge as something unique. What I am arguing for is a dialectic:

> Reverting to the Hegelian formula, we may say that the Zionist "synthesis" stood directly opposed to the "antithesis," modernism, and sought a *rapprochement* with the original "thesis,"

traditionalism. For with modernism, Zionism shared the general principle that the Jewish problem required an immediate, rational solution. . . . With traditionalism, Zionism shared, as an emotional bond, the common vision of a solution by which Exile would be transcended. (Halpern 1961:76)

It is from this second source, the sought-after rapprochement of the Zionist synthesis with the traditionalist thesis, that one may trace the other symbols of Zionist nationalism, those of exile, redemption, the coming, and chosenness.

There are many illustrations of this synthesis. A most general one may be found by examination of the structure of the Zionist movement. Although from its inception Zionism was rarely characterized by a monolithic stance towards any issue of importance (rather the reverse), once can still discern three main groupings within the movement at any one time. These are centrist general Zionists; socialist labor Zionists on the left; and religious Zionists on the right.[2] Through time, alliances have formed and dissolved, and factionalization was and is rampant. However, historically, the function of labor Zionism and religious Zionism seems clear. Taken together, these Zionist variants allowed the movement as a whole to face both ways, that is, towards modernism and traditionalism, and to respond to (Jewish) anti-Zionist criticism originating in either sphere. On the left, labor Zionism (under the influence of Syrkin and Borochov, especially) responded to those radical Marxists who saw the solution of the Jewish problem as epiphenomenal to the solution of the class struggle in capitalist political economies. These critics condemned any nationalism (but especially, it seemed, a Jewish nationalism) as regressive and reactionary. Borochov in particular argued that the class struggle would never be resolved until each nation had its own "strategic base" wherein intra- as well as inter-class conflicts could be ameliorated. Intraclass conflicts were national conflicts; thus the resolution of national struggles must precede the resolution of class struggles.

On the religious right, Zionism faced a different criticism. Here the movement responded to Orthodox or ultra-Orthodox construals of tradition that condemned Zionism as a heresy which sought to force the end, abrogate the divine timetable, and hasten redemption. Such figures as Rabbi Shmuel Mohilever and Rabbi

A. I. Kook defended the movement against this charge. Rav Kook, for example, held that Jewish settlement of the Land of Israel was in fact "the beginnings of Redemption," and that pious Jews could work with secular, even antireligious, Zionist pioneers, since the secular and antireligious—no matter what *they* thought—were in fact acting as agents of the divine will.

Whatever the forms of debate and compromise taken by labor and religious Zionism within the larger Zionist arena, what concerns us here is the role played by each in speaking to a larger Jewish consensus. For both served to present, with varying degrees of success, the Zionist synthesis as a meaningful solution to both modernist and traditionalist critics.

A second illustration of the Zionist synthesis may be found in the so-called Uganda affair. In 1903, in the aftermath of the Kishinev pogroms, Herzl presented to delegates of the Sixth Zionist Congress a proposal offered by Great Britain. Britain proposed to open British East Africa (Uganda) to organized Jewish settlement. From the beginning, Herzl had argued for the importance of a publicly recognized charter, one that would sanction Jewish settlement, and against settlers' desultory or ill-organized "infiltration" tactics. Britain's proposal was, therefore, a major diplomatic victory for Herzlian Zionism, since it indicated a form of recognition by a major power of the Zionist organization and its aims. Ironically, this victory served to split the movement, instigating a crisis that threatened to destroy it. On Herzl's insistence the proposal was bound over to an investigative committee; but only on Herzl's personal appeal did a faction that stormed out of the congress return.

Herzl died in 1904. A year later the Seventh Zionist Congress defeated the so-called Uganda scheme, and with it the notion of Jewish settlement outside the Land of Israel. At this Congress a group led by Israel Zangwill, calling itself the Jewish Territorial Association, did split from the Zionist organization to pursue advocacy of organized and autonomous Jewish settlement wherever the opportunity might arise. Within two years, the Uganda offer was withdrawn by Britain.

At issue in this debate was nothing less than the status of the fundamental characteristic of Jewish nationalism, that which gives to Zionism its name and its mission. I am speaking here of the attachment of Jews to Zion, *Eretz Yisrael* ("The Land of

Israel"). "It is a commonplace observation frequently made about Zionism" writes Halpern, "that its bond to Zion is an irrational attachment, not a rational conclusion." For, essentially, "the tie of the Zionist idea with Zion is not theoretical at all. It is an 'existential' reality, a historical fact which Zionism does not question but knows itself to embody" (1961:95, 103).

My second illustration of the Zionist synthesis is focused, then, on Herzl himself. This modern, cosmopolitan Jew of the West had argued for a Jewish homeland in the most positive and rational of terms. Failing in the West, he turned to the East, where his ideas captured the popular spirit and his "countenance" and "personality" raised "messianic hopes."[3] For a time, Theodor Herzl embodied the Zionist synthesis: a man of modernity harnessing the energies and yearnings of tradition. And despite his personal charisma, he thus became bound to the symbols of that tradition. The Uganda affair demonstrated the limits of charisma, for although Herzlian Zionism succeeded in redefining exile as a condition that could be ended by men, it still worked within the framework of "exile"—and exile made sense only if its opposite was Zion. When Herzl attempted to disengage Zionism from its attachment to Zion, even in the service of suffering Jews of Kishinev or of victories of political diplomacy—even in the name of reason—he was bound to fail. The tie of the Zionists to Palestine was a primordial tie, not amenable to the canons of reason.

Thus, while these two examples illustrate the Zionist synthesis of traditionalism (as "thesis") and modernism (as "antithesis"), they (and especially Uganda) illustrate also something unsettling about the synthesis. The dialectic seems imperfectly achieved. For while Zionism opposes both traditionalism and modernism, it appears, in Halpern's phrase, to seek rapprochement not with the latter but the former. It had to: for its mass appeal lay with the Jews of Eastern, not Western, Europe. In the West it was argued by many Jews that they were not a separate nation, a separate people, but only a religious denomination like Christian denominations. Like any nationalism, Zionism had to succeed in elevating the attributes of the nation to "ultimate values" (Katz 1973:11), and in the West, among Jews, the very attribute of "nationhood" was denied or undermined. In the East, however, were Jewish communities "whose myth still perceived Jewry as an ethnic entity" (Halpern 1961:81), as *ethnos* rather than *demos*.

The rapprochement of Zionism with traditionalism was inevitable, for traditionalism offered meaning to the ties of "ethnicity" that would bind Jew to Jew in a Jewish nation. Thus there existed the only conception of a Jewish entity that made Zionism meaningful and possible. At first, in its broad appeal, in Eastern Europe, but eventually in Western Europe as well, tradition provided a conception of Jews, after enlightenment, emancipation, reform, and *embourgeoisement,* as being an ethnic group. And, as Halpern says (1961:103), it is in its celebration of these ties of ethnicity that Zionism's "fundamental movement . . . emotionally even more than intellectually, is . . . back toward tradition."

Aliya: Zionism and the State

In ideological terms, the State of Israel is the product of Zionist nationalism; it is also, like the United States of America, a nation of immigrants. Immigration to Israel is called *aliya* (pl. *aliyot*), from the Hebrew root meaning to "go up," or "ascend" (as used, for example, in Numbers 32:11 or , in the context of the Babylonian Exile, in Ezra 1:3 and 2 Chronicles 36:23). Some of the earliest battles within the Zionist movement were fought over the nature of the program that was to guide Jewish immigration to Palestine: Herzl rejected haphazard infiltration and sought a political charter to guarantee and legitimize aliya. But while these battles were over the nature of the program, at no time after the Territorialists left the movement was aliya divorced from Zionism: often it was at the center of Zionism. When it was not, as in America, then it was the very absence of its centrality that served to define the contours—and points of stress—of the movement. Modern Israel began as a nation of immigrants, but the ideological exigencies of Zionism sought expression in the development of a specific kind of immigrant society. Set down (or returned) in the "traditional setting of the Middle East," the Jewish *halutzim* ("pioneers") segregated themselves and "attempted to transplant into their own frameworks various European institutions" (Eisenstadt 1967:4–6). The Jewish condition in Europe made of Israel an immigrant society; ideological Zionism demanded it be a modern, colonizing society.

It is possible, then, to make aliya mediate between two histories: that of the development of Zionism, and that of the development of the state. Thus it is we find that the history of modern Israel, in the period before statehood, is usually written in terms of five main "waves of aliya." Each wave represented different forces in Europe (and elsewhere) that impelled Jews to migrate, brought different sorts of Jews to the *Yishuv* (the pre-state Jewish community in Palestine) and, in general, marked off different periods in the society's pre-state development (e.g., "the Russians of the Second Aliya brought ideology and idealism, the Germans of the Fifth Aliya capital and 'culture'," is an Israeli commonplace). (Table A1 in the Appendix summarizes some of the main characteristics of these aliyot.)[4]

In the period from the beginning of the British mandate (1919) to the establishment of the State of Israel (1948), aliya accounted for 71.8 percent of the total increase of the Jewish population of Palestine (Matras 1965:27; see also table A2 in Appendix). Through the Fourth Aliya (1882–1931, inclusive) the great majority of immigrants came from Eastern Europe—not Western Europe, the Americas, Africa, or Asia. By the Fifth Aliya (1932–38), the rise of Nazi power and the closing of national borders to Jews elsewhere in the world made of Palestine, for the first time, a genuine haven for refugees, and gave to aliya the characteristics of a mass migration movement (see table A3, Appendix). No longer were the immigrants predominantly young, single persons, in self-selected groups of Zionists come to Palestine consciously to create a new Jewish society. Among refugees, older individuals and whole families immigrated, the non-Zionist along with the *halutz* ("Zionist pioneer"). In the years during and after World War II, in the face of mounting Arab opposition to continued Jewish immigration and efforts by Britain to limit this immigration, aliya continued in a clandestine or semi-clandestine way (*aliya bet*). These operations (including the running of a Royal Navy blockade) lasted until 1948. The advent of the state did not lessen the importance of aliya.

With the achievement of sovereignty one of the first issues to be addressed by the new state was that of aliya. Israel's Declaration of Independence held the state to be open to Jewish immigration and *kibbutz galuyot,* the "ingathering of exiles." It contained a specific appeal to Diaspora Jewry to aid in the task (see Laqueur 1976:125–28). The state's position on immigration

was institutionalized with the passage by Israel's parliament
(*Knesset*) in 1950 of the Law of Return. This law grants to every
Jew the right to settle in Israel as an *oleh* ("immigrant"). In 1952
the Nationality Law was passed, which grants to every oleh (pl.
olim) Israeli citizenship.[5] As recently as 1971 the Knesset, re-
sponding to the plight of Soviet Jewry, passed legislation extending Israeli citizenship to any Jew living abroad who expresses
his desire to settle in Israel.[6]

In the wake of independence came a period of mass immigration, extending through 1951 and bringing, in these four years,
some 687,000 additional olim (Matras 1965:33). These immigrants
came from the British detention camps on Cyprus, and from Poland, Rumania, Yugoslavia, and Bulgaria. Many were survivors
of concentration camps. And, for the first time, very large numbers came from African and Asian countries: almost the entire
Jewish populations of Yemen, Aden, Libya, and Iraq. This latter,
"Oriental" immigration,

> changed the character of the Jewish population of Israel consid-
> erably. . . . Of the total number of Jewish immigrants in this
> period, no less than 35 percent were Jews from Asian coun-
> tries . . . and 14 percent from African countries. Only half, 51 per
> cent, came from European or American countries, compared to
> 90 pecent from these countries among the immigrants of the
> Mandatory period. (Matras 1965:35)

This trend, moreover, was to intensify: in the 1952–53 period
Afro-Asians constituted 70 percent of all immigrants, and in the
period 1954–57 (following the Sinai Campaign and turbulence in
French North Africa) African-born Jews constituted 63 percent of
the total immigration (see table A4, Appendix).

The massive influx of Afro-Asian Jews did more than change
Israel's population characteristics. For the first time, in Alex
Weingrod's words, "ethnicity emerges" as a salient feature of
Israeli society. No longer was degree of involvement in *halutziut*
(the "pioneering spirit") the major discriminator between groups,
as it had been in previous aliyot. Now, differences among groups
could be drawn on "civilizational" lines:

> The experience, customs, and even appearance of Middle
> Eastern Jews differ fundamentally from their European

brethren. Long resident in Muslim lands, their life-style closely resembled their Muslim neighbors. For many of them—the Yemenites and Kurds, for example—Israel represented their first contact with modern Western civilization. . . . For all of these newcomers Israel represented a social revolution: it introduced them to a different technology, new kinds of social and political relations, and a novel system of social values. (Weingrod 1965:13–14)

In order to absorb these immigrants, large "transition camps" (*ma'abarot*) were established, staffed, and supported by a growing bureaucracy. Settlement was then encouraged either in new moshavim[7] or in so-called "development towns." Both were attempts to disperse the Jewish population from the thickly settled coastal strip (especially around Tel Aviv), and to fill out hitherto sparsely settled areas: the Galilee, the reclaimed Hula Valley, and the Negev. There was a unifying theme behind all these "absorption strategies"; its major motif can be discerned in Weingrod's assertion that, for many of these Middle Eastern Jews, Israel was their first contact with Western, modern civilization. Immigration was a break from tradition. Absorption into Israeli society presupposed a special sort of acculturation, and that is, the willingness or the ability, on the part of these Oriental Jews, to "modernize" in harmony with their new home.

The foundations of the Jewish state were laid by successive waves of immigrants. The question of continued immigration underlay much of the conflict among Jews, Arabs, and the British in Mandatory times; the establishment of the state signalled the beginnings of mass immigration from African and Asian lands. In the history of modern Israel aliya becomes a sort of root metaphor, much as American history finds its metaphorical root in the idea of the expanding (and then receding) frontier. I said that aliya mediates between the history of Zionism and that of the state; more mechanically, one may say that Zionism represented the idea of the state and aliya made possible its reality. The problem, however, with these formulas is that they freeze their major components (Zionism, aliya, and the state) in but one aspect of their development and interaction. To put it differently: after statehood, Zionist history and Israeli history converge—often to the distress of certain Zionists—and aliya can no longer mediate

between the two. Instead, aliya became one of the several symbols of the tension between the encroaching routinization of
Zionism's charisma and the demand that Zionism continue to
bring a modern state (and people) towards, in Ben-Gurion's
words, "the fulfillment of its historic mission in redeeming man-
kind" (in Leon and Adin 1972:58). It should not surprise us, at
this point, that even a staunchly secular labor-Zionist like Ben-
Gurion would use the language of mission and redemption: for
here again (Ben-Gurion wrote these words in 1964) was the
sought-after rapprochement discussed above. My aim here, however, is to underscore the ideological crisis that engulfed Zionism
after the advent of the state, and to place aliya in the context of
this crisis.

What were the dimensions of the crisis? Charisma, in the
Weberian sense of that which is *aussertäglich* (outside of the
everyday), can be applied to things—to movements—as well as to
individuals (cf. Zald and Ash 1966). Zionism developed into a
movement whose appeal, authority, and mission were imbued
with charismatic qualities (not to mention those qualities accorded to individual Zionists, beginning with Herzl). This was
especially true when the magnitude of the European Holocaust
became known, and in the critical days immediately preceding
and following the establishment of the state. The movement was
not merely future-oriented; it aimed at creating in Palestine an
entirely new order of human society and a new order of Jewish
individuals. Straddling the purely rational and the purely traditional, its aims were transformative. But with the actual
establishment of the state, Zionism began to face a long period of
heightening ideological crisis. The crisis was based on the im-
pending routinization of the movement, in the face of demands
it remain charismatic.

Where could Zionism stand after the advent of the state? If the
sole aim of Zionist nationalism lay in the establishment of the
state, then with establishment its work ought to have been over
and done with: routinization (or the coming of "normalcy," in the
Zionist's own parlance) ought to have been welcomed. But it was
welcomed neither by the secular Left nor by the religious Right.
The way to counter routinization was to deny that the work of the
movement was over. But while the secular Ben-Gurion could

speak rhetorically of mission and redemption, as above, the parties of the Israeli Left could never quite bring themselves to institutionalize either into party platform or ideology. There were, after all, problems of consistency and dissonance to face. Instead, Ben-Gurion and the Left made another impossible (i.e., messianic) task the primary focus of Zionist attention. This was *kibbutz galuyot*, the in-gathering of exiles towards the complete dissolution of the Jewish Diaspora.

It should now become clear what role aliya was given to play in the poststate development of Zionism. Aliya constituted the means to the achievement of *kibbutz galuyot*, which was itself the means to the achievement of a yet greater end.

To return now to my earlier formulation, between what, and how, would aliya mediate? If at all, it would have to mediate between the state and world Jewry, supplanting "diaspora Zionism" in this role. In its turn, the state would relate to all Jews in a special way: such was the meaning of the Law of Return. Ben-Gurion, as prime minister, introduced a draft of this law to the Knesset with the following words:

> This law lays down not that the State accords the right of settlement to Jews abroad but that this right is inherent in every Jew by virtue of his being a Jew if it but be his will to take part in settling the land. This right preceded the State of Israel, it is that which built the State. (In Silverstone 1973:75)

In the terminology of the social theorist Henry Maine, one could say that the state desired to relate to all Jews in all places on the basis of "status," not "contract." Implicit in the Law of Return—and explicit in Ben-Gurion's commentary—is also an invitation to Jews to activate this special relationship by making aliya. And as the years passed, Ben-Gurion and his supporters strove to turn the invitation into an imperative. Finally, to the chagrin of many Zionists living in the Diaspora, he declared that only an immigrant to Israel had the moral right to call himself a Zionist. Ben-Gurion strove to make of aliya a metonym for Zionism itself. And prominent among those who expressed their chagrin were the Zionist representatives of American Jewry.

The Role of American Jewry

Despite the early activities of such singular men as Mordecai Noah, the son of a soldier in Washington's army who founded, in 1825, the city of "Ararat" on Grand Island on the Niagara River to be a "City of Refuge" for persecuted Jews until Palestine was ready, Zionism was not born fully formed on American shores. It was brought to America part and parcel with the massive immigration of nearly three million Eastern European Jews in the years between 1881 and 1925. Here it was one piece from a large baggage train: Orthodoxy or ultra-Orthodoxy in religion, atheism, radical socialism, the Yiddish language and culture. For a time it looked as though the debates held in dissolving shtetls or in revolutionary Odessa would continue unchanged on the Lower East Side of New York. This, however, was illusory, for two existential facts of Russian Jewish life had been ineradicably altered.

In the first place, these Jews were no longer living in Russia, hemmed within the Pale. America, *di goldenah medinah,* "the golden land," constituted their new environment and provided opportunities for mobility—social, cultural, and psychological—that were unheard of in Paris, much less Minsk, Pinsk, or Petersburg. In the second place, they soon learned that their new environment included other, previously settled Jews, with whom relations were not at all unproblematic.

For in the years between 1840 and 1880, some 200,000 Jews from Central Europe had emigrated to America. They arrived staunchly Germanic in their culture, and changed the face of postcolonial American Jewry, which had hitherto had a Sephardic, Iberian hue. By the time the Eastern Europeans began to arrive en masse, however, the Germans had already achieved a secure middle-class status in the U.S. and, as Dinnerstein writes, "They had made every effort to appear indistinguishable from the more prosperous gentile Americans" (1977:225). And in America, more so than in all of Europe, such efforts did not go unrewarded.

These German (and Austrian) Jews had brought with them their Reform Judaism, built decorous temples, and, by 1875, founded a seminary (Hebrew Union College) for the training of American rabbis. Before the influx of Eastern Europeans, Reform was the dominant American trend,[8] and it was expected that Reform would remain the single expression of American Judaism (as perhaps the word "Union" in the seminary's name suggests). Reform had, after all, a chance to work in America that it had not had in Western Europe. The United States was the first new nation to develop free of the direct impact of Jewish Emancipation and of the reaction of romantic nationalism. There had been no highly articulated ancien régime to be overthrown. "Emancipation" and "nationalism" were, in effect, American givens: two sides of the same coin.[9] The equality of citizens (Emancipation) was addressed in the Declaration of Independence, and the American Revolution (nationalism) had been fought to uphold that very document. A nationalism put in the service of Emancipation, and not proferred in reaction to it, meant that the Jew was finally removed from that status of pawn between warring ideological camps, a position he had conveniently filled in all of continental Europe. America demanded of her Jewish immigrants not apostasy but only that they accept the values embodied in her Declaration of Independence: values that Reform was eminently adapted to espouse. For, finally, here was a land where Jews might be full (American) citizens of the Mosaic sect; where, in keeping with Protestant denominationalism and the developing separation between church and state, a Jewish citizen would differ from a Gentile citizen by his religious affiliation only, not by something so base (and basic) as his ethnicity.

With this understood, it ought not surprise us that most settled German-American Jews viewed the mass arrival of their hard-pressed coreligionists with ambivalence, if not outright hostility. The Eastern Europeans brought with them their Orthodox Judaism, a medievalism Reform was meant to reform; they brought their socialism; or they brought their radical, freethinking atheism: this was not American, either. The Zionists among them brought a nationalism that threatened to compete with American nationalism for the loyalties of Jewish citizens. Worst of all, adherents of all these positions screamed forth their views in a proliferating number of newspapers, pamphlets, and plays published in that most barbarous of tongues, Yiddish. The Germans saw the Russians to be a threat to their security. They feared—ironically, as Herzl argued—that mass Jewish immigration would lead to mass American anti-Semitism.

An examination of the stereotypes held by each group about the other indicates that, at the beginning, differences between them were held to be both base and basic. An English-language newspaper of the "uptown Yahudim," the Germans, wrote in 1894 that "the thoroughly acclimated American Jew . . . is closer to the Christian sentiment around him than to the Judaism of these miserable darkened Hebrews" (in Dinnerstein 1977:225). The German-American Jews found the new immigrants "primitive and clannish, unwilling to take on American ways, insistent on maintaining 'Asiatic' and 'medieval' forms of religion and social life" (Gartner 1969:45). Even efforts to reach out to these "unassimilable Orientals" were often tinged with irony. At a dance of Russian Jewish immigrants, "The guest of honor, an American Jewish lawyer of German origin, began his speech with the comment, 'Who would believe this is a gathering of Russian Jews. Everyone looks handsome'" (in Urofsky 1975:60).

The Russian, "downtown Yiddin," had their own ideas about the "uptowners." To them, "The German Jew was hardly a Jew, but a 'yahudi,' a 'deitshuk.' His Reform Judaism was a sham as Judaism. . . . [M]ore damning than the Reform Judaism. . . . was the seeming absence among them [the Germans] of folk-feeling, that sense of mutuality, of common fate and kinship. . . . It grated . . . [on the Russians] that Jew should hold aloof from other Jews" (Gartner 1969:45).

How to characterize these different perceptions? To the settled German-American Jew, the Russian newcomer was far too "ethnic" for everyone's good; to the Russian, newly arrived and for a time dependent on the charities of his Yahudi brethren, the cold German Jew was simply not ethnic enough.

One of the legacies of Emancipation was the historic split of European Jewry into western and eastern components. In continental Europe (though not in Britain after 1880) these Jewries remained, in the mass, physically separate. In the United States they found themselves sharing the same arena for the first time. And despite the divisive stereotypes, reflecting a basic level of tension and mistrust, within the arena they did interact. When it was clear that the immigrant tide would not abate, the Yahudim spared little in their efforts to aid their coreligionists; and the Yiddin, though resenting the aid-cum-paternalism, needed and accepted the help in the tacit knowledge that, when the chips were down, it was only right and proper that Jew should aid Jew. It was from this interaction, taking place in the pervasive American environment of opportunity and mobility, that American Jewry, Judaism, and Zionism began to take form.

In the United States, Zionism faced an array of critics like those it had had in Europe, ranging from the Reform contingent, who believed that a nationalism aimed at establishing a Jewish homeland was seditious folly, to the ultra-Orthodox, who believed it was sinfully "forcing the End," to the radical socialists, for whom it was a wasteful regression in the course of world revolution. In the U.S., however, there were also important differences in the array.

First, the Reform, despite their numerical inferiority, were economically established and socially fluent in the ways of America. They strove to act as *shtadlanim* ("back-door petitioners"), brokers or middlemen, to "Americanize" the Eastern Europeans even as they aided them, and to act as damper on what they considered to be manifestations of the Yiddins' more "Asiatic" tendencies.

Second, the Yiddin themselves had made, on one level or another, their decision to immigrate to the Golden Land rather than to the Promised Land. The most dedicated European Zionists were those who went to Palestine in one of the first three waves of aliyot. The dynamic vanguard of Zionism was likely to be—as Ben-Gurion later argued—on Kibbutz Degania rather than Delancey Street.

Third, and finally, there was America herself. While the poverty and hardship in the immigrants' first areas of settlement might have restricted their daily involvement in causes other than those related to their own survival, it was also true that social and economic advancement usually awaited those who survived. Industrializing America needed the labor and skills of her immigrants, and she rewarded them. Nothing "Americanized" immigrants quicker than their own perceptions of the rewards to be gained by being Americans. It was not only that Palestine could claim little priority in the context of a sixteen- or eighteen-hour sweatshop work day but that, paradoxically, as conditions improved and as individuals and families began to move "uptown," Palestine could be thought of as that haven for "the poor, persecuted Jews of Europe." Thus, even as financial or political support for Jewish settlement in Palestine would begin to increase, thoughts of one's own aliya would fade further and further away.

At first, however, as America beckoned with open if not quite inviting arms, even many traditional Eastern Europeans, whose emotional ties to Eretz Yisrael were deep, began to wonder if one could be a Zionist and a good American at the same time. The result: prior to 1914 Zionism in the U.S. was moribund. Out of 1.5 million American Jews, the vast majority of whom were Yiddish-speaking Eastern Europeans, "combined membership in all Zionist groups totaled less than 20,000" (Urofsky 1975:104).

By 1914, however, a man who had joined the Federation of American Zionists two years earlier began to become active in its affairs. He would soon assume leadership positions. Louis D. Brandeis was the seminal figure in American Zionism. He was born in 1856 in Louisville, Kentucky, and attended Harvard Law School. He practiced law with great success in Boston, championed progressive social reform, and was a confidant to President Wilson. In 1916, he was named by Wilson to the U.S. Supreme Court.

Brandeis, like Herzl, was a successful, assimilated Jew who was "converted" to Zionism later in life. The similarities between Brandeis and Herzl are fascinating and, also, essential to an understanding of Zionism's American career. Against those powerful Jews who argued that a Jewish nationalism was unpatriotic and seditious, Brandeis put forth the contrary notion: "Zionism is the Pilgrim inspiration and impulse over again," he began, and continued:

> The highest Jewish ideals are essentially American in a very important particular. It is Democracy that Zionism represents. It is Social Justice which Zionism represents, and every bit of that is the American ideals of the twentieth century.... to be good Americans we must be better Jews, and to be better Jews, we must become Zionists. (In Urofsky 1975:128–29)

The contention was that, far from being antithetical to basic American principles, Zionism was eminently compatible with them, was, in fact, yet another expression of these principles.

Brandeis became the leader and spokesman of American Zionism. For a time he was the symbol of that Zionism. He had won prestige in American terms and, through Wilson, he had access to American power. He gradually assembled about him a particularly able group—many, like himself, were uptowners. For the first time an efficient Zionist apparatus was organized in America. But the mass support for this apparatus, as for Brandeis himself, came not from fellow Yahudim but from the Yiddish-speakers of downtown. To them, Brandeis was able to represent—and reconcile—what was echt-American with what was echt-Jewish: the yearning for Zion.

Within ten years this came to an end; to understand why, we must look more closely at the parallels between Brandeis and Herzl. Herzl, an assimilated, cosmopolitan journalist, formulated a Zionist idea and was rebuffed by fellow Jews in the West. He turned from the West and found his support among the masses of Eastern Jewry. Although he argued for Zionism in the most rational of terms, his message (and his countenance) awakened Eastern messianism based upon traditional Jewish conceptions of exile, redemption, and the end. Louis Brandeis, an assimilated uptown Yahudi, went against his fellow Yahudim and was able to galvanize the downtown Yiddin. While the application of a messianic simile did not occur, nevertheless Brandeis, in arguing his Zionist case in the most progressively libertarian of American terms, was accepted by the Jewish masses as a meaningful synthesis of the Americanism they strove for and of the Zionism they so deeply felt.

I have spoken of "synthesis" before, in the case of Herzl. Like Herzl, Brandeis was "the man of modernity" who harnessed the energies and yearnings of traditional men; and, like Herzl, Brandeis was to find himself bound by the symbols of that tradition. For Herzl it had been the Uganda affair that demonstrated the limits of charisma; for Brandeis it was the more complicated, drawn-out fight which he lost to European Zionists led by Chaim Weizmann and represented in the U.S. by Louis Lipsky. Substantively, the two fought over the disposition of certain funds to be used in building the Yishuv, and more generally over the "practical" approach of Brandeis versus the more ideological, "political-cultural" definitions of Zionism that Weizmann and the Europeans demanded. But in 1921, at the Cleveland convention of the Zionist Organization of America, Brandeis lost to Weizmann and Lipsky not over the issue of funds or even definitions, but over the issue of *Yiddishkeit*, "Jewish spirit." Where Herzl lost because, at the critical moment, he was seen to represent

Vienna over Zion, Brandeis lost because he was accused of representing Washington and Boston over the shtetl. Addressing the mass of American Yiddish-speaking Zionists in Cleveland that year,

> Chaim Weizmann tapped an emotional reservoir closed to the rational approach of the American [Brandeis's] leadership. . . . There is perhaps no better word to use than *Yiddishkeit*—an all-pervading sense of Jewishness—to describe the key to that appeal. Had Brandeis had it, he would not have been able to legitimize Zionism in America; once he had accomplished that task, however, then Weizmann, the Jew from Motele, could exploit the resources—financial and emotional—of American Jewry. (Urofsky 1975:297–98)

As it had in Europe at the turn of the century, Zionism in America developed from a dialectic of modernism and traditionalism and—as in Europe—the dialectic was imperfectly achieved. The rapprochement, as Brandeis learned and as Herzl had learned before him, was to be sought on the side of tradition. Nevertheless, conditions in America were sufficiently different from those in Europe to affect the degree of rapprochement with tradition American Zionism could achieve. It was less than could be achieved in Europe, and this gave to American Zionism its peculiar character. It is also, perhaps, why European, Palestinian, and finally Israeli Zionists never quite trusted the depth of feeling of American Zionists in matters other than fund-raising, or cash flow. For even those Yiddish-speakers who voted against Brandeis's lack of Yiddishkeit in 1921 only went on, themselves, to become more American: to move uptown or out to the suburbs. The great majority of American Jews came to share neither the Orthodox world view of traditional Judaism nor the socialist world view of Poalei Zion. In a short time American Jews were neither pious nor ideological; to the Europeans, and later the Israelis, this indicated something essentially *goyisch* ("Gentile") about them.

The conclusive proof of this, so far as the Europeans and Israelis were concerned, was the part aliya played in American Zionism. Aliya was never at the center of American Zionism. Since Brandeis, the Zionist movement in America functioned effectively as banker for the world movement and as a fulcrum for the political leverage sometimes needed to mobilize American presidents and public opinion in the support of the Jewish cause. The American Zionist establishment, however, steered a middle and moderate course, eschewing both Left and Right. This American "non-ideologicalness" was never quite understood—or forgiven—by European and Israeli Zionists. Ironically, even those who voted against Brandeis's "practical" approach, in 1921, found themselves forging a movement in America that avoided "political-cultural" definitions. Nor did the Europeans and Israelis understand the difference, in America, between a "non-Zionist" (who might support the movement financially) and an "anti-Zionist."

The American leadership strove, above all, for a kind of respectability in the American context. "America is different," it was claimed, and American Zionism must reflect that difference, it was demanded. Thus, aliya from America came to be viewed by American Zionists without enthusiasm or, indeed, with mistrust. Aliya brought up questions of dual or divided loyalties, if not the denial of America herself. It was against such charges that Brandeis had to defend Zionism in the early years of its American career.

How was America different? We have seen how Israeli Zionism, after statehood and under Ben-Gurion, sought to revivify itself by making of aliya a metonym for the whole movement. Goals were shifted: the aim of post-state Zionism was to be the complete dissolution of the Jewish exile. There was but one problem. The Jewish exile, especially in the free West, stubbornly resisted its own dissolution. Thus, soon after the establishment of the state, it became evident that American Zionism and Israeli Zionism were on a collision course. The state took as its charter *kibbutz galuyot,* the in-gathering of exiles, and in its view all Jews living *hutz-la'aretz,* outside The Land, were living in exile. American Jews, while willing to support the new state financially, politically, and even emotionally, did not believe, for the most part, that Levittown was exile: especially as Levittown ended the long climb from Brownsville.

After the advent of statehood, the very meanings of Zionism and Zionist had to be refurbished. The iconoclastic Ben-Gurion angered many Americans when he declared that only an immigrant to Israel had the moral right to call himself a Zionist. At the same time, the Israelis wanted to see all Zionist organizations (especially the World Zionist Organization and the Jewish Agency) based in Jerusalem and under the moral authority of the new state; the Americans wanted these organizations to remain separate from, and complementary to, the state.

All of these battles were complicated by (if not predicated on) the strivings of both sides to define the terms of their relationship. The enormous sums of money given by American Jewry towards keeping the state afloat have defined a relationship of profound ambivalence. Israel, collectively, is the *schnorrer*, Yiddish for "beggar," while American Jewry plays the role of patron. This gross material dependence upon the largesse of brethren is one the Israelis—like other people—do not suffer gladly. And they have sought to redress the balance, regain parity, by pointing to the less material, but no less real, goods that Israel offers in return for financial support: a center of gravity for modern Jewry; indeed, the sine qua non of Jewishness and the post-Holocaust Jew. More cynically, Israelis point out that giving by Americans serves to expiate a guilt they "must" feel for not participating in the center directly: for not making aliya. If this be the case, American Jews are getting much for their money. In fact, as with the prototypical schnorrer of the European shtetl, there is an arrogance present because the recipient knows that the donor, by giving charity, is amassing credits (*mitzvot*) for the world to come. Whatever else he may be, in the shtetl, as Zborowski and Herzog (1962:211) write, "the beggar is an instrument of grace." More than occasionally, Israelis have invoked a very similar argument.

To return to our question: America is "different," ultimately, insofar as it is not seen to be exile. And American Zionism is "different" insofar as it fails to connect with the only conception of a Jewish entity that, earlier, made Zionism meaningful and possible; and that is a conception of a Jewish entity as not merely religious or denominational but as *ethnic*. Those American Jews who hold, or come to hold deeply, to this ethnic conception, and act on it, are the subject of this study, for some of them immigrate to Israel. Given the centrality of aliya to Israeli Zionism, and given the noncentrality of aliya to American Zionism, it should not be surprising that such immigrants are a distinct minority— and hardly a typical cross-section—of America's Jews.

The Demography of American Aliya

The Volume of American Aliya

One of the first American olim of note was Ward Cresson, the first United States consul for Palestine, a Protestant appointed in 1845. Within a year, Mr. Cresson converted to Judaism and, as "Michael Boaz Israel," founded an agricultural colony outside Jerusalem. Supported by the American philanthropist Judah Touro, this colony grew to a population of more than two hundred. At least a quarter were American Jews (Lapide 1961:37ff). In the period before the First Aliya (1882), however, most American Jews in Palestine were settled, characteristically, in one of the four holy cities (Jerusalem, Safed, Hebron, and Tiberius). Here they lived off halukkah funds and studied Torah. By 1902, some one thousand U.S. citizens were registered under the protection of the consulate in Jerusalem (Lapide 1961:45).

According to official statistics, during the period of the British Mandate (1919–48), some 6,613 American citizens immigrated to Palestine. Almost two thousand came as part of the Fourth Aliya (1924–31), almost four thousand as part of the Fifth (1932–38). The highest estimate puts American aliya in this period at 11,195. Even this higher estimate, however, sets the level of American aliya at about 3 percent of total immigration, coming at an average rate of three hundred per year. If American *yerida* (out-migration) in this period had been consistent with that of other European groups in Palestine, it would have constituted 20 to 40 percent of the total (Goldscheider 1974:348–51).

These olim of the later Mandatory period were different from the pious immigrants of the 1800s. Many came imbued with the pioneering ideals of the developing, secular Zionist movement in

35

Europe and America. They were attracted to the agricultural re-
settlement of the land, to kibbutzim. By 1937 the first American
kibbutz, Ein HaShofet,[1] was formed, the settlers having spent six
years in training in Palestine. By 1952 there were fourteen American kibbutzim, some settled by individuals who had fought as
volunteers in Israel's War of Independence (see Morris 1953).

Within the first two years of Israel's sovereignty some additional thousand Americans immigrated under the Law of Return.
Annual data on arrivals between 1950 and 1975 are summarized
below, in table 3.1.

As used in these tabulations, an "immigrant" is a person en-
tering Israel to take up residence under the Law of Return (1950).
Under this law, such a person gets automatic Israeli citizenship.
A "potential immigrant," according to newer regulations of the
Ministry of Interior valid since June 1969, is "a person entitled to
an immigrant visa or an immigrant certificate under the Law of
Return, who intends to enter Israel and stay there for more than
three months" (Ministry of Immigrant Absorption, Special Series
No. 416, 1973: IX–X). Such a person enters on an "A-1 type visa"
valid (normatively) for three years. This status, which replaced
the older category "temporary resident,"[2] gives the entrant all
the rights and subventions allowed "new immigrants" (*olim
hadashim;* see Chapter 4), but allows also a three-year "wait-
and-see" period before any decision about accepting or rejecting
Israeli citizenship need be made.[3] The new category was instituted in direct response to increased aliya from the West, following the Six-Day War. The great majority of American immigrants, between 1969 and 1975, chose to enter Israel as "potential
immigrants" (about this I shall have more to say in later chapters).

Table 3.1 indicates that some 45,426 Americans immigrated to
Israel between 1950 and 1975 ("American" by country of residence; by "country of birth" the figure would be approximately
25 to 30 percent smaller). In 1950 American immigration accounted for 0.4 percent of total immigration; in 1971 American
olim constituted more than 17 percent of all immigrants. In general, immigration to Israel occurs in periodic cycles (see Ministry
of Immigrant Absorption, Special Series No. 489, 1975:V), and
the same pattern is evident in the American case. After falling to a
low in 1956, aliya from the U.S. began steadily to increase; by

Table 3.1 Immigrants and Tourists Settling, from U.S. (as "Country of Residence"), 1950–75

Year	No. of Immigrants	No. of "Potential Immigrants"	Total
1950	761	NA	761
1951	568	NA	568
1952	292	NA	292
1953	202	NA	202
1954	294	NA	294
1955	321	NA	321
1956	187	NA	187
1957	277	NA	277
1958	378	NA	378
1959	330	NA	330
1960	413	NA	413
1961	313	NA	313
1962	619	NA	619
1963	868	NA	868
1964	1,006	NA	1,006
1965	924	NA	924
1966	749	NA	749
1967	665	NA	665
1968	932	NA	932
1969	671	5,068	5,739
1970	639	5,785	6,424
1971	1,049	6,315	7,364
1972	805	4,710	5,515
1973	659	3,734	4,393
1974	465	2,624	3,089
1975	373	2,430	2,803

SOURCES: For 1950–72, *Immigration to Israel, 1948–1972,* speical series no. 416, pt. 1 (Jerusalem: Israel Central Bureau of Statistics, 1973), table 4, pp. 23–25; for 1973, *Immigration to Israel, 1973,* special series no. 457 (Jerusalem: Israel Central Bureau of Statistics, 1974), table 2, p. 4; for 1974–75, *Immigration Statistics,* vol. 6, no. 12 (in Hebrew) (Jerusalem: Israel Central Bureau of Statistics, 1975), table 2, p. 4.

1962 it reached the level, once again, of 1948–50 immigration. For the next six years aliya averaged about eight hundred persons per year. Then, in 1969, it took off, reaching an all-time high of more than seven thousand in 1971. The following year it fell 25 percent; 1973 saw a fall of 20 percent compared to 1972, and aliya in 1974 was down 30 percent from 1973.

Despite the decrease in aliya relative to its 1971 high, it is clear that American immigration underwent a significant change, beginning in 1968. The role of the Six-Day War in effecting this

change is an important one, and will be discussed in greater detail
in coming chapters. But it is also important not to overvalue the
direct influence of the 1967 war, or to forget that events in the
U.S., as well, in this period, were important factors in influencing
aliya. What is most important to understand, however, is that the
increased volume of American aliya in the post-1967 era cannot
be traced to a single event, either in Israel or the United States.
(By 1976, for example, in a group of recently arrived Americans
surveyed, fully 53 percent indicated that neither the Six-Day nor
the Yom Kippur wars had "direct influence" on their decision to
migrate [Berman 1977:32]). Rather, the changing volume of migration is itself reflective of a change in the relationship between
American Jewry, American Zionism, and Israel. The events of
June 1967 (and later of October 1973), played an important part in
redefining the nature of the relationship. In these particular times
of crisis, a small proportion of younger American Jewry responded in a way other than the traditional avenue of massive
fund-raising. At the outbreak of the 1967 war, and in the months
following, some 750 Americans (among 7,500 others) came to
Israel as volunteers, working in hospitals, kibbutzim, and construction (Zinger 1973:66). It is estimated that about a third stayed
on after their time of volunteered service, and many others left
Israel to return eventually as olim. These younger volunteers, and
the thousands that followed under the aegis of formal programs
quickly instituted by the Israeli government, responded, in effect,
to the old appeal of Ben-Gurion that American Jews take an active and direct part in the building of Israel. The logical extension
of such direct participation is one's own aliya. Of the total American immigration between 1950 and 1975, fully 80 percent came in
the years following 1967. The Six-Day War did not cause this
aliya: the part it played is to be found in the reaction of a segment
of younger American Jewry to it. This reaction, in time of crisis,
took the form of active participation, initially of volunteerism.
The effects of volunteerism (as opposed to fund-raising) transcended the relatively small number of volunteers. Returning
volunteers became *shlihim*—emissaries of information—to an
American Jewish population whose concern and interest in Israel
had been intensified as a result of the war. Some older assumptions about the relationship between American Jewry and Israel
began to change. These assumptions were discussed in Chapter 2;
they are summarized by Goldscheider:

In the pre-1967 era, American Jews and among them American Zionists, assumed that aliya would come from other countries, where Jews faced persecutions and hostility. The role of American Jews was at most to provide adequate economic support and effective political aid to Israel. Paradoxically, the American Zionist expressed great opposition to the idea of American aliya; the thought of his own immigration to Israel never seriously entered his mind while the idea of aliya on the part of his children "struck him as fundamentally absurd in theory and entirely to be rejected in actual practice." It is against the background of these assumptions that the radical change in the character of American aliya [after 1967] must be viewed. (1974:338)

For the remainder of this chapter, I shall focus on the social and cultural character of this post-1967 aliya.

Regional Distribution

The regional distribution of American olim who arrived in Israel in the years 1969–70, and 1976, is compared to the 1968 distribution of the U.S. Jewish population in table 3.2. A comparison of the 1969–70 data with the U.S. Jewish distribution reveals no significant differences: there is a slight over-representation, for olim, of the Northeast (probably from New York City) over other regions. Berman's survey of newly arrived

Table 3.2   Regional Distribution: American Olim and U.S. Jewish Population

Region	U.S. Jewish Population 1968 (%)	American Olim 1969–70 (%)	American Olim 1976 (%)
U.S., Northeast	64.0	66.2	56
U.S., North Central	12.5	12.8	10
U.S., South	10.3	9.7	6
U.S., West	13.2	11.3	20
U.S., unspecified	—	—	1
Canada	—	—	8
Total	100.0	100.0	101

SOURCES: U.S. Jewish population and 1969–70 olim, from Goldscheider 1974: 359. American olim of 1976, from Berman 1977:19. The size of Goldscheider's sample was N = 167; Berman's, N = 132.

olim in 1976, however, points to a clear overrepresentation of the West (probably California) over all other regions. These latter data might reflect, of course, a redistribution of the American Jewish population westward. Berman also includes 8 percent of his sample as "Canadian." If we base our comparison on the estimate closest in time to the U.S. data—to olim arrived in 1969–70—we would say that regional distribution does not appear to be significantly selective of American aliya.

Generational Status

Table 3.3 summarizes the findings of several surveys on the question of the generational status of the olim. As used in this table, "first generation" refers to individuals born outside the United States, to non-U.S. citizens; "second generation" to individuals, born in the U.S., at least one of whose parents were foreign-born; "third generation" refers to native-born Americans both of whose parents were also born in the U.S.

Table 3.3   American Olim, Generational Status

Source	First Generation (%)	Second Generation (%)	Third Generation (%)	Total (%)
Goldscheider 1974:361 Olim: 1969–70 N = 167	30.4	29.4	40.1	99.9
Jubas 1974:98 Olim: 1967–71 N = 1,178	25	39	36	100
Avruch (survey conducted in Jerusalem) Olim: 1968–76 N = 100	14	59	27	100
Berman 1977:19 Olim: 1976 N = 138	9	34	57	100

Jubas and Goldscheider's data (covering the years 1967–71) indicate some 70–75 percent of all olim were born in America, with 35–40 percent being third-generation Americans. Berman's

survey indicates, for 1976 olim, that less than 10 percent were
foreign-born, with 57 percent being third-generation. My own
survey—conducted in Jerusalem—puts the majority of olim (arrived between 1968 and 1976) in second-generation status, reflecting in the main, I suspect, the higher median age of my sample (at 38.1) compared to Goldscheider's (at 25.9) and Berman's
(at 27.5). In my sample, the median age that first-generation olim
came to the U.S. was 9.5 years. Finally, official aliya statistics for
1975 indicate some 83 percent of all American olim of that year
were born in American (see Israel Central Bureau of Statistics,
Immigration Statistics [in Hebrew], vol. 6, no. 12 [1975] tables II
and III, pp. 4–5). According to Goldscheider, generational status
is not "conspicuously selective" of American aliya (1974:361).

Age, Sex, and Family Status

Generational status for American Jews is, of course, closely
correlated to age. Table 3.4, with data on olim arrived in 1973,
indicates clearly that age is selective of American aliya. The median age for 1973 American olim is 28.0; for American Jews (in
1957) it is 36.7. Almost 60 percent of all American immigrants are
below the age of thirty; after thirty the largest age-group is
sixty-five or older: individuals living in Israel on their pensions,
savings, or social security benefits.

Table 3.4 points also to the demographic selectivity of sex.
Males, in general, are underrepresented among olim, and especially so in the age bracket 15–29. There is parity of representation in the age group 30–44, and a slight overrepresentation of
males among those olim sixty-five or older: it appears widowers,
rather than widows, are more likely to immigrate. Antonovsky
(1968) found selectivity in favor of women to be characteristic of
American immigrants in the pre-1967 era, as well.

Table 3.5 shows marital status to be selective of American
aliya. The percentage of "singles" among olim is almost double
that among the U.S. Jewish population. Among olim there seems
to be a slight tendency for women, rather than men, to be un-
married. Berman's 1976 data indicate an increase in the proportion of divorced individuals (undifferentiated as to sex) making
aliya.

Table 3.4   Age and Sex Distribution of North American Olim,
                   All Olim, and U.S. Jewish Population

	North American Olim (1973)		Total Olim, 1973		U.S. Jewish Pop., 1957	
Age	%	% Male	%	% Male	%	% Male
0–14	15.3	49.2	21.6	51.0	23.2	NA
15–19	7.5	39.2	9.1	49.8	6.9	45.7
20–29	33.9	42.7	20.2	46.9	} 32.2	50.1
30–44	14.0	50.6	18.2	49.2		
45–54	6.4	45.5	11.5	45.2	} 27.7	50.1
55–59	3.3	40.6	4.1	44.2		
60–64	5.4	47.3	5.0	43.5		
65+	14.2	51.9	10.3	46.3	10.0	45.7
Total	100.0	46.2	100.0	47.9	100.0	NA
Median age	28.0	—	29.6	—	36.7	—

SOURCES: Data on olim adapted from *Immigration to Israel, 1973*, special series no. 457 (Jerusalem: Israel Central Bureau of Statistics, 1974), table 7, p. 10. Data on U.S. Jewish population adapted from Goldcheider 1974:363.

NOTE: In this and all the following tables using 1973 Israeli census data on immigrants, "North American" is a composite category. The total number of "North Americans" arrived 1973 was 5,104. This total includes, however, 711 olim from Canada, Australia, and New Zealand. The number of immigrants from the U.S. in 1973, out of 5,104 "North Americans," was 4,393.

Data for 1973 immigrants point to an even higher percentage of "singles," slightly more than half (see table 3.6). Here the comparison between American olim and all (1973) olim is even more

Table 3.5   Marital Distribution of American Olim, All Olim, and U.S. Jewish Population

	American Olim 1970		All Olim 1970		U.S. Jewish Population 1957		American Olim 1976
Marital Status	% Male	% Female	% Male	% Female	% Male	% Female	% Male/Female
Single	44.2	45.2	42.4	38.8	23.5	17.7	44
Married	49.3	43.5	52.9	46.7	73.0	67.4	41
Widowed	3.4	7.4	2.7	11.1	2.5	13.4	12
Divorced	32.	4.0	2.0	3.4	1.0	1.4	3
Total	100.0	100.0	100.0	100.0	100.0	100.0	100

SOURCES: 1970 data and U.S. Jewish data from Goldscheider 1974:365 (N = 167). 1976 data from Berman 1977:18 (N = 141).

Table 3.6   "North American" and All Olim, by Status in
Family and Size of Family, Arrived 1973

	"North American"	All Olim
Family head	17.9%	25.6%
Accompanying		
person	31.9	56.9
Singles	50.2	17.5
Total	100.0%	100.0%
Families (by size)		
2	60.9%	35.7%
3	14.3	29.0
4	12.5	21.2
5	8.2	8.6
6	2.6	3.0
7	0.9	1.2
8	—	0.7
9+	0.6	0.6
Total	100.0%	100.0%
Average family size,		
including singles	1.5	2.3
Excluding singles	2.8	3.2

SOURCES: Adapted from data in *Immigration to Israel, 1973,* special series
no. 457 (Jerusalem: Israel Central Bureau of Statistics, 1974), table 14, p. 20.
NOTE: On "North Americans," see note to table 3.4

striking. As might be expected, the average family size (excluding
singles) for American, compared to all, olim is smaller: 2.8 versus
3.2.

Education and Occupation

Table 3.7 indicates that educational attainment is highly selective of American aliya. Compared to the Israeli Jewish population, all olim show a higher level of education, but this is
particularly striking in the American case. As well, American
olim attained higher levels of education than the American Jewish
population from which they came (keeping in mind the limitations
of comparing data collected in 1957 with those collected in
1969–70). My own survey work, conducted in Jerusalem, showed
an even higher level of educational attainment (see table 3.8).

As Goldscheider correctly points out, "The relatively small
number of olim from the United States precludes any real quan-

Table 3.7   Years of Schooling Completed

Years of Schooling Completed	Jewish Pop. of Israel 1970 (%)	All Olim 1969–70 (%)	American Olim 1969–70 (%)	American Jewish Pop. 1957 (%)*
Less than 9 years	49.7	35.7	9.3	28.7
9–12	35.5	31.7	23.8	39.0
13–15	9.2	14.9	25.2	12.7
16+	5.6	17.7	41.7	17.3
Not reported	—	—	—	2.3
Total	100.0	100.0	100.0	100.0

SOURCE: Adapted from data in Goldscheider 1974:369–70.
*1957 data for persons aged 25 and older; 1969–70 data for persons aged 18 and older.

titative impact of educational... selectivity on the American Jewish community" (1974:367). But this is not necessarily the case vis-à-vis Israeli society. Here, the Americans constitute an educational elite, a situaton which—given the relationship between educational attainment and occupational distribution patterns—is also true for the Americans' placement in the occupational structure of Israel.

Table 3.9 provides a detailed breakdown, by "occupation abroad," of North American olim compared to all olim who arrived in 1973. Table 3.10 provides a summary of these data in a slightly broader classificatory scheme, and includes data on employed persons in the Jewish Israeli labor force.

These tables indicate that fully 64.4 percent of all employed North Americans were working in scientific, academic, professional, or technical fields before their aliya. This compares with 44.0 percent of all olim, and 17.9 percent of the Jewish Israeli

Table 3.8   Level of Education Completed, American Olim, Resident in Jerusalem, Arrived 1968–76 (N = 100)

Last Level Completed	%
Elementary school	—
High school	8
Some college, no degree	15
College degree	32
Postgraduate (professional or graduate training)	45
Total	100

SOURCE: Avruch, Jerusalem survey (1976–77).

labor force. In the United States in 1967, about 13 percent of the total labor force were employed as "professionals," including teachers (Engel 1970:173). Data from 1957 on the U.S. Jewish population indicate some 18 percent of American Jews were employed as "professionals" (Goldscheider 1974:372). Even given, therefore, the overrepresentation of Jewish professionals in the U.S. labor force, it is clear that occupation—especially for the category "professional"—is highly selective of American aliya. Within the category "professional," the selectivity seems to operate especially on teachers at the primary and intermediate levels, and to a lesser degree on engineers, architects, and medical workers (including nurses). While American aliya is overselective of professionals, however, Goldscheider cites evidence that it is underselective of "managers and proprietors" (1974:371–73). Jubas confirms this, adding, "It can be noted that to become an entrepreneur in a new country ... is not an easy matter" (1974:112). About this point, entrepreneurship, and about Americans' occupational change in general, I shall have more to say in Chapter 7.

Surveys undertaken by Antonovsky (1969) of pre-1967 American aliya indicate that the proportion of professionals to other occupational categories is increasing with time. Impressionistic data in Isaacs (1966:48–53) confirm this view.

Finally, a look at the combined data on educational attainment and occupational distribution indicates clearly that American olim, once in Israel, constitute an educational and occupational elite. Two-thirds have spent some time in college; more than 40 percent have undertaken some kind of postgraduate work. The more substantive ways in which this elite status is manifested by Americans is to be the subject of coming chapters.

Religiousness, Zionist Involvement, and Jewish Education

Tables 3.11 and 3.12 summarize data, from various sources, on the religiousness of American olim. In table 3.11 these data are compared to those from a community study of Jews in Providence, R.I. (Goldstein and Goldscheider 1968). On the basis of this comparison it is clear that American aliya is overselective of

Table 3.9   "North American" and All Olim, by Occupation
Abroad, Arrived 1973

	"North Americans"		All Olim	
	Absolute Nos.	%	Absolute Nos.	%
Total	5,104	100.0	54,886	100.0
No occupation	2,038	39.9	22,053	40.2
Not specified	1,310	25.7	7,595	13.8
Occupation stated: total	1,756	34.4	25,238	46.0
Scientific & academic workers	385	21.9	5,651	22.4
—in life sciences	15	0.8	99	0.4
—in sciences	29	1.7	280	1.1
Engineers & architects	97	5.5	2,486	9.9
MDs, dentists, and dental assistants	60	3.4	1,100	4.4
Pharmacists & veterinarians	13	0.7	215	0.9
Jurists	29	1.7	162	0.6
Academic: social sci.	66	3.7	752	3.0
Academic: humanities	31	1.8	277	1.0
Teachers in higher educ.	33	1.9	79	0.3
Teachers & principals in secondary institutions	12	0.7	201	0.8
Other professional, technical & related workers	747	42.5	5,457	21.6
Teachers & principals in primary, intermediate schools	397	22.6	1,619	6.4
Auditors & accountants	12	0.7	73	0.3
Workers in religion	32	1.8	72	0.3
Authors, artists, composers, & journalists	133	7.6	1,137	4.5
Social workers, probation & related officers	55	3.1	94	0.4
Nurses & para-medicals	74	4.2	1,035	4.1
Physical science technicians	7	0.4	263	1.0
Engineering: technicians and practical engineers	7	0.4	810	3.2
Systems analysts & computer programmers	16	0.9	47	0.2
Other professionals, & related tech. workers	14	0.8	307	1.2
Managers & clerical	261	14.9	2,926	11.6
—managers	43	2.5	193	0.8
—clerical	218	12.4	2,733	10.8
Sales workers	118	6.7	1,829	7.2
Service workers	32	1.8	1,139	4.5
Agricultural workers	17	1.0	49	0.2
Skilled workers in building, industry, mining, and transportation	153	8.7	7,062	28.0

Table 3.9 (continued)

	"North Americans"		All Olim	
	Absolute nos.	%	Absolute Nos.	%
Unskilled workers	5	0.3	852	3.4
Not known	38	2.2	273	1.1
Total: occupation stated	1,756	100.0	25,238	100.0
Total: no occupation	2,038	100.0	22,053	100.0
Housewives	390	19.1	3,298	15.0
Students	1,103	54.1	11,540	52.3
Pensioneers, supported, and children up to 5 years old	545	26.8	7,215	32.7

SOURCE: Adapted from data in *Immigration to Israel, 1973,* special series no. 457 (Jerusalem: Israel Central Bureau of Statistics, 1974), table 18, pp. 26–27.

Jews affiliated with the Orthodox movement. Berman (1977) and Goldscheider's (1974) data indicate no conspicuous selectivity of Reform Jews, while Jubas (1974), Engel (1970), and my own survey point to an underselection of Reform. All the sources indicate an underselection of the most populous of the three major American trends, Conservative Judaism. The contrast between aliya

Table 3.10   1973 Olim by Occupation Abroad and Israeli Labor Force by Occupation, 1973 Average

Occupational Category	"North American" Olim (%)	All Olim (%)	Israeli Labor Force (Jews) (%)
Scientific & academic workers	21.9	22.4	6.2
Other professional, technical & related workers	42.5	21.6	11.7
Managers & clerical	14.9	11.6	20.7
Sales workers	6.7	7.2	8.0
Service workers	1.8	4.5	12.5
Agricultural workers	1.0	0.2	6.1
Skilled workers in building, industry mining, and transportation	8.7	28.0	28.5
Unskilled workers	0.3	3.4	5.6
Not known	2.2	1.1	0.7
Total	100.0	100.0	100.0

SOURCES: On olim, adapted from data in *Immigration to Israel, 1973,* special series no. 457 (Jerusalem: Israel Central Bureau of Statistics, 1974) table 18, pp. 26–27. On Jewish Israeli labor force, adapted from data in *Statistical Abstract of Israel, 1974,* no. 25 (Jerusalem: Israel Central Bureau of Statistics, 1974), table XII/1, p. 305.

Table 3.11   Religiousness: Self-Identification with Trend
              in U.S.

Source	Orthodox (%)	Conservative (%)	Reform (%)	Other (%)	Total (%)
Providence, R.I. study (Goldstein & Goldscheider 1968; in Sklare 1974:210)					
All ages, all generations	19.8	54.1	21.2	4.9	100.0
25–44 age group, 3d gen. only	4.5	51.9	36.7	6.8	99.9
American olim, 1969–70 (Goldscheider 1974:380)					
All generations	37	20	22	21	100
3d generation only	28	18	28	26	100
American olim, 1968–76, resident in Jerusalem (Avruch)	44	35	4	17	100
American olim, 1967–71 (Jubas 1974:105)	37	29	12	22	100
American olim, 1976 (Berman 1977:24)	25	42	18	15	100

from Orthodox and Reform trends is sharpest in my own work (44 vs. 4 percent). This survey was based on olim resident in Jerusalem, and I think it is clear that that city holds a special attraction for Orthodox immigrants; this accounts, possibly, for the extreme contrast.

In table 3.12 religiousness is expressed in a different manner. While "Orthodox," "Conservative," and "Reform" make sense in the American context, religiousness in Israel is expressed by a different set of terms: *dati* ("observant") and *lo-dati* ("not observant"). "Observance" refers to the following of *halakhah,* rabbinic law, based on the 613 *mitzvot* ("injunctions") of the Torah. The middle term in the opposition between *dati* and *lo-dati* is either the medial "not so observant" (literally: *lo kol-kakh dati*), or the more complex category *m'sorati* (literally, "traditionalist"). About these categories—and especially *m'sorati*—I shall have more to say later. For the present I follow the categorization uniform to all the sources listed in table 3.12; they use the medial, and less descriptive, category of "not so observant."

Examining table 3.12 by itself, we find that American olim classify themselves as "observant" in proportions higher than

Table 3.12   Religiousness: Self-Identification by Observance

Source	Observant (%)	Not So Observant (%)	Not at All Observant (%)	Total (%)
Israeli sample (Antonovsky 1963; cited in Matras 1965:98)	30	46	24	100
All olim, arrived 1974 (Ministry of Immigrant Absorption, *Annual Report, 1974*, p. 4)	27	31	42	100
American olim, 1969–70 (Goldscheider 1974:380)				
All generations	46	30	24	100
3d generation only	43	37	20	100
American olim, resident in Jerusalem, 1968–76 (Avruch)	51	31	18	100
American olim, arrived 1976 (Berman 1977:23)	41	42	18	101

either a sample of Israelis (Antonovsky 1963), or all olim who arrived in 1974 (Ministry of Immigrant Absorption, *Annual Report for 1974*, Jerusalem, 1975). Once again the contrast is sharpest in my own survey, based on Americans living in Jerusalem: more than half considered themselves "observant," and less than a fifth identified themselves as "not at all observant."

Examination of tables 3.11 and 3.12 together, however, tells us more; two additional points are revealed. First, note that the proportion of "observant" American olim is consistently higher than the proportion of "Orthodox" Americans, in the works of Goldscheider, Berman, and myself. The American classification of "Orthodox" is, thus, not strictly synonymous or congruent with the Israeli classification "observant" (*dati*). The direction of noncongruence—the higher proportion of observant over Orthodox Americans—is to be explained, I suggest, primarily by reference to Conservative American olim. An oleh affiliated with the Orthodox movement in the U.S. moves easily into the category *dati* in Israel. An oleh affiliated with the Reform movement moves—less easily and with some exceptions—into the Israeli categories "not so observant" or "not at all observant." The oleh affiliated in the U.S. with the Conservative movement, however, finds himself to be liminal with reference to the *dati/lo-dati* opposition. In the U.S., followers of the Conservative movement exhibit the widest behavioral range of religious praxis; some blend into Orthodoxy (or Orthopraxis), others into Reform.[4] Once in Israel, it is the Conservative oleh, who leaned towards Orthodoxy in the U.S., who is most likely to intensify his observance of *halakhah* (by wearing a skullcap and maintaining strict observance of the Shabbat, for example), and reclassify himself—along with the Orthodox—as *dati*.

The second point to emerge from examination of tables 3.11 and 3.12 is to be found in Goldscheider's data, which are presented with a generational breakdown. In the Providence, R.I. study, a clear decline is evident in Orthodox affiliation between "all-generation" (19.8 percent affiliated), and the third generation of the 25–44 age group (4.5 percent of whom have Orthodox affiliations). The "all-generations" figure includes, of course, individuals who were not born in the U.S. (i.e., first generation); it is their continued affiliation with Orthodoxy that brings the proportion up to close to a fifth. The same trend is evident—though less sharply—for American olim who arrived in 1969–70 (table 3.11). If all the generations are counted, 37 percent of these olim are Orthodox, while 28 percent of third-generation olim are so affiliated. Moving to table 3.12, however, we find that with the classification "observant" (*dati*), etc., the age/generational trend all but disappears: when all generations are counted, 46 percent of these American olim classify themselves "observant," while fully 43 percent of all third-generation olim identify themselves in the same manner. It seems, therefore, that for those Americans who make aliya it is the case that affiliation with the Orthodox movement decreases with succeeding generations—a situation strongly characteristic of American Jewry in general—but it is *not* the case that self-identification as a religiously observant Jew suffers the same generational decline.

A very similar situation exists for the next demographic factor, the oleh's involvement with Zionist organizations in the United States. In one view, as has been discussed, personal aliya is conceived to be the highest expression of an individual's commitment to Zionism. As data from various sources, summarized in table 3.13 indicate, however, anywhere from 40 to 65 percent of all American olim were not members of any Zionist organization in the United States. If one leaves aside my own Jerusalem data, and compares Engel's pre-1967 data to Goldscheider's post-1967 generational breakdown and to other sources, it appears that

Table 3.13   Zionist Activism and Organizational Affiliation in the U.S.

Source	Active Member (%)	Not So Active Member (%)	Nonmember (%)	Total (%)
American olim, 1969–70 (Gold-scheider 1974:377)				
All generations	39.3	11.4	49.4	100.1
3d generation only	28.3	11.3	60.4	100.1
American olim, 1968–76, resident in Jerusalem (Avruch)	43	18	39	100
American olim, 1967–71 (Jubas 1974:102)*	21	18	61	100
American olim, arrived 1976 (Berman 1977:25)	23	12	65	100
American olim, 1950–66 (Engel 1970:164)**		57	43	100

*In Jubas (1974) I have recalculated percentages based on his frequency distribution to be "adjusted percent," i.e., the percent minus the "no response" category.

**Engel (1970) queried his respondents on their Zionist youth group affiliation only.

membership in Zionist organizations decreased proportionally in the post-1967 era, and decreases proportionally with successive generations. Antonovsky (1968:5) reports a similar decline in Zionist affiliation for Americans arriving in each of three periods prior to 1967 (pre-1948 olim; olim arrived in 1948–56; those arrived in 1956–66).

Jubas summarizes this trend simply: "Zionism, today, attracts fewer young people to its organizations" (1974:103). (Why this is the case is a problem in the sociology of contemporary American Jewry.) In the past, the majority of American olim were styled as coming out of various Zionist organizations and their youth groups (see, for example, Morris 1953); today this seems no longer to be the case. For my purposes, however, it is important to understand that commitment to Zionist ideology can exist quite separate from a concomitant commitment to Zionist organizations. Indeed, in the responses to a different question in his survey, Jubas found 84 percent of his sample to "agree strongly" or to be "sympathetic with" Zionist ideology—compared to the 39 percent of the sample who were actually members of Zionist youth groups (1974:103). In my own interview and survey work, I found commitment to Zionist ideology to be quite strong, regardless of youthful or adult organizational affiliation.

The Zionist ideologies espoused by my own informants or respondents were not, therefore, limited to the party lines of one Zionist organization or another. In a sense, these individuals were "observant" Zionists but not necessarily "Orthodox" Zionists. My use of the religious terms, and the implicit comparison between religiousness and involvement with Zionism, is intended. In the case of religiousness, we saw a generational stability in the category "observant" and an instability in the category "Orthodox." I suggest that there is a similar stability, for these American olim through successive generations, in their espousal of Zionist ideology—however much instability there is in their organizational affiliation. I am also arguing that the Zionist ideology felt and expressed by these post-1967 olim seems to be, as Goldscheider suggests, "much less 'Zionist' in the narrow, formal sense and much more 'religious' in its broadest, sociological meaning" (1974:375). The ramifications of thinking of these post-1967 Zionists as religious individuals is something I shall discuss in some detail in Chapter 5.

Given the relatively high levels of religious observance and Zionist (ideological) involvement, relative to the American Jewish population in general, it ought not surprise us that most of these olim have had some Jewish or Hebrew education in the United States. From his survey of pre-1967 olim, Engel concludes that, "The one characteristic common to most American settlers was Jewish education. Ninety-one per cent had some Jewish schooling in America. . . . The proportion of day-school attendance was much higher for settlers (37 percent) than for all Jewish children in the United States (13 percent)" (1970:165). Jubas, for olim who arrived in 1967–71, found that 84 percent had some Jewish schooling in the U.S., while 24 percent had attended all-day schools (1974:107). Goldscheider's sample of olim who arrived in 1969–70 included 85 percent who had had some Jewish education, of whom a third went to a Hebrew day school (1974:377–78). Berman's survey of 1976 arrivals indicates some 87 percent had some form of Jewish education in America, of whom 21 percent attended a Hebrew or Yiddish day-school (1977:23). The proportion of those receiving Jewish education, and attending day schools, appears to have declined slightly in the post-1967 era. Goldscheider, however, on the basis of a generational breakdown of his data, discounts this trend: "Very little generation change may be noted in the proportion [of olim] . . . with at least six years of exposure to some form of Jewish education" (1974:378). For the olim who arrived in 1969–70, and through all three generations, the proportion with at least six years of Jewish education ranges narrowly between 63 and 66 percent.

Residential Dispersion in Israel

Table 3.14 summarizes data on olim who arrived in 1973, according to selected localities to which they were first referred. Some of the mechanics of referral are to be discussed in the next chapter; for now, several general aspects of Americans' residence in Israel will be presented.

First, more than three-fourths of all American olim move to towns and other urban localities. But this proportion is smaller than that for all olim (84.4 percent), and smaller still than that for the Jewish Israeli population, 90.6 percent of whom lived in urban areas by the end of 1973.[5] The city that attracted the largest proportion of American olim was Jerusalem (19.7 percent), followed by Tel Aviv-Yafo (Jaffa), with 12.7 percent. Jerusalem also received the largest single proportion of all olim in 1973, 7.2 percent. Although the urban population of all olim was proportionally higher than that of North American olim, the latter were concentrated in relatively fewer localities: olim of 1973, in toto, were dispersed more widely than were the North Americans among them.

The reason for the relatively smaller percentage of urban North American—compared to all—olim becomes clear if we look at the proportions of olim settling on kibbutzim. Almost 14 percent of all Americans settle, at least initially, on a kibbutz, compared to little more than 5 percent of all olim and little more than 3 percent of the Jewish Israeli population.[6] Although the percentage of Americans settling on kibbutzim has fallen since the pre-1967 era— some 28 percent of pre-1967 Americans lived on the kibbutz (Antonovsky 1968:4)—it is still the case that American new immigrants comprise a very large kibbutz-dwelling group in Israel.

Table 3.15 presents, under a different format, a longitudinal

Table 3.14   "North American" and All Olim, Arrived 1973, by Selected Locality to Which They Were First Referred

Locality	"North American" Olim Absolute Nos.*	%	All Olim Absolute Nos.	%
Total olim, 1973	5,104	100.0	54,886	100.0
Of total, those settled in towns or urban localities	3,890	76.2	46,300	84.4
Thereof:				
Jerusalem	1,006	19.7	3,979	7.2
Tel Aviv-Yafo	648	12.7	2,711	4.9
Haifa	285	5.6	2,540	4.6
Ashdod	37	0.7	2,399	4.4
Ashkelon	20	0.4	971	1.8
Be'er Sheva	101	2.0	2,130	3.9
Bat Yam	95	1.9	921	1.7
Dimona	3	0.1	1,906	3.5
Hadera	8	0.2	1,287	2.3
Holon	67	1.3	540	1.0
Tiberius	4	0.1	576	1.0
Karmiel	30	0.6	1,248	2.3
Lod	13	0.3	635	1.2
Mevasseret Zion	155	3.0	810	1.5
Nahariyya	14	0.3	1,873	3.4
Nazareth Illit	33	0.6	1,989	3.6
Netanya	305	6.0	2,328	4.2
Akko (Acre)	5	0.1	606	1.1
Afula	1	—	1,095	2.0
Arad	77	1.5	1,105	2.0
Pardes Hanna	72	1.4	1,063	1.9
Petah Tikva	62	1.2	553	1.0
Tzefat (Safed)	8	0.2	736	1.3
Kiryat Bialik	6	0.1	928	1.7
Kiryat Shemona	1	—	548	1.0
Kiryat Yam	35	0.7	892	1.6
Rishon LeZion	27	0.5	506	0.9
Ramat Gan	202	4.0	734	1.3
Kibbutzim: total	711	13.9	2,828	5.2
Other rural localities	159	3.1	1,499	2.7
Not known	344	6.7	4,259	7.8

SOURCE: Adapted from data in *Immigration to Israel, 1973,* special series no. 457 (Jerusalem: Israel Central Bureau of Statistics, 1974), table 22, p. 34.

*The absolute numbers do not sum to total (1973) immigration because "localities" were selected for inclusion in this table by those to which 500 or more persons (for all Olim) were referred. Percentages, however, were computed on the basis of "true totals": for "North Americans" 5,104; for all olim 54,886. On the category "North American" see note, table 3.4

view of American residence patterns. From this table comes a
clue to why American olim are more narrowly dispersed than all
olim. First, three and five years after their aliya, one-fifth to one-
quarter of all Americans continue to live in the Jerusalem District.
This compares with a stable 10 percent of all olim who live in the
district, and with the 10 percent of the Jewish Israeli population
that resides there.[7] Thus, both as new immigrants and, years
later, as Israelis, Americans are proportionally overrepresented
in Jerusalem.

Table 3.15 also indicates that relatively few Americans (5 to 7
precent) live in Israel development towns, compared to all olim
(of whom one-quarter to one-fifth reside in such towns). The difference in urban dispersion discussed above (Americans relatively narrow, all olim relatively wide) surfaces here. The Israeli
government encourages its citizens to settle in these development
towns, in order to disperse the population from the coastal region,
and offers special allowances and dispensations (in taxes,
mortgages, etc.) to those citizens who do settle in one. These
areas, however, are not among the most popular in Israel; to most
Americans, moreover, they lack the *halutzic* ("pioneering") appeal of kibbutz life and, being towns, they lack the romantic
appeal of working the land. Compared to new immigrants in general, the American comes to Israel with a lot of capital, and in
most cases he need not choose his residence solely on the basis of
government subventions. There is less often, for the American,
an economic need behind his decision to move from Tel Aviv or
Jerusalem to a development town. If he does make the move, it
will be because he wants to. Then, too, unlike other new immigrants, the American cannot be placed in a development town,

Table 3.15   Area of Residence, North American and All Olim

| | Olim of 1971–72 3 Years after Aliya | | Olim of 1969—70 5 Years after Aliya | |
| | North Americans (%) | All Olim (%) | North Americans (%) | All Olim (%) |
Area				
Coastal region	75	64	67	70
Jerusalem district	20	10	26	10
Development towns	5	26	7	20
Total	100	100	100	100

SOURCE: Adapted from data in *Annual Report, 1975* (in Hebrew) (Jersualem:
Ministry of Immigrant Absorption 1976), table 3.18, p. 116.

against his will, by a bureaucratic apparatus. For, more so than his co-immigrant from the Soviet Union or from Chile, the American, if he is displeased or dissatisfied, can pack up and leave. Many do.

Emigration from Israel

For a variety of reasons, accurate information on the level of *yerida*, or emigration from Israel, is difficult to come by. Here, more than for any other aspect of the migration process, estimates (which are very often correlated to Israeli political stances of one sort or the other) predominate over detailed survey statistics. For the same ideological calculus that made of aliya a metonym for Zionism—or at least asserted its centrality to the Zionist idea—has made of yerida the symbol for the negation of Zionism. The Hebrew language has a word for mere migration (*hagira*); but it has another, older word for migration to the Land of Israel: aliya. "Aliya" came from the Hebrew root meaning to "ascend," or "go up." The oleh, or "immigrant to Israel," is thus literally "one who has ascended." Those who emigrate from Israel are called *yordim* (sing., *yored*), from the root meaning to "descend," but also to "decline" and to "deteriorate." This is just one indication of the attitudes towards immigration and emigration, if not always towards immigrants and emigrants.

The stigma attached to yerida attaches most often and strongly to native-born Israelis who emigrate rather than to new olim who return, after a short time, to their countries of origin. The estimate for the number of sabras who have taken up permanent residence outside Israel has been put at about 300,000; of this number perhaps two-thirds to three-quarters live in the United States. The "absorption" of these Israeli immigrants into American society, and the relations between them and American Jewish communities in which they settle, constitute issues that are, in essence, complementary to the concerns of the present study. For the analysis of the complex relationship between American Jewry and Israel, even if focused on migration alone, must take account of the existence of a variety of migratory streams.[8]

To return to the yerida of, specifically, new immigrants, research conducted by the Israel Central Bureau of Statistics indicates that the following demographic factors are selective for emigration.

1. Immigrant visa status. The extent of emigration among "potential immigrants" is about four times the extent among "immigrants."

2. Emigration is highest among individuals aged eighteen to twenty-nine.

3. Emigration is higher among single than married individuals.

4. Emigration rates vary inversely with length of residence in Israel (measured, thus far, through the first three years of residence).

5. Emigration is higher among those who attain a high level of education than among those who have primary or secondary educations only (see Israel Central Bureau of Statistics, *Supplement to the Monthly Bulletin of Statistics*, no. 1 [1973]: 125–28).

It will be noted that this demographic profile for emigration corresponds very closely to the profile drawn for American immigrants in the preceding pages. As a glance at table 3.16 shows, a sixth factor may be added to the emigration profile:

6. Emigration is highest among individuals of "Western origin."

If we take those olim surveyed over the greatest time-span (olim who arrived in 1970–71), we see that by the end of their first year in Israel one-fifth had left. Within the next two years, however, only an additional 12 percent emigrated. By the end of three years, close to a third of the 1970–71 arrivals had emigrated from Israel. I take this official estimate of one-third to be conservative: a statement, perhaps, of the lower limits of American yerida. Another estimate, based on Canadians only, puts the proportion of yerida at about 40 percent of the 3,000 to 5,000 Canadian *families* that live in Israel.[9] Many of my informants were firm in their assertion that up to three-fourths of all American olim return eventually to the United States, while the sociologist Leonard Weller quotes a "conservative estimate" of one-half (1974:31).

Nevertheless, one final point about yerida should be made. Of the olim I surveyed, some four-fifths had visited Israel at least once prior to their aliya; of this number well over half had spent at least six months in the country. The migratory stream between America and Israel, for many individuals, has the characteristic of a long-term commuter flow. Young persons spend a summer volunteering on a kibbutz; some study a year in one of the country's universities; many professionals spend a sabbatical year there; others, thinking of eventual aliya, take pilot trips of moderate duration. Any one of these individuals may have lived in Israel under a potential immigrant's visa, or may have identified himself as an *oleh hadash*, a new immigrant, rather than a *tayyar*, a tourist. Because of this, the perception of American yordim may by unduly high: these individuals were, properly speaking, never immigrants to begin with. More intriguing, however, is this fact: about one in every ten olim with whom I spoke had attempted aliya before and had "failed." Here, the pattern was clear: these individuals, on their first aliya attempt, were typically aged under thirty, and they were single. They returned to the United States and worked, saving money, with the goal of trying aliya again. In a few cases, two unsuccessful attempts preceded a third try.[10] Whatever the level of American yerida is, whether a third or much higher, it is clear that the loss to Israel is not quite absolute. People try again. One oleh—himself such a repeater—summed up the situation simply: "Israel gets in your blood like a microbe. People stay infected for a long time."

Summary

Between 1950 and 1975 some 45,000 American Jews immigrated to Israel. There was a significant increase in aliya in the years following 1967.

American aliya is selective by three major demographic factors: age, sex, and marital status. Olim tend to be young, aged under thirty; more women than men make aliya; more single than married persons make aliya. Compared to the American Jewish population, olim have attained a high level of education and are concentrated in professional occupations. Compared to the American Jewish population, more Orthodox-affiliated individuals make aliya and, regardless of affiliation, a plurality of olim consider themselves to be religiously observant. They do so, indeed, in proportions higher than those of the Jewish Israeli population. Olim were not conspicuously active in Zionist organizations in the U.S. (but perhaps more so than the American Jewish average), though most espouse a broadly Zionist ideology. They are

Table 3.16   Emigration from Israel

Last Continent of Residence	Arrived 1972–73*	1971–72		1970–71		
	Duration: 1 yr.	2 yrs.	1 yr.	3 yrs.	2 yrs.	1 yr.
North America	13%	22%	17%	32%	25%	20%
South America	5	12	7	20	17	13
Western Europe	13	19	15	29	26	21
Eastern Europe	3	3	2	5	2	1
USSR	3	3	2	5	(2)**	(1)
Asia-Africa	(3)	9	5	9	8	5

SOURCE: *Supplement to the Monthly Bulletin of Statistics*, no. 12 (Jerusalem: Israel Central Bureau of Statistics, 1975), p. 56.

*The division of calendar years reflects the Jewish lunar calendar that is used in some Israeli census reports. The Jewish calendar year runs from September to August, typically.

**Percentages in parentheses are based on estimates with sampling errors of at least 30 percent.

characterized, compared to the American Jewish population, by a high level of Hebrew or Jewish schooling.

In Israel, American olim are clustered in a narrower range of urban settlements than are either new olim, in toto, or Israelis. Proportionally, Jerusalem attracts the most American olim; proportionally, Americans are overrepresented on the kibbutz (compared to new olim, in toto, and to Israelis).

The official estimate for the level of American yerida, after three years residence in Israel, is one-third. Some proportion of olim, however, have attempted aliya more than once; some 80 percent had visited Israel at least once prior to their aliya.

In sum, in the words of Goldscheider, "olim from the United States clearly do not represent a demographic cross-section of the American Jewish population" (1974:366).

Klita
Institutional Support and the Absorption of Immigrants

The Idea of Absorption

Klita is the Hebrew word for "absorption," and in this context it refers to a broad range of notions having to do with the integration, acculturation, assimilation, and adjustment of new immigrants to Israel. One can speak of social absorption (*klita hevratit*), economic absorption (*klita kalkalit*), linguistic absorption (*klita lashonit*), and so on. Another meaning of klita has to do with "retention," and this meaning is also germane. For the end result of "successful klita" is, in the words of one government official, "An aliya that stays. You cannot separate 'aliya' from 'klita.' You cannot speak of aliya if the olim leave Israel." While social scientists find it useful to differentiate between such concepts as adjustment and acculturation (e.g., Eisenstadt 1954: 12–15), or between subjective adjustment and objective adjustment (e.g., Antonovsky and Katz 1970:77–78), in Israel it is the single idea of absorption, klita, that covers the complex process of—as the official put it—"immigrants becoming Israelis." In this chapter, I use the word in its omnibus, Israeli, sense.

The olim who arrived in Palestine during the first and second waves of aliyot were not absorbed by the already settled, long-resident Jews of Eretz Yisrael. The latter were religiously Orthodox, organized under the Turks under the broad divisions of Ashkenazi and Sephardi, and then by communities or by their following of particular rabbis within communities. There was much antagonism between the pious members of the Old Yishuv and the secular Zionists of the post-1880 era, constituting the New Yishuv. The Zionists, then, absorbed themselves, and each other. Reacting in some measure against the culture and society of the Old Yishuv, they aimed to create, in Palestine, a new conception of Jewish culture and society. The environment in which—and against which—they worked was foreign and hostile; pursuit of their specific goals, however, demanded not merely their adaptation to this environment but their transformation of it. It is their success in these endeavors that determined the character of absorption of future waves of immigrants: by the beginning of the Fourth Aliya, the environment that faced new immigrants was one that had been molded, in large measure, by the olim of the preceding forty years. The character of "successful absorption" had been set by the first new immigrants. The idealized Israeli society into which later new immigrants were expected to be absorbed had been already defined by the time Israel's Declaration of Independence was signed.[1]

With the advent of statehood came the period of mass immigration bringing, in four years, some 700,000 immigrants. Given this scale, it is not surprising that absorption policies demanded a greatly increased bureaucratic apparatus to deal with olim. Increased bureaucratization is the hallmark of post-1948 klita. This bureaucratization took place both within the Israeli government and the extragovernmental Jewish Agency; the latter was directly responsible for transporting the olim to Israel and settling them. These tasks were made more difficult by the relative scarcity of resources available to the fledgling government and the Agency. Nevertheless, while in May 1952 there were 113 ma'abarot ("transition camps") with a population of 250,000, by the end of 1953 some 350 new settlements were established—including 251 moshavim and 96 kibbutzim—with a population of over 20,000 families. By 1954 the development towns of Yeroham, Migdal HaEmek, Kiryat Shemona, and Dimona were in their first stages of growth. By the time the next large influx of North African Jews began (after 1956), direct "ship-to-settlement" absorption was favored. The ma'abarot were largely eliminated within a decade (Zinger 1973:58–62).

Even as the immigration of Jewish refugees, fleeing from "lands of stress," began to abate, Israel turned towards the great reservoir of Diaspora Jewry in the West. Partly the battle for Western immigration was fought in ideological terms; the goal was to make aliya central to a Western conception of Zionism. It was also understood, however, that different approaches to klita would be necessary if Western olim were to be successfully integrated. The problem was not the lack of a bureaucratic apparatus for dealing with immigration and absorption, for this existed. The problem was, as a Ministry of Immigrant Absorption official told me, "The 'orientation' this bureaucracy would take." In a general way, this problem of "orientation" is the subject of the present chapter.

The Jewish Agency

ʼ Historically, both aliya and klita were handled by departments within the Jewish Agency. The Agency was first mentioned in Article Four of the British Mandate for Palestine under the League of Nations. In part, the article read:

> An appropriate Jewish agency shall be recognized as a public body for the purpose of advising and cooperating with the Administration of Palestine . . . to assist and take part in the development of the country. The Zionist Organization . . . shall be recognized as such agency. (Laqueur 1976:35)

In the Mandatory period the Agency pursued relations on three fronts. First, it represented the Jewish National Home to world Jewry. Second, it represented the National Home to the British—both to the colonial apparatus in Palestine and to the Foreign Office in London. Third, as an international organization, it represented its own interests to the intranational *Va'ad Le'umi,* the Executive Jewish Council of the Yishuv.

With independence in 1948 the *Va'ad Le'umi* became the nucleus of the first government of Israel. With the coming of sovereignty, the Agency relinquished many diplomatic, developmental, and governmental functions to the newly established government of Israel. But the division of labor between the extragovernmental Agency and the Israel government did not occur without conflict; the Agency had been too powerful a force to accept its obsolescence in the context of a sovereign nation-state.

The Twenty-Third World Zionist Congress, meeting in 1951, voted to continue the Agency, and ratified its status as an entity one and the same with the World Zionist Organization. In 1952 the Knesset passed the "Law on the Status of the World Zionist Organization-Jewish Agency," which read in part:

> The State of Israel recognizes the World Zionist Organization as the authorized agency which will continue to operate in the State of Israel for the development and settlement of the country, the absorption of immigrants from the diaspora, and the coordination of activities in Israel of Jewish institutions and organizations active in those fields. (Zwergbaum 1973:144)

In 1954 a further covenant was signed by the government and the WZO-JA. This recognized the latter as the representative of world Jewry in relation to immigration, absorption, land settlement, and the channeling of Diaspora Jewry's financial support to Israel. In the area of immigration, the Agency maintained a network of offices outside Israel, arranging transportation, shipment of possessions, medical examinations, and so on. The the area of absorption, the Agency ran intensive language schools (*ulpanim;* sing. *ulpan*) and vocational training programs, and administered grant and loan funds. For a period of time construction costs of immigrant housing were shared by the government and the Agency. Finally, the Agency supported certain cultural, educational, and, later, religious Israel-oriented programs in the Diaspora.

Conflict continued. Even with the existence of parliamentary law and other formal agreements operating between the government and the WZO-JA, and even given the existence of ties that bound one to the other—especially shifting personnel—their relationship remained in a state of flux. With respect to each other, both labored under certain advantages and disabilities. On the face of it, of course, the Israel government had priority. But the government has always needed some nongovernmental agency to represent its aliya interests abroad, especially in the West. A consular section in an Israeli embassy was, simply, not sufficient. In 1950, for example, Ben-Gurion (after some hasty remarks on the responsibilities of Diaspora Jews to Israel) had to make clear to certain influential, and nervous, Jewish organizations in the U.S. that Israel represented its own citizens only, and made no dual loyalty claims on Jewish citizens of other nations. Thus the government needed the extra-governmental WZO-JA—and

American Zionists were able to resist the complete centralization of Zionist authority in Jerusalem. On the other hand, these American Zionists labored under difficulties of their own. Since 1929 the Jewish Agency had included non-Zionists, especially from the U.S., among its executive and membership; the Agency had been thus enlarged to make it more representative of world Jewry as a whole—and to give some of the heavier financial contributors, who considered themselves non-Zionists, a voice in the councils. But the 1952 Knesset law had combined the World Zionist Organization and the Jewish Agency, and for this reason Ben-Gurion was able to attack the Agency on the grounds that the expectation that the WZO would become the major link between Israel and the Diaspora remained unfulfilled, especially in the U.S. where non-Zionist groups maintained control of fund-raising and turned a deaf ear to Israel's call for the in-gathering of exiles. In other words, so long as parliamentary law identified the Agency and the World Zionist Organization as one and the same entity, the government could attack the Agency by claiming it was not Zionist enough.

When aliya from the West, and particularly the U.S., did increase after the 1967 war, the government was determined to limit some of the power of the Agency. First, in 1967, three Agency departments—Immigration, Absorption, and Economic—were merged into a single department and combined in a joint government-Agency Authority on Immigration and Absorption. A year later, the government announced plans for establishing a new ministry, the Ministry of Immigrant Absorption, which would assume direct responsibilities for klita. The Agency would remain responsible for arranging aliya only. With regard to immigration and absorption, then, the basic guideline for separation was to be that the Agency would function abroad, in the service of immigration, and the new Ministry of Immigrant Absorption would function in Israel, in the service of klita.

This division, too, proved illusory. In large part this was because the complex tax laws of the United States demanded that the financial contributions of Americans to Israel be disbursed in Israel by nongovernmental agencies, if they are to enjoy a tax-exempt status. Thus, even in the face of a government ministry, the Agency was able to retain control of ulpanim, immigrant hostels, absorption centers, and some social-welfare programs for new immigrants. Meanwhile, to complicate matters even further, an internal agreement reached in July 1969 separated the World Zionist Organization from the Jewish Agency, stipulating that the Agency would undertake "practical" work in Israel—development, immigrant welfare, etc.—while the WZO would undertake "ideological" tasks in the Diaspora—educational and organizational work.

In short, by 1970 the situation looked like this: with respect to the government, the Agency was responsible for promoting aliya, and based itself in the Diaspora. Government handled klita, in Israel. But, with respect to the World Zionist Organization, the Agency was responsible for "practical"—i.e., absorption—work, and it was based in Israel!

If this state of affairs appears confusing, it was often no less so for officials involved in one organization or the other. I asked D., an executive of the Jewish Agency in Jerusalem, to explain the difference between the Jewish Agency and the World Zionist Organization, adding that it appeared that many staff members held positions in both organizations. I had asked this question of other staff, and had received as replies: "I don't know"; "It's very complicated"; "There is no difference." D. explained that the difference was understandable only in terms of tax and foreign policy considerations. The U.S. and some other governments contribute—and allow contributions of—money to the Agency under a tax-exempt status. But in the eyes of the U.S. government the "official charter" of the Jewish Agency is to help Jewish refugees from "lands of oppression" only: to get them to Israel and help absorb them. The Agency is not supposed to work in the U.S. on aliya. Thus, the official arm in the U.S. for aliya is the World Zionist Organization. Now the WZO also gets money from private individuals (though not from the U.S. government), but these monies are not tax-exempt.

The difficulties created by this situation were exemplified by D. with the story of a full-page ad that was placed in the English-language *Jerusalem Post* welcoming a British group for two weeks of aliya seminars in Israel. The ad was signed with the name of a director of the Jewish Agency, on the assumption it would not be seen outside of Israel. D. said that, at this point, "Everything hit the fan." The ad ought to have been signed by one of the directors of the World Zionist Organization even

though the same person also held a similar title in the Jewish
Agency. Apparently, the British government has a similar tax
arrangement with the WZO-JA as the American, and because
the *Jerusalem Post* is distributed and widely read abroad, the
notice of welcome to a group of British subjects on an
aliya-related subject (their *own* aliya, that is) ought to have been
a WZO notice of welcome, not a Jewish Agency notice of welcome! The official responsible for placing the notice had assumed
incorrectly that it was for "internal," Israeli, consumption only.
D. added: "What's the difference? Outside of Israel it's the WZO
and not the Jewish Agency."

On one level—not that of tax laws—the intricate, and sometimes tangled, division of labors among the Jewish Agency, the
WZO, and the Ministry of Immigrant Absorption reflects the
complex, and sometimes tangled, relations between Diaspora
Jewry, Zionism, and the State of Israel. For the individual immigrant or his family, however, the division of labor has other, more
concrete ramifications. For one, it means that responsibility for
his klita falls on several different organizations, each representing
somewhat different interests and each, as well, buttressed by its
own bureaucratic structure. Whatever else may be involved in
absorption to Israel, a confrontation with its bureaucracy is in-
escapable.

"Making Aliya": Institutional Support and Apparatus

In North America, there were in 1977 eighteen offices of the
Israel Aliya Center (affiliated with the World Zionist Organization). The majority are concentrated on the East Coast, including
four in New York City (of which one is the main office and one is
devoted entirely to kibbutz-bound aliya). There are centers in
New Jersey, Boston, Chicago, Houston, Los Angeles, San Fran-
cisco, Cleveland, Miami, Michigan, Philadelphia, and Washington, D.C. Three centers are in Canada (Vancouver, Toronto, and
Montreal). The placement of aliya centers runs roughly parallel to
that of Israeli consulate-general offices. These centers perform
two related functions. One is to inform American Jewish com-

munities in a general way about aliya and life in Israel: to provide speakers and material to Jewish groups, *hugei-aliyot* ("aliya circles"), and so on. The second is to provide information, counselling, and facilitative support to specific individuals who plan to make aliya. This function is served by the *shaliah* ("emissary"; pl. *shlihim*).

The institution of *shlihut* ("emissary mission") dates to the patriarchate following the destruction of the Second Temple (70 C.E.), and there is mention of the practice in the Talmud. These emissaries travelled abroad soliciting funds from Jewish communities in the Diaspora. In the earliest days, typically, one shaliah went abroad on behalf of a specific town in Eretz Yisrael, e.g., Jerusalem, Hebron, or Safed. After the seventeenth century it was customary to send two, one Ashkenazi and one Sephardi. Certain families of Eretz Yisrael were known for providing generations of shlihim (see David 1972:1358–68).

Given the conditions of travel and the times, a shaliah, usually abroad for two years, had to be many things: a professional fundraiser, an adventurer, and, not the least, an appropriate representative of the Holy Land. He carried a variety of authorizing documents, from a formal, general letter of authorization and introduction (*iggeret k'lalit*), to the contract setting forth the arrangement between himself and his principals—salary and expenses deductible (from a fourth to a third of all monies collected)—to the *pinkas ha-shlihut*, the "account book of the mission." Usually he was treated very well in the communities he visited, as it was considered a great *mitzvah* to support fellow Jews in Eretz Yisrael. If he was treated poorly—and if he had the authority of great rabbis or *dayyanim* ("judges") behind him—he had powers of *herem* ("excommunication") at his disposal.

In 1976 there were about thirty shlihim in North America concerned specifically with aliya.[2] They were employees of the World Zionist Organization (Jewish Agency); none had powers to invoke *herem*. Although, each year, there are some number of tourists to Israel who change their status to immigrant in that country, and some who immigrate without any previous contacts, the great majority of olim have contacted, at least once, an Israel Aliya Center and a shaliah for information or guidance.[3] Contact with a shaliah is required if one wishes to take advantage of the loans and subsidies that are available to new immigrants. These loans cover the costs of transportation and the shipment of possessions. The shaliah also arranges accommodations in absorption centers, hostels, or ulpanim.

As with most aspects of aliya, the shlihut system has had its share of political and ideological controversy. Many olim complained that the position—with its two years abroad—is given as reward for faithful service to one political party or another, without regard to the qualifications of the individual. Others complain that certain American Jewish organizations are denied shlihim if—in the words of one—they "incur the wrath of the Jewish Agency Executive."[4] Meanwhile, the Agency is itself under pressure to send shlihim who will represent every shade of Zionist ideology in Israel; in December, 1977, for example, it was announced that two shlihim representing the religious, right-wing Gush Emunim movement would travel under Agency auspices for a brief mission in the United States.[5]

Most of my informants had strong feelings about "their shaliah," and in many cases the feelings were negative. Shlihim were charged with misinforming, with outright lying, with being indifferent or even hostile to aliya. A long-resident oleh, however, had this to say about these kinds of complaints:

Many of these complaints are justified, but they must be put in perspective. These olim need to vent their frustration somewhere, and since the system is so amorphous they pick the person who had initial importance in aliya, the shaliah.

Shlihim, of course, have their own complaints. One, recently returned from two years in the U.S., told me: "Aliya is still a frightening word to most American Jews. Sometimes I spoke to groups and felt afterwards that the mothers in the audience thought I had come to America to steal their children." Another said:

People complain of our "qualifications," but think about it: We must be immigration officers, social workers, psychological counselors, orators, financial advisers and, on top of everything else, seers: judges of who we think will make it in Israel, and who won't.

Sometimes, it is true, I tried to dissuade someone from coming, but then I thought—and I am not *dati* ["observant"]—"It is a sin to discourage a Jew from coming to Eretz Yisrael!" In the end, anyone who really wanted to come could convince me to fill out the appropriate forms.

Another former shaliah provided this insight:

What happens to the shaliah, in his post, is really very similar to what happens to the oleh. In my first post many years ago, in England, I felt like I was going out on a glorious mission. I lasted two weeks before I quit—and I felt terribly ashamed of quitting, just as many olim feel terribly ashamed if they leave Israel.

So I went out again. My hopes were a little less high, so my disappointments were a little less strong. But I was plenty disappointed. There is a parallel with the oleh: he must deal with Israeli bureaucracy; I had to deal with the indifference of the American Jewish establishment, and of most American Jews, to aliya. . . .

How does Israel attract American Jews? How to induce immigration from a country of wealth to one of less wealth? From a Western country to a country of Middle Eastern culture? From a modern, democratic regime to Israel—a Polish country with Turkish laws? Obviously, the shaliah must be more than an immigration officer, sitting in his office with annual reports and questionnaires. He must reach out to the communities. I remember, after I'd been in America several years, writing a friend in Tel Aviv to tell him that I was "spreading the *gospel*" in the U.S. He wrote back that I was tired—culture shock, you know—and that I should come home.

In July, 1976, the Jewish Agency and WZO announced that all future shlihim would be chosen by public tender (to eliminate charges of political favoritism) and that all candidates would undergo "ten hours of psycho-technical tests" and a period of specialized training before setting out on their mission (to eliminate the "qualifications" criticism). In the meantime, other Jewish organizations have established their own shlihut, some under Agency auspices and some not. The American and Canadian immigrants' association, the AACI, has sent selected members on brief, two-month missions to North America. The official arm of Conservative Judaism, the United Synagogue of America, has an "aliya desk" in New York and an "absorption affairs office" in Jerusalem. Rabbi Meir Kahane's Jewish Defense League ran an aliya organization called *Tsuva* ("Return"), and so on. While the official Agency system of shlihut continues under attack and remains the object of criticism, it is probable that the shaliah, in some form, will continue to be the first contact the future immigrant makes with the bureaucracy of Israel.

Final Arrangements: Institutional Support and Apparatus

In the U.S., the potential immigrant meets with a shaliah.[6] The shaliah compiles a dossier on the immigrant's background: education, technical skills, motivation for aliya. On the basis of this information, the shaliah counsels the potential immigrant on aspects of klita, such as job opportunities within his field, necessities for retraining, instruction in Hebrew, and so on. In some cases the shaliah may discourge aliya, but it is unclear if there exists a uniform set of criteria that is applied by all shlihim. From my interviews it appeared that potential olim above the age of forty, or with children already in high school, were more likely to encounter discouragement than others; this does not apply, however, to olim sixty or older who go to Israel to retire on pensions, savings, or social security benefits. There seemed to be some differential encouragement according to profession—a lawyer might encounter less encouragement than a physician—but I have no evidence that professional criteria were applied uniformly by all shlihim. It does appear that in some aliya centers (in New York City, for example) Orthodox and non-Orthodox olim are routinely handled by different shlihim.

The shaliah, however much discouragement he offers, cannot prevent an individual from making aliya. Under the Law of Return, the final decision on matters of citizenship or status rests with the Ministry of Interior or, under appellate conditions, with the Israel Supreme Court. The shaliah may block, however, the granting of Jewish Agency loans and subventions for a new immigrant, and this in turn may effectively dissuade an individual from immigration. On the other hand, I encountered several persons who, in the face of this kind of discouragement, entered Israel as tourists and changed their status to immigrant through the Ministries of Interior and of Immigrant Absorption. At that point they were eligible for government loans and subventions.

More commonly, however, the potential immigrant does not encounter this degree of discouragement. As the remarks by shlihim cited above indicate, many view their "mission"—at least initially—in very idealistic terms; they are reluctant to block the aliya of an individual by invoking bureaucratic measures, even though they may not encourage it. When the shaliah feels comfortable with the individual's decision to make aliya, he forwards the dossier to the American Desk of the Aliya Department, Jewish Agency, in Jerusalem.[7] The desk sends out feelers on the immigrant's behalf, especially towards permanent housing and employment. The desk arranges for temporary accommodations and Hebrew instruction, for example, in an absorption center, residential ulpan, or hostel. In some cases, schooling for the immigrant's children is arranged by the desk.

The potential immigrant then reviews the desk's arrangements and suggestions with his shaliah. In the area of employment, rarely is anything finalized in this manner: Israeli firms usually respond: "We'll hire on condition of interview." For this reason, an alternative exists in the "Pilot Trip" (*Tour V'Aleh*). The potential immigrant comes to Israel on a partly or mostly subsidized (by the Agency) trip. He is not a tourist. He has a schedule of appointments and interviews with firms in Israel, and the conditions of the subsidy demand he keep them. Sometimes more concrete arrangements for employment are effected in this manner. If the oleh knows he will be working in Haifa, for example, he can arrange with his shaliah temporary accommodations in that city.

Finally, a date is set; loans are secured for personal and baggage transportation ("lifts"); a place in an absorption center or hostel is reserved.[8] The act of aliya is done. In Israel—if it did not already begin in the oleh's dealings with his shaliah and the Jewish Agency bureaucracy—klita commences.

The First Stages of Absorption: Institutional Support and Apparatus

There are a variety of settings, most of them including temporary accommodation, for the initial absorption of new immigrants. Referral to particular settings depends upon, among other things, the age, marital status, and professional-educational attainments of the immigrant. In Jewish Agency parlance, the main division lies between "direct" and "indirect" absorption. Behind this distinction lie certain bureaucratic assumptions about language-learning (Hebrew) and competency requirements.

In brief, "direct absorption" is favored for the nonprofessional" (in U.S., "blue-collar") immigrant; "indirect absorption" for the "professional." In practice, any individual with a bachelor's degree is considered professional. All the settings under the heading of indirect absorption exist to teach the new immigrant Hebrew. They are all "transition frameworks" built around intensive, daily language-instruction. It is assumed that the nonprofessional immigrant can work and learn Hebrew on the side, that is, from co-workers or in ulpanit (less intensive night schools, often run by municipalities).[9] After his aliya, the nonprofessional immigrant is handled directly by the Ministry of Immigrant Absorption, not by the Jewish Agency. He is directed to permanent housing immediately, generally in a development town where there is—more or less—guaranteed employment. Through the Labor Exchange, employment is found, and his absorption is expected to take place on the job and in his community. The theory is that a nonprofessional does not need immediate language competency to operate, for example, a lathe or press. It should be noted, however, that the nonprofessional is eligible for all the rights—loans, mortgages, and subventions—that the new professional immigrant is.

The resources of indirect absorption, then, are not considered rights but necessities. They exist to teach Hebrew to immigrants who need the language immediately, for employment. The most widespread such resource, or setting, is the "absorption center" (merkaz klita), developed following the 1967 war to accommodate increased aliya from the West. Each center is open to immigrants with professional status and is reserved usually for families with children. Occasionally couples without children, or even single individuals aged over thirty, are admitted, although technically the "immigrant hostel" (*ma'on*) is reserved for these categories. Another difference is that one is charged nominal rent in the ma'on (therefore, the assumption is, an individual with employment is directed there), while in the merkaz klita rent is deferred or waived (see n.8).

Both absorption center and hostel are semiclosed immigrant communities. Flats with kitchens are usually provided; half-day language classes are held on the premises, and child-care is provided during Hebrew instruction (typically from 8 A.M. to 1 P.M.). Older children are encouraged, however, to attend local schools immediately and transportation to them often is arranged. Some centers offer language instruction with emphases in particular professions; there is, for example, a center in Dimona established for immigrant engineers, with language instruction that stresses technical Hebrew. There is another center especially for physicians and health specialists. Technically, one is allowed a tenure of five months in a center (a year in a hostel) but, according to one official, "There are housing and construction problems in Israel which allow the Jewish Agency to turn a blind eye to people who remain in a merkaz klita for a year or more."

There are a handful of residential ulpanim, located in cities, and intended for younger, single olim. Accommodations are of a dormitory type, with a common dining room. Tenure is five months and it is, typically, more strictly enforced than in a center or hostel. A fee covering room, board, and language instruction is charged. Classes meet six days a week for five hours a day; the total fee in 1976 at Ulpan Etzion, in Jerusalem, was 600 IL (approximately $75).

More numerous are kibbutz ulpanim, also intended for young (allowable ages between seventeen and a half and thirty-five) and usually single immigrants. No fee is charged. Students are lodged two to four to a room and eat in the kibbutz dining hall. They devote half the day to language study and the other half to labor on the kibbutz. The course is six months long. The kibbutz is subsidized by the student labor and by the Jewish Agency on a per capita student basis.

In the case of indirect absorption, then, the Jewish Agency plays a large role. In the residential ulpanim the Agency shares responsibility with the Ministry of Education; in absorption centers with the Ministry of Immigrant Absorption. In both centers and hostels there are, ideally, representatives of older, pertinent ministries (Labor, Health, Education, etc.). Most are staffed with social workers, and an education director responsible for coordinating cultural and historical programs. Occasionally specialists are called in: "In the case of Soviet immigrants we have bankers who hold seminars on banking—on what is a 'check' and how to write one." This same official added, ruefully: "Obviously we don't need to teach the American immigrants that. They want to know why it is they can't use their MasterCharge cards here. They end up lecturing the bankers on what is 'revolving credit'!" In some sense this wry observation on Americans summarizes much of what I shall have to say in Chapter 7; for now it can serve to point up one simple fact. The centers, even as they are semiclosed immigrant communities, are by no means culturally homogeneous communities. At times over seventeen nationalities may be represented in one center or hostel. In this way they provide the immigrant, if indirectly, one salient measure of klita to Israeli society.

Table 4.1 summarizes data on these settings of indirect absorption. Note that the category "hostel" is divided into four types. The total occupancy in all settings (excluding kibbutz ulpanim), as of February 1, 1976, was 9,416 persons. This was characterized as, "almost to capacity."

According to table 3.10, over 60 percent of all North American olim are professionals. On this basis the common framework of initial klita is one of indirect absorption. In practice, many olim without a bachelor's degree are reserved places in absorption

Table 4.1   Number and Occupancy of Absorption Centers, Hostels, and Ulpanim, as of February 1, 1976

Type	No.	Occupancy
Absorption centers	26	3,726
"Regular hostels"	24	2,935
Student hostels	9	1,411
Hostels for aged	17	981
Singles' hostels	3	127
Residential ulpanim	4	236
Total occupancy & number	83	9,416

SOURCE: *Monthly Report* (Jerusalem: The Jewish Agency, January 1976), p. 3, and interview data.

centers, especially if children are involved. The shaliah's recommendations in this matter are almost always followed; moreover, anyone can appeal for a place in a center or hostel, and each case is then considered individually.

The consensus of most of the officials from the Agency and the Ministry of Immigrant Absorption with whom I spoke was that these centers, as language-teaching institutes, did their job. Olim, as well, had praise for the "ulpan" aspects of the centers. But several officials complained that, "Although these centers were designed to teach Hebrew and to cushion the first shocks of Israel, sometimes olim set up a semipermanent life within the merkaz klita, and are reluctant to leave it for the real world." Some, on the other hand, had an opposite complaint: "Many Americans are not used to living in a community as varied or intense as a merkaz klita. They leave too soon, just to get out. They don't finish the language course, and this is their biggest mistake: it will go on to haunt them." One official of the Ministry of Immigrant Absorption, himself an immigrant from the U.S. in 1960, sketched with some sympathy the first few months of indirect absorption:

Most olim who land in Israel have made some arrangements. They have documents from their shaliah, and he has reserved them a place in a merkaz klita. But although close to 80 percent of all olim from North America have been to Israel previously, the average oleh does not know where his absorption center is. To him it is just a place on the map. Usually he is brought there in the middle of the night. The next morning, immediately, he has many things to attend to: language proficiency testing, and registration for the ulpan; arranging schooling for his children. Increasingly, there are facilities for registering his children at the ulpan itself; if there aren't, he must go into town, speaking little or no Hebrew. This is a problem. In this area, also, parents must decide to which trend of schooling they want their children to go—*dati* ["religious"] or *lo-dati* ["nonreligious"; the state supports both trends]. If they are unsure, there is usually no one to help them decide or, worse, they are "helped" with propaganda for or against one trend.

After a month or so, the woman has adjusted somewhat to the problem of housework, shopping, and so on. Within two or three months the man begins to worry seriously about employment. He writes to the contacts his shaliah suggested. No one answers him. He registers with the Ministry of Labor at the

center or in town. No one responds. At the same time, there is
continuing anxiety over permanent housing—but without a firm
idea of where he will work, how can he decide where he will
live? As anxiety over employment mounts, the average oleh
begins to take days off from the ulpan to track down jobs all
over the country. This is very bad, because the primary job of
the oleh in this period is to learn Hebrew. His anxiety over
housing and employment interferes with this. Even if he finds a
job, there are sometimes problems: the job is in Tel Aviv and
his merkaz klita is in BeerSheva.

   Finally—let us say he finds a job and housing and leaves the
center. Now, I would say, his problems begin.

In the area of housing the new immigrant has two basic
choices—whether to buy on the public or the private market.
(Rental housing is scarce and relatively expensive in Israel: a
perennial problem.) Demands for public housing on the part of
immigrants of the 1950s and 1960s have decreased its availability
to new immigrants. In addition, the average four-room flat in
public housing ranges in size from 72 square meters (in Jerusalem
and the main centers) to 84 square meters (in development areas);
such flats are intended for families of from six to eight persons.
Because of the flats' small size—and also because of such factors
as the attractiveness of the neighborhoods and the quality of the
local schools—many Americans reject public housing and look to
the private market. As new immigrants they are entitled to special mortgages; the size of the mortgage, however, is inversely
related to the total cost of the apartment, in order to avoid government subsidies of "luxury apartments" for new immigrants at
the expense of housing for sabras or veteran settlers.[10]

One final aspect of the institutional apparatus for the absorption
of immigrants should be noted here. In the past, it was the policy
of the Jewish Agency, and later of the Ministry of Immigrant
Absorption, to encourage the dispersion of new immigrants into
communities of different and varying "ethnic" composition. This
was motivated by a fear of ghettoizing immigrants of similar
backgrounds, and by the belief that such dispersion aided immigrants' integration into the mainstream of Israeli society. It is now
felt that this approach has failed, "making for yordim rather than
integrated olim," in the words of one Agency bureaucrat. At
present, therefore, there is a new interest in "group aliya" and

settlement in urban areas, comparable to the *garinim* ("nuclei") that in the past established and settled kibbutzim and moshavim. There is one such settlement in the coastal city of Ashdod, composed of French-speakers, and there were plans for another settlement of English-speakers at Gilo, a suburb of Jerusalem. The scope of the Gilo settlement was greatly reduced, however, because of conflicts between the World Zionist Organization, which represented the interests of olim, and the Ministry of Housing, which sought to represent the interests of all Israelis in a period of acute housing shortage. The future of the urban group-settlement scheme is therefore in doubt; the fate of the Gilo project illustrates well the tensions between the government and the Jewish Agency-WZO discussed earlier.

The American Immigrants' Association

The existence of immigrants' associations, or *landsmann-schaft*, as part of the phenomenon of migration has been well documented (see, for an anthropological view, Fallers 1968). They were an important part of the Jewish immigrant's early experience in America, tending, however, to decline in importance in the second and third immigrant generations. In Israel—at least a decade ago—there were about thirty such associations, showing a decline in number from the earliest days of statehood (Isaacs 1966:63). One of the associations that has grown in membership, due to increased migration, is the Association of Americans and Canadians in Israel (AACI).

Established in 1951, the AACI claimed, in 1976, a membership of 11,145, of whom 10 percent were spread among 69 kibbutzim and 22 moshavim. The association views its principal activities as being: (1) the counseling of members; (2) lobbying on behalf of new immigrants to obtain better conditons; (3) encouraging aliya from the U.S. and Canada; and (4) providing for its members' social and cultural activities (cf. P. Katz 1974:231).

The counseling function is illustrated in table 4.2. The greatest number of counseling interviews dealt with loans and mortgages, followed by sessions on housing, employment, and "status" (citizenship queries, visa queries, etc.). Membership in the association is a prerequisite for availing oneself of its counselors.

Table 4.2   AACI Counseling Interviews, Subjects
                  Discussed (1975)

Subject	No. of Interviews
Army	776
Customs	461
Employment	985
Hityashvut (settlement on kibbutz or moshav)	400
Housing	1,229
Loans and mortgages	1,582
Personal counseling	411
Social activity & volunteering	409
Social Security (U.S.)	454
"Status"	985
Total	8,433

SOURCE: *Report to Delegates,* Twenty-Fifth Anniversary Convention, AACI
(BeerSheva: March 23–24, 1976), n.p.

Although there is no way to tell, from table 4.2, how many separate
interviews were held with the same individual, it is probably fair
to say that, given a total number well in excess of 8,000, at least
half of the membership of AACI availed itself of the association's
counselors. The AACI would seem to serve well its counseling
function. Yet, it must be remembered that the membership figure
of 11,145 does not represent the total number of American and
Canadian immigrants in Israel. The association has its critics, and
we should briefly examine some of the bases of their criticism.

First, and most simply, some critics charge that the AACI is
little more than a "social club" that is ineffective in aiding klita or
encouraging aliya. Others question the ultimate good of the
landsmannschaft concept, arguing it creates irrelevant divisions
among Israeli citizens. Many, finally, resent the direction (or intensity) of AACI's lobbying on behalf of American immigrants,
claiming it engenders hostility on the part of other Israelis towards a group they come to see as twice privileged: once, for
having come from "wealthy America" and, second, for enjoying
preferential treatment as new immigrants in such matters as
taxes, customs, housing, subsidized schooling, and so on.

While the AACI see its major goal as aiding *klita hevratit,* the
"social absorption" of the new immigrant, at least one social
scientist adduces evidence that the association fosters "the separation of American immigrants from Israeli society"; that, in her
sample, those "American immigrants who were active in the

AACI were not well acculturated to Israeli society" (P. Katz 1974:241, 238). Katz would maintain that the AACI is not a support for the absorption of immigrants, but rather a hindrance. This is the case because the association leadership constantly stresses American values in an Israeli setting. Harold Isaacs made a similar point in a different way, noting that the Hebrew name of the association is *Hitahdut Olei America Ve-Canada Be-Yisrael,* "The Association of Immigrants from American and Canada in Israel"; in the official English version of the title the reference to "Immigrants" (*olei,* a plural construct form) is eliminated. "In this difference between the name in Hebrew and the name in English," Isaacs writes, "lies the heart of the story of these American Jews . . . the dilemma in which they have placed themselves and the ambivalence in which all but a few of them painfully live" (1966:65).

The dilemma—among others—of expressing American values in the Israeli context is something I shall discuss in greater detail in coming chapters. As to the American landsmannschaft, it is not simply a matter of deciding whether it constitutes support or hindrance in klita. Like the Jewish Agency and the Ministry of Immigrant Absorption, the AACI is established as an organizational presence on the aliya and klita scene. More than occasionally, the association offers critiques of its own, loudly and publicly opposing policies of the other two. The association is an American forum for criticizing aspects of Israeli society. And it is, whatever else, another resource for the oleh. Some olim ignore it, some selectively exploit it, others use it as a crutch. One immigrant, long resident, put the matter in pragmatic terms:

I am no fan of the AACI, and withdrew my membership after my first year in Israel. I don't like the leadership, and the people who are most active in it are not the people I feel most comfortable with. But I resent people saying it hinders absorption, because no one has ever defined what "absorption" to this crazy country really is. Or maybe those of the Second Aliya did, from Minsk. But do you think the German Jews living in Netanya and speaking German for thirty years agree with them? I know there are people who absorb only to the little society of the AACI, and speak English and miss Wheaties. But will their children? No: *they* will be Israelis. So do not criticize the AACI or these people. They are, after all, living in Jerusalem or Savyyon, not Miami Beach.

Klita: Politics, Ideology, Bureaucracy

Klita is the Hebrew word for "absorption," and most Israelis view it as inseparable from aliya: only with "successful klita" can the nation attract "an aliya that stays."

The state is committed to Jewish immigration, and in aid of it has developed an increasingly complex apparatus to insure the integration of new immigrants. It was often the case that this apparatus was fashioned in response to and in times of severe crises, ranging from the underground immigration network set up during World War II (*aliya bet*), to the special problems of absorbing thousands freed from the death camps of Europe, and hundreds of thousands from African and Asian lands. Some of the elements of the apparatus—for example the shaliah system—were old institutions set new tasks. Other elements—the ma'abarot and, later, absorption centers—were newly fashioned for the tasks at hand. Taken as a whole, the apparatus was never merely concerned with the pragmatics of immigrant integration; it was forged according to stringent, if not always consistent, ideological (Zionist) principles. Thus, for example, Hebrew competency was stressed, not only because Hebrew was the language of the land, but because it was the language of the Land of Israel; because revival of the language was seen as a prerequisite for the revival of the people. In the ulpanim, new immigrants were not simply taught Hebrew—as the following recollection of an American indicates:

> I remember my very first day in ulpan, what words they taught us. We learned the difference between "immigrant" and "tourist." Even before we learned to say, "My name is.... What is your name?" we learned to say: "Ani oleh hadash, ani *lo* tayyar" ["I am a new immigrant, I am *not* a tourist"].

Even where Hebrew competency was concerned, the difference was early taught between the competence of a Diaspora Jew in Israel for a brief sojourn over Passover, and the competence of a Hebrew-speaking "new Israeli."

The strong ideological component behind klita was sparked by the first waves of immigrants who, as I noted, absorbed themselves. They came in small, nonfamilial primary groups (*garinim*, etc.), with a strong sense of elitism. "Their aims in migration," writes Eisenstadt, "were not purely adaptive and instrumental—as was the case with most of the Jewish immigrants to overseas countries—but mostly solidary and cultural, i.e., the establishment of a totally new type of communal life" (1954:217). This was in contrast to the later waves of immigration, especially the Oriental ones, following the establishment of the state. The primary group for them was familial; a sense of elitism was absent; often the chief motive for migration was based on "the traditional-Messianic pattern" (Eisenstadt 1954:220). While the first, European-Zionist immigrants absorbed themselves in an environment of minimal bureaucracy, later immigrants were expected to be absorbed in an environment of increasing bureaucratization. Indeed the bureaucratization was designed to produce an absorption apparatus that would insure that klita took place along the lines of the "type of communal life" the first pioneers had envisaged.

In this chapter, I have tried to outline the elements of the absorption apparatus and the kinds of institutional supports available to new immigrants. The emphasis was on the post-1967 period, with reference to American olim. I have tried also to give some idea of the development of the apparatus, with historical reference to the many-faceted conflict between the Jewish Agency-World Zionist Organization and the government of Israel. The conflict between these institutions is concrete and specifiable: it is centered around policies, goals, and programs. But the institutional conflict is also a cipher, symptomatic of larger tensions between Diaspora Zionism and Israeli Zionism; between *Galut* ("exile") and Zion; between, in a sense, the identities "Jew" and "Israeli" (cf. Herman 1970).

The outcome of the tension—at whatever level we wish to apprehend it—is also specifiable and concrete. The ideological components of the absorption apparatus become politicized, that is, they are thrown open for negotiation, used as resources in a public arena of debate and compromise (cf. Bailey 1969, 1973; Swartz 1968). This is what happened, we have seen, with Ben-Gurion's usage of the Zionist principle of *kibbutz galuyot*, the in-gathering of exiles.

With regard, specifically, to klita, the outcome has been not merely a burgeoning bureaucracy but burgeoning *bureaucracies:* one serving the interests of government (the Ministry of Immigrant Absorption), one serving the interests of the extragovernmental Jewish Agency-WZO, and a host of lesser ones serving other interests (the AACI, the Conservative Movement of America, and so on). Supposedly, of course, all the bureaucracies exist only to serve the immigrant. Whether they do so in an efficient manner, given the sometimes intense competition among them, is open to question and doubt.

In October 1976, a long-awaited report on the status of aliya and klita was made public. The so-called Horev Report (named after the chairman of the special commission, Amos Horev, president of Technion) advised the abolition of the Ministry of Immigrant Absorption and of the Aliya and Absorption Department of the Jewish Agency. In their place a "Supreme Council for Aliya Absorption" would be established, headed by the prime minister. But the day-to-day decisions on programs and policies would fall into the hands of the Jewish Agency executive. In practical terms, the loser would be the Ministry of Immigrant Absorption and the government. Responsibility for both aliya and klita would revert almost entirely to the Jewish Agency—as was the case in pre-state days.

To the present, the Horev Report has been the center of deep and bitter controversy. The fate of its recommendations is uncertain. Usually, the debate is centered on such questions as whether the immigrant will benefit (the Agency position) or suffer (the ministry position) if the report's recommendations are implemented. Occasionally, however, the terms of the debate shift, and one sees more clearly the politicization of ideological principles—their use as resources.

Several months before the report was made public, the then-minister of immigrant absorption, Shlomo Rosen, warned his critics "against playing into anti-Zionist hands by implying that immigrant absorption . . . [in Israel] has failed." [11] Mr. Rosen was saying, if effect: Criticize the ministry's apparatus and you criticize the Zionist enterprise upon which the Jewish state is founded; criticize the apparatus and you commit treason. [12] As the terms of the debate are raised (or fall) to this level, it becomes increasingly unclear where, precisely, the needs of the immigrant fit in.

Israel
Tradition and Modernity

5

Ethnic Identity and Aliya

...the patient of today suffers most under the problem of what he should believe in and who he should—or, indeed, might—be or become; while the patient of early psychoanalysis suffered most under inhibitions which prevented him from being what and who he thought he knew he was....

And so it comes about that we begin to conceptualize matters of identity at the very time in history when they become a problem. For we do so in a country which attempts to make a super-identity out of all the identities imported by its constituent immigrants; and we do so at a time when rapidly increasing mechanization threatens these essentially agrarian and patrician identities in their lands of origin as well. The study of identity, then, becomes as strategic in our time as the study of sexuality was in Freud's time.

Erik Erikson, *Childhood and Society*

Aliya and Economics: Aliya as Migration

The Hebrew language, and many who speak it, make the distinction between migration in general (*hagira*) and migration to Israel (*aliya*). Why this is the case—and the place of aliya in Zionist and Israeli history—was discussed in some detail in Part One. But for the social scientist or historian the distinction, at some level, may be reasonably ignored: aliya is an instance of the class "international migration." In this section I want to consider briefly aliya as such an instance; thus we shall see how the movement of American Jews to Israel is similar to, and different from, other instances of migration.

Migration is not a monolithic phenomenon. One of the early typologies of migration, that of Fairchild (1923), distinguished among several types: invasion, conquest, colonization, and immigration. Petersen (1958), among others, offers a cogent critique

85

of this scheme, and a classification of his own. Migration is divided into several classes: primitive, forced, impelled, free, and mass. Each class is distinguished by the migratory force behind it (primitive, for example, by "ecological push"), and each class is associated with a different migration type, characterized according to its conservative or innovative effects.

When not specifically concerned with the elaboration of typologies, however, much of the migration literature accepts a basic division of migratory movements into those involving primarily "pull" factors, and those involving primarily "push" factors (see, e.g., Taft and Robbing 1955). The "push-pull" framework is adapted by Pierre George (1959), who divides contemporary migration into two broad categories: migration caused by "necessity" or "obligation"—usually political or religious in nature—and migration caused by "needs." The needs are economic, for example, the need for particular types of labor in countries of ultimate destination. This need creates a labor market that attracts migrants. The first category is characterized usually by push factors—famine, political perscution, and so on. The second category is characterized by a combination of push from country of origin and a usually more salient pull from the country of destination. I shall consider shortly some of the implications of the push-pull models in studies of American aliya.

Like the class of international migrations of which it is an instance, aliya is not monolithic. In the premodern era it was a movement of predominantly pull factors; individuals were motivated by religious desires to live and die in the Holy Land. Through the Third Aliya the Zionist pioneers were—although pushed from Europe—pulled to Palestine by ideological and nationalistic motivations (and their intentions were innovative and not conservative). Through the Fourth and Fifth Aliyot, as conditions in Europe worsened and national borders throughout the world closed to fleeing Jews, aliya became a movement impelled by pushes: Palestine became a haven for refugees in a migration of mass proportions. This idea of push can be extended to the Jewish immigrants from Arab lands after 1948, if not unequivocally so.[1] But in the case of voluntary immigration from Western countries—"free aliya" in the parlance of the Israeli government and the Jewish Agency—the distinction between push and pull becomes problematic.

Where migration is a voluntary matter, where the decision to migrate is made by individuals in a context of more or less free alternatives, we no longer need consider elaborate typologies that include such movements as pastoral nomadism, flights from disasters, and the mass exodus of entire populations (cf. Shaw 1975:8). The movement that concerns us here—that of American Jews, especially in the post-1967 period—cannot be classified under the headings of nomadic, refugee, or mass migrations; neither is it immediately obvious that American Jews migrate because of religious or political discrimination or persecution. We may assume that the migrants are motivated by needs. We cannot assume, with Pierre George, that these needs are to be adequately described as economic.

In cases of voluntary migration, models utilizing, as independent variables, economic factors of various kinds have predominated. As Helen Safa (1975:1) writes in her introduction to a collection of anthropological studies of migration:

> Migration is normally viewed as an economic phenomenon. Though non-economic factors obviously have some bearing, most studies concur that migrants leave their area of origin primarily because of a lack of employment opportunities and in hopes of finding better opportunities elsewhere.

In voluntary migration, the economist's model of why, and whither, people migrate has proven forceful and attractive. So long as one pays a modicum of attention to certain noneconomic variables—climate, for example—it appears that most migrations of the voluntary type can be accounted for using economic or pecuniary independent variables. Shaw (1975:134) notes that "work related and economic considerations appear to be the major motive in up to 50–60 per cent of the decisions to migrate" within U.S. borders.

In this regard, American aliya contrasts sharply. Jubas's (1974:121ff.) survey of more than a thousand American immigrants who arrived between 1967 and 1971 indicates only 3 percent held that "a better job or position in Israel" was their major reason for immigrating; 4 percent noted general fears of unemployment as a major reason; but only 2 percent related these fears to their own job or profession. The immigrants themselves come to view economic opportunities in Israel wryly; this riddle was asked of me often: "How do you make a small fortune in Israel?" The answer is: "You come with a large one."

Aliya from America is not primarily an economically motivated phenomenon; this is not to say that aliya is unaffected by the general economic situation in the U.S. or by the absorptive capacity of the Israeli economy. Clearly these are relevant factors. First, I suspect economic considerations are selective of Americans who—perhaps thinking about possible aliya—do not migrate. Many olim with whom I spoke shared and reflected this viewpoint:

> Ask anyone—the average individual is not going to leave a home and a job and security for another language, another job, another life, and everything else. It must be somebody who's off his rocker somehow, who's got some loose marbles some place—or, who wants something very badly.

Second, the most commonly given reason for "making yerida," leaving Israel, is the economic: "I was unable to live on an Israeli income"; "I could not make ends meet." Survey data support this view (Engel 1970:178–79; Jubas 1974:196ff.). A third way in which economic factors are relevant is that they appear to influence the selectivity of certain professions among those who do migrate. Goldscheider (1974) notes an increase among olim who are engineers, an increase that coincided with an employment slump for that profession in the U.S. A former shaliah told me he was amazed by the number of New York City schoolteachers who attended recent aliya seminars, arranged by the Jewish Agency, in that city. Many, he said, expressed fear for their jobs or dissatisfaction with teaching in the city's system.

In this sense Israel, to an unemployed New York schoolteacher, may indeed present opportunities, and he might well articulate these in naming his reasons for aliya. But these are also reasons either to leave New York and seek a teaching position elsewhere in the U.S., or to remain in New York and seek employment in a field other than teaching. Indeed, this is how most people—Jew or non-Jew—would perceive and solve this particular problem. As one oleh put it:

> If you want to better your material lot and leave the U.S., everyone knows you'd be better off going to Australia. And if

it's adventure you want, if you're crazy about tackling another language at the age of thirty, then for sure you're best off in Brazil—there's a country that's booming!

In addition, there exists a group of professionals, American rabbis ordained at Reform or Conservative seminaries, who make aliya with the knowledge that in Israel they must abandon most of the rights, privileges, and prestige of their ordination. These individuals are automatically out of work when they come to Israel, and they must seek employment outside the Israeli "Orthodox"-controlled rabbinate. All have given up a source of supplementary income in two areas of rabbinical work, marrying and burying. In Israel they seek employment in related professions (e.g., education), or in new areas entirely. And finally many olim have explained their aliya precisely as a reaction against what they perceive to be America's overinvestment in the values of "money and materialism," especially in relation to their children's "moral development."

In the case of engineers or New York schoolteachers, economic considerations may indeed motivate a decision to migrate—but why to Israel? Such considerations might as well motivate a decision to change professions, while remaining in the U.S. In the case of Reform or Conservative rabbis, aliya is hardly, on the face of it, a way to maximize economic advantage. And finally, those olim who react against money and materialism seem to be striving to maximize other advantages at the expense of the economic.

Not all olim left behind the position or the income of Allan.[2] Accept him as a limiting case; he is speaking about what an economist would perhaps call foregone income or opportunities:

I said I paid a price to live here, and you ask me what the price was. Let me say, my last salary in the States, in Chicago, was way over $100,000 a year. I don't know if you call this "price" or not—that's part of the price. I had a lifetime position, as vice-president, with an international company. I lived in a fourteen-room house with a pool, and with all the conveniences anyone wanted; and I had every year my Cadillac, and a Jaguar, had three automobiles around the house. Everything that anyone could want: money, the pleasures of life. I loved sailing so I had a sailboat. But I loved sailing still more so I bought myself a bigger sailboat. These things—that's part of the price. In fact every time I'm by the sea my heart breaks; I can't afford a boat here; I haven't been sailing since I've been in Israel. That's all part of the price. What I was once able to do for myself, for my family, financially, I can't do today because if you don't have the income you don't spend it. I'm certainly far from being a charity case, but if you don't earn any money you just don't spend it. You live on...on...as good as you know how. (Forty-eight years old; married; four children; first-generation American; aliya 1968)

All of these cases—schoolteachers, engineers, Reform and Conservative rabbis, and Allan—argue for the nonprimacy of pecuniary considerations in motivating a move to Israel (though some argue for a pecuniary primacy *in* Israel). These cases point to something else, for in all of them one question of import becomes not why migrate, why change professions, why forego this income or those opportunities, but why *Israel*? The beginnings of an answer lie in the grumblings of one unhappy oleh, a physician who immigrated in 1968. He was dissatisfied with the Israeli government and its policies at home and abroad; he expressed great dislike of Israelis themselves. He said: "If there was another Jewish state, I'd live there."

Motivations for Aliya

What motivates certain American Jews to migrate to Israel is a question that has received much attention in each of the several surveys on American aliya. In the preceding section I cited some surveys to assert the nonimportance of pecuniary motivations; the lack of importance of such motivations distinguished the American case from others of the voluntary migration type. But the process by which American aliya was distinguished from other cases of migration did not render the ideas of migration theorists useless. George (1959) was correct when he identified a kind of migration caused by needs; he erred in limiting these needs to the economic. Similarly, it is possible to retain the economist's notion of utility—and some of what it implies—if we broaden its definition beyond goods, commodities, and services to include the utility of places. And indeed such a notion has been introduced to the migration literature (Wolpert 1965). Here I would say that Americans move to Israel because it is perceived as the "place of highest utility," Finally, we may still find it useful to ask, with the economist, what it is these olim are trying to maximize. For based upon his perception of increased opportunities, the contemporary Moroccan migrant to France, or Turkish migrant to West Germany, moves to maximize some economic advantage. What was Allan trying to maximize with aliya?

These points should be kept in mind, as in this section, I examine motivations for aliya. I begin with the findings of survey research. Their broad statistical base, as well as their general agreement on the motivation problem, allow me to make certain generalizations about why Americans migrate. But by their nature such surveys often suppress the stories of individuals, and with them a finer sorting of immigrant types. In the last part of this section, turning to my own interview data, I shall attempt to fill in this lacuna. Then I shall consider these findings in light of certain issues in the study of social and ethnic identities.

The extent of agreement among all the survey researchers on the problem of motivation makes it possible to preface their findings with this statement by Jubas (1974:124): "If the motives for coming to Israel of this population were to be summed up in one word it would be unquestionably 'Jewishness'." It remains to be seen what the substance of this "Jewishness" is.

In the period before 1967, most of the reasons American olim gave for their aliya may be classified as "Zionist" reasons. That is they were self-consciously ideological and nationalistic in content, and referred often to "the Jewish People" or "the Jewish homeland." A striking example is the reason, "I made aliya to build the Jewish homeland," which is connected closely to the Zionist principle of *halutziut* ("the pioneering spirit"). Antonovsky (1968:9) found that, of fifteen motives for aliya, this reason ranked highest by percentage of respondents—63 percent called it "very important" in their aliya decision. By the time Jubas conducted his survey of post-1967 olim, however, the attraction of "pioneering spirit" had fallen, by rank-ordered percentages, to seventh place. Only 28 percent of his sample chose it as a "very important" motive for aliya (1974:122). Jubas's ranking of the top seven of fifteen "very important" motives in an aliya decision was as follows: "At home as a Jew in Israel" (51 percent); "A sense of belongingness in Israel" (49); "A sense of purposeful existence" (45); "Israel is a better place for my children to grow up" (43); "Jewish national life in Israel (35); "Jewish cultural life in Israel" (30); "I like the pioneering spirit in Israel" (28). At the bottom of the ranking was the economic motive cited earlier: only 3 percent migrated because of a better job or position in Israel. The religious motivation ("to live a fuller religious life in Israel") ranked ninth: 23 percent of the sample called it a "very important" motive in their decision to make aliya.

While the "nationalist" motive is still a strong one, it is less self-consciously "Zionist" among post- compared to pre-1967 olim. Indeed, we might have expected this in light of the decline in Zionist organizational affiliation (see table 3.13). What is more interesting, however, is to consider what elements of Jewishness replaced the clear statements of Zionist principles that characterized pre-1967 immigrants.

First, there are religious motives. Antonovsky's sample was weak in religious motivation: only 7 percent listed this as their most important reason for aliya. In contrast, 23 percent of Jubas's sample indicated a primary religious motivation. Here we should recall the larger percentage of post-1967 olim who classified themselves as "observant" (see table 3.12).

Second, motives involving clear statements of Zionist principles—like *halutziut*—were superseded in the rankings by much more personalistic motives, having to do with Jewishness: "at home in Israel"; "a sense of belongingness"; " . . . of purposeful existence," and so on. It is not that motives such as these cannot be given a Zionist interpretation. They can, and many olim do give one. Thus, even a recent survey such as Berman's (1977) notes "Zionist identification" to be the most frequently mentioned motive. But the substance of this identification seems to have changed for a significant proportion of olim. Before 1967 this Zionism was ideological—in the sense that different Zionist youth groups served to inculcate variant Zionist ideologies in their members—and it was objective, that is, motives were formulated in such terms as "for the sake of the Jewish people." After 1967, Zionist identification became less organizationally ideological and much more subjective, that is, motives were formulated in such terms as "for my own sake as a Jew" (cf. Antonovsky 1968; Antonovsky and Katz 1969).[3]

We begin to see why it is insufficient simply to label the immigrants "Zionist," and to say they immigrated for "Zionist reasons." Little light is shed here on the problem of motivation; for we see that after 1967 the Zionist idiom is personalized. Shorn, in a sense, of the party lines that characterized the Zionism of many pre-1967 olim (cf. Morris 1953), the new Zionist idiom is freer to express, in a self-conscious manner, Zionism (and aliya) as a personal solution to a personal dilemma. And this is why we see the importance olim attach to such motives as "a sense of belongingness in Israel," a "sense of purposeful existence," and a sense of "at-homeness." We can, finally, put this in a different way: The rhetoric of classical Zionism dealt with "the problem of Jews" or, sometimes, with "the problem of Judaism." The rhetoric of a large proportion of contemporary American immigrants takes its substance, self-consciously, from a different source. It deals with the individual coming to grips with "*my* problem as a Jew."

In addition to factors which pull the immigrant to Israel, several surveys investigated factors which push the immigrant from the U.S. Engel (1967:167ff.) notes that 65 percent of his sample were disturbed by assimilation in the U.S. Jubas (1974:137) presents a finer sorting of push factors, including crime rate (61 percent), racial tensions (60), fears of assimilation (57), the undesirability of the U.S. as a place to raise children (55), drug problems (54), and anti-Semitism (53).[4] Both of these researchers maintain that pull factors to Israel are more salient for olim than are push factors from the U.S.; but by doing so they fail to consider adequately the basic question of the rootedness of these immigrants in American society.[5] What is striking is that the reasons for leaving the U.S. are cast in terms of objective social dilemmas: crime, drugs, racial problems, and so on; while the reasons for going to Israel are cast in terms of subjective personal dilemmas: at-homeness, belongingness, and the like. But here the push-pull dichotomy, in a questionnaire/survey format, obfuscates. For surely the person in Israel who says "I feel at home" or "I have a sense of belongingness" is also telling us something of his feelings of at-homeness or belongingness in the United States.

I am arguing that what is implied in the obverse of the pull-factors to Israel is a critique of American society different from complaints about crime, drugs, and the rest. It is a critique whose dimensions are subjective and personal. Here we see the olim criticizing not American society, objectively, but their perceived places in that society. There is an important difference between the two critiques. The objective says, "I didn't like America because of what it was." The subjective says, "I didn't like America because of what it was and who I was (or who my children would be) in it."

Let us return to the problem of motivation. It is descriptive, but not sufficient, to characterize the motives for aliya in one word—Jewishness, or Zionism. For Jewishness is used by olim to formulate related conceptions about self and about societies: "who I am (was) in America; who I am (will be) in Israel." The surveys are able to tell us that American Jews who become American olim have made a great and intense investment in their Jewishness. Less directly, the surveys tell us something else: these olim are individuals for whom Jewishness goes a long way in answering the question, "Who am I?" Their Jewishness is a central construct of their total social identity. And, these olim are individuals for whom the answer to the question, "Who am I?" gives rise to a more disturbing question, and that is, "Given who I am, can I be that person in America?"[6] Many people today are disturbed about, and critical of, aspects of American society, including crime, drugs, racial tensions, materialism, and so on. Few ask themselves, "Given all that, do I belong in America?"

Jewishness, for the great majority of olim, is the central factor in motivating a decision for aliya; but it is at once a push and a pull. For having defined themselves to be a certain kind of person, these olim then seek a place where that person belongs, feels at home, and has a sense of purposeful existence. One sometimes hears of a society in search of an identity. Here we are presented with identities in search of a society.

If one looks at Jubas's ranking of "very important" pull motives, one sees, in fifth, sixth, and ninth places, below the personalistic and subjective motives discussed earlier, three other motives: Jewish national life in Israel; Jewish cultural life in Israel; and fuller religious life in Israel. Taken together, these motives may be used to designate certain immigrant types. Each type is defined by reference to the primary objective motive given for aliya. The types may be named: nationalist (Zionist), culturalist, and religious.

During interviews, it was fairly easy to pick out the types; most olim stressed one cluster of motives over the others. Nevertheless, it is important not to confuse "types" with "persons." As persons, most olim were some composite of these types. And it is important to recall that behind all the types lay the subjective motivations ("belongingness," etc.) discussed earlier. The point is that people may express their feelings of belongingness, or the lack thereof, with reference to different aspects of their Jewish identity—religious aspects over "cultural" aspects, and so on. But precisely because I am speaking of the kinds of ethnic identifications that, in part, compose an ethnic identity, it would be folly to claim that my typology is exhaustive. The dynamics of identity formation and maintenance defy any typologizing that freezes different identifications in unalterable patterns or relationships. It is not only that, as some social anthropologists claim, identity is "situational" (Barth 1969), and consciously so, but that an identity as complex, or rich, in identifications as Jewishness allows a person many combinations and permutations of differential investments in sets of identifications. It is all well and good to differentiate, on the basis of questionnaire or interview data, the "Zionist" from the "religious" immigrant. But persons are not so monolithic. One can speak to a religious person who, because of his beliefs, is vehemently anti-Zionist. In the next interview, however, one is faced with a religious person who is—just as vehemently—pro-Zionist.

Having made these important caveats, I turn now to my partial typology. Unlike Jubas, but consistent with our earlier discussion, I divide each type into push as well as pull components. The types are illustrated with interview material.

Religiously Observant (Usually "Orthodox" in U.S.)

Pull. The attraction, often, is less to the State of Israel than to the "Land of Israel" (*Eretz Yisrael*). This person migrates to fulfill religious injunctions (*mitzvot*); he interprets these injunctions as demanding his presence in Eretz Yisrael. Because of this, the religious oleh often suffered from a sense of "hypocrisy" in the U.S.: a cognitive and emotional dissonance. In part, this constituted a push.

Push. "Not only," one oleh, Dov, said,

is it easier to live a religious life in Israel than in the States, but if you're a religious Jew you pray every day to God, that he should gather you from the four corners of the earth and bring you back. How can you *pray* that, in the U.S., and not be a hypocrite? Twenty-eight years ago, maybe, Jews had a reason for not going home. But for thousands of years the Jewish people waited. And *you,* in your lifetime, have the privilege of fulfilling that mitzva. I thought about that a lot. I decided I couldn't live with myself—as a religious Jew—if I stayed in America.

Note, here, the progressive decline of distancing that Dov exhibits. That is, what began the excerpt is a statement of "fact": it is easier to live religiously in Israel. Next, the pronoun "you" is used to assert the hypocrisy proposition. Finally, Dov reverts to "I." Here he makes a statement about identity: having defined himself as a certain kind of person, a religious Jew, he could no longer live with himself in America.

Even the initial statement of "fact," however, has its identity substratum. I asked Dov why it was easier to live religiously in Israel. He replied:

In the U.S. I had to compartmentalize my Jewishness, and especially my religiousness. I'm a chemist. Everyone thought of me as a chemist who is Jewish. I thought of myself as a Jew who happens to be a chemist. Here in Israel I *happen* to be a chemist. But in religious terms—all the holidays in America were Christian holidays, like Christmas and Easter. Here all the holidays are Jewish religious holidays. Take Hanukkah. It celebrates our victory over the Hellenists, over their defamation of the Temple. It's *my* holiday. (Forty-two years old; married; two children; second-generation American; aliya 1969)

The issue of compartmentalization of Jewishness in relation to other aspects of identity—e.g., class or occupational identities—is something I shall consider shortly. As a problem, compartmentalization is not limited to religious olim.

Nationalist (Zionist)

Pull. The individual makes aliya with reference to Zionist principles, for example, "to live in Israel, to build there and to be

rebuilt there." It will be noted that this principle subsumes what I
have called objective and subjective motivations. To build Israel
refers to the fashioning of a new Jewish society; to be rebuilt is
reflexive; it refers to the fashioning of a new kind of Jewish person. The Zionist oleh often feels himself to be fulfilling the logical
extension of his Zionism. Implicitly, he accepts the formulation of
Ben-Gurion: a Zionist is one who lives in Israel.

Push. If I have defined an immigrant type pulled by nationalist
motivations, I should be prepared to find these same motivations
designating a push from the U.S. This immigrant leaves the
United States because he is unable to identify with America as a
"national community," and because he needs to invest in some
sort of national identification. The interviews, here, are rich:

> *Naomi:* I never felt any attachment to America. I never felt
> American. I was raised in an Eastern European home; my par-
> ents never did speak English properly and I always felt embar-
> rassed about how they behaved in public because they behaved
> like Eastern Europeans rather than Americans. So I always felt
> alienated, never a part of the American community. I was
> raised in a slum, and the whole American idea of outdoor grills,
> garages with two cars—or even one—were all foreign to me. I
> was never American. My parents could never write a note to
> the teacher. They'd always ask me to write it and they'd sign it;
> and now *I've got the same thing with my son.* I tell him to write
> the note, in Hebrew, and I sign it [laughing]; but I always felt I
> didn't belong over there. (Thirty-five years old; married; two
> children; second-generation American; aliya 1971)

Naomi's last remark, about her son, has implications for belongingness in Israel that I shall consider in coming chapters. For
the present, however, lest one suspect such feelings as these are
limited to American children of European immigrants, here are
some remarks by a fifth-generation American Jew, a Zionist.

> *Scott:* I never heard Yiddish as a child, and not Hebrew until
> my fourth year of college. I became a Zionist through civil
> rights and SDS—or maybe in reaction to them. The blacks told
> whites to "go home," and I thought about that: where is my
> home? SDS was my home for awhile—America, with her in-
> volvement in Vietnam, wasn't. But then SDS and the Left
> started calling Israel "racist" and "imperialist." By that time,

around 1971, "Israel" meant "Jewish" to me, and *I* was
Jewish. So SDS and New-Left America wouldn't be my home,
either. I guess I needed a country a lot. I've been here [in
Israel] four years; just got out of the Army. I think I've found
one. (Twenty-six years old; single; fifth-generation American;
aliya 1972)

As in the religious case, little identification is exhibited with
"American holidays." Said one Zionist:

Christmas, Easter—those are American holidays. I always had
to explain to my kids why we didn't celebrate them, why we
were *different*. But even July Fourth, or Thanksgiving—*my*
ancestors weren't Puritans on the Mayflower; *my* history isn't
in England or even Valley Forge. Here all the holidays are
Jewish national holidays—like Hanukkah; the victory of
Macabbean freedom fighters over the Syrian Greeks.
(Twenty-nine years old; married; two children; second-
generation American; aliya 1970)

In the Hanukkah citations, one can see why it is reasonable to
speak of immigrant types. The religious oleh, Dov, named
Hanukkah to be a victory of Judaism over Hellenism, over the
defamers of the Temple. For the nationalist oleh, Hanukkah
commemorates the victory of the "freedom fighters," on behalf
of the Jewish nation, over another national group, the "Syrian
Greeks." Thus, any two informants (or respondents) who say they
are attracted by the celebration of "Jewish holidays" in Israel,
may mean different things with regard to the same holiday.
    Finally, the following remarks indicate that, while some olim
feel the lack of identification with America as a national community, their identification with Israel is felt to be something more
than one with an Israeli national community:

Yehuda: You ask an American Jew who is completely assimilated, has no sense of his Jewishness—is just-like an American goy—why he is loyal to America, and he'll tell you, like
the goy: "It's my country." Now if you ask an American Jew,
who is aware of his Jewish heritage, that question, he'll answer:
"Because America is free and democratic, and in it Jews can
live in peace." But notice how this is *conditional* loyalty—what
if America stopped treating Jews well? Should he be patriotic?

Now ask me, an American Jew who made aliya, if I'm loyal to
Israel. The answer is yes. Ask me if it's because Israel treats
me well. The answer is no: it has treated me horribly. But you
see, asking me if I'm loyal to Israel is like asking me if I'm loyal
to my family. "Why are you loyal to your family?" It's my
family! You aren't loyal to your family because it's democratic, or because it treats you well; because your family gives
you steak every Thursday night, and if it stopped giving you
steak you'd reconsider your loyalties. No, no way. I'm here
because it's my *family*. (Thirty-nine years old; married; three
children; first-generation American; aliya 1971)

The notion of investment in Israel as an investment in "family" is
one I shall examine shortly.

"Culturalist"

Pull. This individual goes to Israel to live in the "center" of
"world Jewish culture." Very often, the culturalist is one who
defines himself as "not religious" and "not Zionist," but "committed Jewishly."

Joshua: I'm not a Zionist, and I'm antireligious. As a result I
felt the only place for me was Israel. Because here, *here,* you
are Jewish. You don't have to be religious; you don't even have
to be a Zionist! Here we're Jewish and our children are Jewish,
and we're involved in Jewish affairs without putting up a front
of being religious.

Push. But there are push components as well; Joshua continues:

Now, in the states, to be Jewish you had to be in a Jewish
community, and in America the Jewish community is—for us it
was hypocritical because it all centered around the shul
[synagogue]. It all had to be through the shul. Here you don't
need that. We're Jewish, we're part of Jewish culture. And
we're part of the [Israeli, secular] mainstream. Whereas in
America we were part of the extreme—everybody thought we
were tremendously religious, because we sent our kids to learn
Yiddish and were active in Jewish affairs. And when they found
out that we didn't even go to shul on the High Holidays, or we
weren't interested in joining this Conservative shul, they

couldn't understand. "How can you be Jewish?" they asked
us. They assumed we were Orthodox; you *had* to be Orthodox.
In fact, when I grew a little beard, once, they thought I was on
my way to becoming a rabbi! (Forty-three years old; married;
three children; second-generation American; aliya 1969)

The other push components of a cultural sort have to do with
the dissatisfaction so many olim feel with American culture.
Sometimes a critique is formulated in terms of the "conformity"
demanded in America, but most often the target is America's
"materialistic values."

> *Victor:* In the States the constant fighting for the buck—it's
> bad for the kids and it's bad for their parents. I went back for a
> visit last year and saw the kids of my old friends—kids that are
> *my* kids' age. They are suffering, in a way that my son, some-
> where on the Golan tonight, will never suffer. Those kids are
> choking on America's affluence. They have no values. (Thirty-
> seven years old; married; two children; third-generation Amer-
> ican; aliya 1971)

As a separate, categorical type, the culturalist is perhaps the
weakest of the three. Joshua's antireligious and anti-Zionist
iconoclasm notwithstanding, very few culturalists fail also to invest in religious or nationalist identifications; fewer nationalists or
religious lack cultural commitments. The criticism of the values
of American society, similarly, is common to all types.

The culturalist type is weakest in another, noncategorical
sense. For many culturalists, the culture in which they have invested has a Yiddish, Eastern European referent (note that
Joshua had his children learning Yiddish, not Hebrew). This they
share, incidentally, more with the religious than with the
nationalists. Regardless of the omnibus, Tylorean conception of
"Jewish culture" that they maintain, these culturalists are sometimes referred to derisively (by other olim) as proponents of
"culinary Judaism"—the Judaism of "bagels, lox, and
pastrami." The culturalists, nevertheless, share with some of the
religious a derisive stereotype of the "typical young Israeli in
sandals and tight pants." They feel, that is, that Israel has de-
stroyed the "Yiddishkeit" of the Jewish people (cf. Friedmann

1967); they forget, perhaps, that a goodly proportion of world Jewry never learned Yiddish, *di mama loshen* ("the mother tongue"), speaking instead a Judeo-Arabic or Spanish dialect. One immigrant feared for her children's children: "As bad as it would be—and this is what I feared for in America—for them to lose, after two or three generations, their Yiddishkeit . . . I realized it would be just as bad to see my kids turn into Israelis . . . arrogant, uncultured, boorish, Middle Easterners." Another immigrant, a culturalist, explained his difficulties in learning to speak Hebrew:

> I had a lot of trouble with it; I just couldn't learn it. Then I realized I didn't want to: that *language is culture,* and I just didn't like Israeli culture enough to allow me to learn the language. (Thirty-three years old; married; four children; second-generation American; aliya 1972)

For both categorical and noncategorical reasons, the culturalist type is a weak one.

My typology needs, finally, a fourth and truly residual categorical type. For some—but not many—individuals did make aliya for essentially non-Jewish reasons. Their spouses made aliya; or their children; or perhaps, in America, they married a returning Israeli. Some small proportion did make aliya for primarily economic reasons. In other cases a personal trauma, divorce or widowhood for example, made a change of environment desirable. Perhaps these individuals had thought of aliya before; perhaps not. Many were among the proportion of American olim who had never visited Israel before their aliya. Some, undoubtedly, are satisfied in Israel, and remain. The common "wisdom" among persons of the first three types, however, is clear on this point: that these are the olim who never stay. But we have seen that the motivations among religious, nationalist, and culturalist types are not so objective as some olim believe. One immigrant spoke scathingly of those who make aliya for non-Jewish reasons, especially personal ones: "So many people come here to 'find themselves,' the government ought to hand out mirrors." But an hour later, at the interview's conclusion, this same person (of the nationalist type) agonized over the "impossibility" of his returning to America:

How could I return to Los Angeles? What would I do there:
preach Zionism? I was *here,* Charlie. Or tell people to come
after I went back? Or send money to Israel? This is why I have
to stick it out here. Because otherwise I have to rearrange my
whole life and face a completely new world. A world that's
different, a world where my Jewishness is bankrupt. And if that
happens, who am I? (Forty-five years old; married; three children; second-generation American; aliya 1969)

The preceding typology described a range of immigrant types,
with reference to their primary objective motive for aliya. These
motives were religious, nationalist, and culturalist. In the Israeli
environment, however, the terms of the typology are altered;
immigrants sort themselves—as they are sorted by others—into
types defined by a single dimension: religious observance. One is
dati ("observant") or *lo-dati* ("not observant"). Here we see
religious Zionists and religious anti-Zionists; nonreligious Zionists and antireligious Zionists. One is religious or nonreligious,
with varying commitments to other aspects of "Jewish culture"
and with critiques of American culture of varying harshness.

There is another classificatory scheme that may be applied to
olim. It is developmental, that is, it refers to the point in a person's life when a high investment in Jewishness is effected. Undoubtedly, the key factor here is the family: we face a study in
Jewish enculturation and identity formation. At present I am unable to offer an elaborate developmental schema; I want to talk
about Jewishness in terms of, simply, "early" and "late" investments. For my purposes, "early" refers to a period from
childhood through adolescence.[7]

The difference between the two periods of investment emerged
in interviews. On the one hand, many informants spoke of having
been raised in "intensely Jewish" homes—whether religious,
Zionist, or culturalist—where the commitment to Israel was very
strong. Some had grandfathers who had fought, in Palestine, as
part of the Jewish Legion. Many of the religious were aware, from
a young age, of the *mitzva* ("injunction") to settle in Eretz Yisrael. Many of the nationalists had been members of Zionist youth
groups in the U.S. And, as data presented in Chapter 3 indicate,
the level of Jewish education among olim was in general very
high. Early investment can be summed up in the words of one
oleh, a nationalist: "Sometimes I think Zionism is in my genetic
code. As far back as I can remember I wanted to live in Israel."

Some olim, on the other hand, spoke of having been raised in homes where, as one put it, "Jewishness was never an issue. Sure, my father told me Christmas wasn't 'our' holiday, but still we had a tree. We called it our 'Hanukkah bush.'" For these individuals, an intense investment in Jewishness came later. The paths to that investment were varied: many, having decided to give their children some Jewish education, found themselves increasingly involved in synagogue or community affairs. One oleh married a Gentile. His parents, he said,

> were never such great Jews before, but suddenly they asked me if Bonnie would convert. I was really surprised, but I asked her. And she seemed excited by the whole thing. So she began studying with this Conservative rabbi, and so did I. And I became more aware then of what it meant to be Jewish. It was crazy: Bonnie and I became Jews at the same time! (Twenty-seven years old; married; one child; third-generation American; aliya 1973)

The hallmark of "late investors" is a fairly rapid, increasing involvement with Jewishness: an intensification of their Jewish identity. The remarks cited earlier by Scott provide some illustration. His dissatisfaction with aspects of American society was reflected in his involvement with civil rights and campus groups of the Left. As he became alienated from these concerns, he "fell onto" (in his own words) his Jewishness. Later in the same interview Scott elaborated on this:

> The Six-Day War—I was in high school at the time—preceded my involvement in radical causes. In college I forgot all about it, almost that it had ever happened—but it must have made some deep impression on me, because I can remember when these SDS guys first started talking about "imperialist Israel," I told them in detail all about how the war started, how Israel had almost been strangled to death before it, and fought in self-defense. At the time I didn't even know where that attitude, and all that information, had come from!

One often sees very clearly, among late investors, the effects of the Six-Day War. For many, it was the seminal experience in the intensification of their Jewishness. Some spoke of "the apathy" of their Gentile friends in the face of Israel's plight. After 1967, as

I pointed out, aliya from the U.S. rose significantly. The effects of the 1967 war, however, ought not be considered in isolation. It must be remembered that certain events, trends, and movements gave character to American society in the middle sixties and early seventies. These, too, had their effects on aliya. The year 1967 is both a convenient and reasonable marking-off point in a study of aliya from the United States, so long as one remains aware of changes in American society that occurred about the same time. Wars in Israel, per se, do not cause aliya. Aliya from the U.S. showed no significant change, in either volume or demographic character, in the aftermath of the Yom Kippur War (1973). For Scott, then, the personal importance of the Six-Day War arose in the context of his alienation from SDS and the Left.

While the paths to late investment are varied, many of the immigrants spoke of their experiences in the Civil Rights move-ment of the 1960s as "clearing the way" for an investment in Jewishness. In some cases it was the blacks telling them to "go home to your own communities" that marked a "turning point." In other cases, experiences with white fellow-workers made the difference.

> *Ruth:* In the summer of 1965 we were deeply involved in a push for black integration into the fancy North Shore suburbs of Chicago. We were very involved with open housing, and the [white] chairman of the project lived with us for the entire summer. We were very active. And at the end of the summer, we were having a bull session—Christians and Jews who had all worked together very hard that year to break all the real estate clauses against open housing. So at the end we had this bull session. And this fellow who had *lived* with us—I don't know how the conversation got around to this—and with whom we'd been very close, started to talk about America, and how America was founded—oh, yes—"for Christians, by Chris-tians, on Christian principles." And I said: "So wait a minute; where does that put *us?* Are we second-class citizens?" He said: "Well...." And I thought: This guy worked so hard for blacks, this great liberal—excuse me—schmuck. And there he was: *that's* what he really thought about us. We weren't equals—we were *Jews.* And I had been a big champion of integration, and assimilation, and getting along with everyone else. And from *that point on* I said: O.K., Ruth, slow down. And I think it was the following year that we yanked, literally,

the kids out of public school and put them into Hebrew day-school. In this lovely WASP community that we'd moved to *because* it was WASP, *we* had our kids in day-school. This was a very big step for me because it represented to me—before, in negative terms—the very ghettoizing that I'd been trying to escape. (Thirty-seven years old; married; three children; fourth-generation American; aliya 1971)

Experiences such as this—and there were many—should not be glossed simply as experiences of "anti-Semitism." Anti-Semitism, per se, was far from the most salient factor motivating an aliya decision. Rather, those olim who had been active in civil rights or, later, anti–Vietnam War groups, were already manifesting their dissatisfaction with aspects of life in America. Active involvement with civil rights or such groups as SDS were ways to maximize marginality in America, while one remained *American*. When white participation in civil rights was spurned by blacks, and when radicals and intellectuals of the Left made Israel an object of attack, these olim lost an important support: a way to criticize America while remaining American. "Falling onto" their Jewishness, they continued to express their marginality; but it became increasingly difficult to continue being an American.

Their investment in Jewishness, coupled with their dissatisfaction in, and alienation from, American society, cleared the way for a particular search. It was a search for consonance between a conception of identity and one of society. As identity became more compellingly Jewish, American society was seen to be—just as compellingly—an inappropriate (if not quite hostile) environment for that identity. The question was asked: "Given *who* I am, where do I belong?" Increasingly, these persons came to believe that their Jewish identity would find consonance only with a Jewish society. If it could not be found in a "society of Jews" in parts of Chicago, New York, or Los Angeles, it must be sought elsewhere: in a Jewish state serving a Jewish society; in Israel.

It is correct to say that Jewishness is the primary motive in a decision for aliya; but one must say more than this. The immigrant types that I described were defined with reference to their primary motive for aliya: religious, nationalist, and culturalist. But in turn, these motives, and their corresponding types, describe kinds of Jewish identifications that, in part, compose a Jewish identity. While identifications are made with objects, the locus of the resulting identity is subjective: it is bounded by the person. The person does not merely identify with, for example, the Jewish religion but with a conception of a religious Jew. His investment is in *himself* as a religious Jew. It is part of an investment in his Jewishness. With aliya, the person has decided to maximize his Jewishness by immigration to Israel. Thus olim say: "I came to Israel to live a fuller Jewish life," or, "I decided that Israel was the only place where I could live a full Jewish life." They say something else: "I came to Israel to come home"; "I came to belong. . . . " For, as a person, one can live a full life as a Jew, in a Jewish community, in America. But for the oleh it is germane that there is only one *Jewish society,* Israel.

The Intensification of Ethnic Identity

In this study ethnic identity revolves around the notion of Jewishness, whether this is characterized by informants according to religious, nationalist, or culturalist criteria. The olim were individuals who, in America, had invested heavily in this identity; their investment preceded their decision to make aliya. In terms of a life-career, in many cases the investment was high from early on; in other cases there was a dramatic increase in investment. The decision to make aliya represents the individual's decision to maximize this investment. Like Helen Safa, quoted earlier, some anthropologists have presented cases where certain "ethnic phenomena" follow migration. When the primary motive behind migration was economic, the ethnic variables were dependent ones. In American aliya, then, we have a case where the ethnic variable is posited as independent. Among other things, we shall want to see how other variables, including economic ones, change as a function of it.

Designating dependent and independent variables is actually a way of stating the obvious: that the isolation of Jewishness as motive is, properly, the starting point of my inquiry, not the end point. Studies in which it is assumed that Jewishness, as an identity, exists in vacuo are, as Seymour Martin Lipset pointed out, insufficient to the task (1970:141ff). Studies that rely for their definition of Jewishness only on such objective criteria as religious, nationalist, or culturalist identifications are, as I have sought to show, insufficient to the task. For the olim use their Jewishness to constitute an image of personhood and self. Their Jewishness goes a long way in answering the question, "Who am I?" The study of this question—of its "answers"—and others that precede and follow it, is a study of social identity (cf. Gordon 1964:19ff).

My starting point here is to posit two identities that are, obviously, part of the potential immigrant's field: "Jewish" and "American."[8] At the highest level we should want to ask: How are these identities interrelated, and to what extent are these relations problematic? "Most American Jews," writes Antonovsky, "have postulated the absence of conflict between being Jews and being American. Retaining the label Jew, they expand their ethnic identity; they seek to define themselves as 'American Jews'" (1960:428–29). Considered just in terms of these two identities, our olim appear to be individuals who, in America, retained the label Jew but failed to expand their identity to invest in the label American. But more is going on; Jew and American are not the only identities in the field. Recall the remarks of Dov: "I'm a chemist," he said. In America, "everyone thought of me as a chemist who is Jewish. I thought of myself as a Jew who happens to be a chemist."

If we admit into the field something called occupational identity, it becomes apparent that a conception, like Antonovsky's, of identity conflict that occurs on the ethnic level only, is insufficient. One may be "ethnically" an American, although this is arguable. In America, however, one cannot be "ethnically" a chemist. It is clear, then, that what we require is some more holistic conception of identity under which "ethnic identity" may be subsumed, may be seen in a subset relationship. At that point we can discover what it means to invest in the ethnic identity. And for our olim, we can discover what the implications are, for a total identity, in the maximization of their Jewishness. For that holistic conception of total identity I propose to use the term "social identity."

About "social identity" one is tempted to say—like Freud about psychoanalysis in America—that it was accepted without being understood. At the least, the notion often has been used by a variety of social and behavioral scientists without sufficient regard to its specific referents. Partly, I suspect, this is because it enables analysis to move in two different directions. One, beginning with the person, goes outward towards society; the other, beginning with certain problems in the study of society, goes inward towards the person. Traditionally, there have been few concepts that have taken account of both directions; that of "role" has been one of them (cf. Sarbin 1954:223; Spiro 1961:100).

The approach to social identity that moves from society inward follows Linton (1936), Parsons (1951), and Nadel (1957). Social identity is conceived under the rubrics "status" and "roles." The concern is macrosociological, that is, with the functioning of the social system as a whole. Recent work refining this tradition includes Goodenough (1965) and Keesing (1970). Implicitly, the social identity of a person is here conceived as the sum and conjunction of his social statuses, of their coordinate roles, of role-sets (Merton 1957), etc. The best of this work does not present social identity as a static set of traits (cf. Turner 1968:556); but even the best limits this identity to the cultural definitions, within a social system, of social positions (cf. Goodenough 1965:312ff). Much of the work, therefore, is still susceptible to an early critique, by Foote (1951:14), of role theory: that it suffers "from lack of a satisfactory account of motivation."

The second approach to social identity—from person outward—has two different sources. One stems from the work of G. H. Mead (1934), with roots in James (1890) and Cooley (1902). Here, a sense of personal identity, the self, is derived from and originates in social interactions with "significant" others. A person's conception of self, his personal identity, therefore, depends greatly on the evaluation of his presentation of self to and by others. This is a presentation of a social identity. Similarly, the person is able to conceive the personal identities of others only as their social identities. The concerns of this approach have been microsociological, though the notion of roles remains. They have issued in, among other things, symbolic interactionism (Shibutani 1961), and problems of impression formation (Asch 1952), impression management (Goffman 1959), and person perception (Bruner and Tagiuri 1954). Goffman summarizes one advantage of this "social identity" over the one linked too closely to "status," namely, that in considering social identity, "personal attributes such as 'honesty' are involved, as well as structural ones, like 'occupation' " (1963:2).

The second source of the person-outward approach is Freud or, more specifically, those of his students and followers who nurtured the growth of a psychoanalytic ego psychology. They include Hartmann (1939), Anna Freud (1936), and Erikson (1959; 1963). Without even attempting a full description of this rich tradition, I offer this. What began, in Freud, with certain problems of reality testing, secondary processes, and object relations— especially with respect to narcissism, the self as object—would develop into a conceptual freeing of the ego, and a formulation of the social identity as it "develops out of a gradual integration of all identifications" (Erikson 1963:241).

The great advantage of this last approach is that it transcends macro- and microsociological concerns; for at root, applied to sociocultural phenomena, its concerns are motivational. Persons establish identifications with objects because the objects are perceived to satisfy certain *needs*. Needs may be overtly biological ones, such as hunger, or culturally constituted ones, such as power or prestige. In any event, all needs are not economic (cf. George 1959). One can imagine, indeed, a human need to feel "belongingness" in one social system, or society, if the person feels little or none in another. One can even imagine a human need to identify more strongly with certain parts of a social identity than with others.

As a concept, then, social identity points inward, to the person (self or ego),[9] and outward, to society. The conditions of its ontogenesis have been described by Erikson (1968:61):

> The gradual development of a mature psychosocial identity . . . presupposes a community of people whose traditional values become significant to the growing person even as his growth assumes relevance for them. Mere "roles" that can be "played" interchangeably are obviously not sufficient for the social aspect of the equation. Only a hierarchical integration of roles . . . can support identities. Psycho-social identity thus depends on a complementarity of an inner (ego) synthesis in the individual and of role integration in his group.

Erikson's description contains not only a sketch of social identity ontogenesis but also clues for finding some sources of social identity conflict. To take but one source: a hierarchical integration of roles implies that some roles are invested with more salience by self *and* others than are other roles. For example: playing

the role of "father," at home, is to be more important than playing the role of "chemist." If, therefore, a person's hierarchical
profile of roles differs greatly from the consensus of others—if it
is too important to him to play the role of "chemist" everywhere, at all times—one can expect conflict. The conflict cannot
adequately be described as role conflict, for insofar as roles are
hierarchically valued, and the hierarchy is itself internalized by
the person, the conflict affects not only the reciprocal role-play of
self and others but also the ego synthesis of self (and perhaps of
others). This synthesis, as Erikson notes, depends on a kind of
complementarity; if this is lacking, we should expect to find social
identity conflicts (cf. Wallace and Fogelson 1965).

I assume, finally, that some high level of this conflict is painful
for the person. He will attempt to resolve it. He has, at least, two
options. He can restructure his hierarchical profile of roles to
regain (or attain) consensus with his community of others; or he
can retain his hierarchy and seek a community of others
where—he believes—his hierarchy is part of the consensus.

It should be clear that my usage of social identity borrows
shamelessly from all three traditions. First, social identity does
refer to culturally constituted social categories (or statuses) which
have objective attributes. Second, social identity originates and
persists in interactions between self and others. Third, social
identity is internalized; it is interdependent with ego identity
(Erikson sees the latter as "anchored" in the former [1963:279]).
This means, finally, that social-identity conflict, change, and
manipulation have psychodynamic correlates.

It is axiomatic that the salience of particular social categories—or identity clusters—varies cross-culturally. In some
cases categories present in one culture (the "lineage" among the
Nuer) will be absent in another (the "lineage" in contemporary
American culture). In other cases categories may be found to
exist cross-culturally ("men" and "women"), but the meanings
ascribed by actors to the categories will exhibit cultural differences. For contemporary American culture I shall follow, with
some modification, Zavalloni's (1973:82) scheme:

The point of departure will be to consider each individual or
society member as "objectively" located in an identity cluster.
Part of such objective location can be read as an identity card:

it includes sex, age, nationality, profession, family status. If we add religious and political affiliation and social class, we have eight basic groups that characterize *objectively,* even if not *subjectively,* all members of society. The study of social identity is concerned with the subjective counterpart of the identity card, that is to say with the meanings of different identity group memberships, for an individual. (Emphases in original)

I propose two modifications. Of Zavalloni's eight categories I wish to extract two, "nationality" and "religion," and combine them. Following Milton Gordon—who includes, incidentally, "race"—I call this an "ethnic" category (cf. Gordon 1964:27). "Ethnicity"—the substance of the ethnic category—is a less exact specification than "nationality" and "religion"; but that is also its strength: it connotes more. Ethnicity subsumes nationality, religion, and race, and also identity clusters of linguistic and other cultural—or culturalist—dimensions. An individual may identify with two or more nationalities (e.g., Greek *and* American), one of which may be more ethnically valenced than the other. Essentially, "ethnic" is a cover term for a kind of category in contradistinction to other categories, for example, "social class" or "political affiliation." On occasion we may still find it useful to tease out "nationality" and "religion" as components of the ethnic category. For my definition of the "ethnic group" which may—or may not—coalesce out of the ethnic category (cf. Cohen 1974), I follow Glazer (1975:8): such groups "consciously share some aspect of common culture" and are "primarily defined by descent." To this I would add that members' loyalty, and its continuing dramatization, are probably equally determinative of ethnic groups.

My second modification is of a refining nature. Where Zavalloni spoke of the "meanings of different identity group memberships for an individual," I should like to specify "meanings" to indicate the differential investments that individuals make in some identity clusters over others. Such differential investments will determine, to paraphrase Erikson, the nature of the hierarchical profile each person internalizes. I am speaking not only of a hierarchy of roles associated with objective statuses but of the subjective counterparts of the roles—what De Vos meant when, speaking of ethnicity, he wrote: "ethnicity cannot be defined by behavioral criteria alone. Ethnicity is determined by what a person feels about himself, not by how he is observed to behave" (1975:17). I would add: "not *only* by how he is observed to behave."

Without attempting to articulate a full field theory, we can conceive of social identity topologically, consisting of different identity clusters. But a dynamic rendering of social identity demands something more, something expressive of force, valence, or vectors; some way in which certain clusters are made more salient than others; some way in which needs are both generated and satisfied.

Those who have worked with a notion of identity as being composed of "clusters" or "subidentities" have recognized that certain of these culsters are often more heavily invested in than others. Zavalloni (1973:86) refers to such instances as "polarized identities." Daniel Miller (1961:282–83) speaks of certain "dimensions" of identity in terms of their "degree of centrality" in a total identity. Those dimensions that enjoy a high degree of centrality, he writes, "are heavily loaded" in a person's "self-evaluation." And Devereux (1975:65ff)—who is more straightforward in his use of investment than some others—speaks of a person's "hypercathexis" of his ethnic identity.

Devereux conceives of an individual's total identity as consisting of "a whole series of class memberships, a series of class identities, one of which is his ethnic identity." Note that Devereux uses, here, "class" in its logical, and not socioeconomic, sense. Different individuals may share some or many class identities; but a complete enumeration of identities will differentiate one individual from all others. Differentiation is possible in another sense, for individuals may hypercathect certain class identities. Devereux sees grave consequences in such hypercathexis:

> When one of A's class identities becomes hypercathected to the point of severely conflicting with, or else totally subordinating to it, all the rest of A's class identities, singularly dysfunctional manifestations of class identity begin to appear. One conflict can arise when what is deemed to be the principal class identity is actually less effective in certain circumstances than are other class identities. . . .

Turning specifically to ethnic identity, when a hyper-
cathected ethnic identity overrides all other class identities, it
ceases to become a tool and becomes...a straight-jacket.
(1975:65)

I want to return now to the problem at hand, in light of the
foregoing discussion of identities—social, ethnic, and others.

As an ethnic identity, Jewishness does not exist in vacuo. It is
part of a total identity, part of a social identity.

The olim are individuals who, in America, intensified their
Jewishness. Intensification is the result—in Devereux's
terms—of hypercathexis: an increased and increasing investment
in ethnic identity over other identity clusters in a total social
identity. In this scheme, maximizing refers to a movement towards the point at which Jewishness overrides, or subordinates to
it, other clusters.

As this point—of maximization—is reached, it becomes necessary to consider fully the subjective counterparts of hyperinvestment in objective, ethnic-Jewish, attributes (religion,
nationality, culture). I have discussed this at some length. The
subjective counterparts are part and parcel of a self-definition of
personhood and self; they go a long way towards answering the
question, "Who am I?" Answers to this question may be seen to
form a hierarchy. Answers may be coded as identities: "I am a
man; I am a Jew; I am a chemist." Those identities at the top of
the hierarchy are the most heavily loaded—the ones in which a
person's investments are the greatest.

The olim are individuals who, in America, invested very
heavily in their ethnic identity. This identity was near—if not
at—the top of their hierarchy of identities.

The hierarchy is internalized: its presentation and evaluation
by self and others has psychodynamic correlates. Psychodynamic
equilibrium is maintained if, among other things, the presentation
and evaluation of a person's hierarchy of identities finds consensus with others'. If consensus, or complementarity, is lacking,
social identity conflicts ensue. The person will attempt—feels the
need—to resolve them. He may attempt to restructure his hierarchy to attain, or regain, consensus in his existing community of
others; or he may seek instead a community of others where—he
believes—his hierarchy is part of the consensus.[10]

The olim are individuals who, in America, unable or unwilling to restructure hierarchies, make aliya in order to find a new community. They search for consonance, consensus, complementarity. They search for a home and a sense of belongingness. They criticize America—on questionnaires—in objective terms (racial, drug, crime problems, and so on), because to criticize it in subjective terms is to recall the roots, and the pains, of the conflict. Unable or unwilling to think and feel themselves to be "chemists," or whatever, who "happen to be Jewish," they seek a community of others where they can be Jews who happen to be "chemists" (or whatever). They conceive Israel to be that sort of community: they decide it is the only one in the world.

For the remainder of this study I deal, in some way or another, with the implications and consequences of that conception and decision. '

Ethnicity and Tradition

This chapter has been built around the explication of two complementary concerns: what motives do olim—as respondents or informants—give for making aliya, and what motivates them to make aliya? I framed the concerns by a discussion of social and ethnic identities, and of differential investments in identities. Because I was interested in motivation, attention was paid to psychodynamic correlates. In this last part of the chapter, I want to look at the nature of these differential investments from a different perspective. What does it mean to make a hyperinvestment in ethnic, over other, identities? How can we characterize such investments? What are their implications for a structural transformation of social identities? For a beginning, let me return to the question of motives, and a brief look at Jubas's (1974:137) questionnaire data.

In the preceding section I discussed the objective nature of the olim's critique of America—what Jubas coded as "push"—compared to the subjective nature of their attractions to Israel—Jubas's "pull" motives. There I was interested in pointing up the personal and subjective dimensions of the olim's critique of America. Now I want to return to the apparent objective and social dimensions of their critique.

Leaving aside for a moment the more specifically Jewish fears of assimilation (ranked third of thirteen push motives), and anti-Semitism (ranked sixth), the olim's ranking of eight top push factors in a decision to make aliya was as follows: "high crime rate in America; racial tensions; America as an undesirable place to raise children; drug problems; political unrest; against war in Vietnam." In interviews, olim enumerated two other criticisms, of America's overinvestment in "materialism" and "conformity." With regard to this, Engel (1970:166), on the basis of his survey, wrote: "They left [America] . . . because they felt a growing anxiety about being part of a society in which materialism and conformity threatened the realization of their human potential." The fear of assimilation may then be, in fact, a manifestation of the larger concern with conformity.

Engel pinpoints clearly an image of American society common among many olim. The image is that of a society wracked by conflict, anomie, and alienation, even in the face of affluence. As an image, it bears a striking resemblance to the darker pictures sometimes painted of industrial, postindustrial, modern, or modernizing societies. C. E. Black, writing of the "agony of modernization," notes that, "Many regard personal insecurity and anxiety as the hallmarks of the modern age, which can be traced directly to the profound social disintegration that has accompanied modernization" (1967:32). In modern societies, as Riesman et al. (1953:26) point out, the individual is "surplus" and "expendable." In traditional societies, he "belongs." Recall, here, the olim's concerns with belongingness. In large measure, the critique of American society American olim articulate, grounded in such issues as crime and drugs, is also a critique of modernity.

With this in mind, let us look at what the substance of investment in ethnicity is. To invest in ethnicity is to invest in certain ties, attachments, or loyalties over others. Insofar as (I follow Glazer [1975] here), the ethnic group is one that is primarily defined by descent, these ties are ascriptive. This feature they share with sex (or gender). But this feature distinguishes them from other, achieved ties: (in America) to class, political groupings, occupational or professional groups, other voluntary associations (unions or guilds), and to "nationality" itself, insofar as one can become a "naturalized American citizen." To invest in

ethnicity is to invest in a radically different cluster of identifications: to region; to kinship; to a mythic notion of race; to a language which, enjoying the ancestral status, takes on the attribute
of sacred; to a place or region to whose topography is also imputed sacred qualities; to a grouping of "fellow ethnics" that
forms, in Durkheim's sense, a "moral community." Above all, an
investment in ethnicity is an investment in attachments that are
mediated by blood.

The difference between these two clusters of attachments, and
the sentiments that underlie them, has been pointed out by
others. Edward Shils (1957) called the first cluster one of "civil
attachments"; the second one of "primordial attachments."
Taking the attribute of kinship, Shils (1957:122) wrote:

> The attachment to another member of one's kinship group is
> not just a function of interaction, as Professor Homans would
> have it. It is because a certain ineffable significance is attrib-
> uted to the tie of blood. Even where affection was not great, the
> tangibility of the attachment to the other person, by virtue of
> our perception of his membership in the kinship group, is
> clearly in evidence.

Geertz (1963) followed Shils in his distinction between civil and
primordial ties but broadened its field—from subgroups in the
various armies of World War II (cf. Shils 1957)—to discuss the
problems of certain "old-new states" in their achievement of
integration as modern states. Geertz (1963:259) wrote:

> By a primordial attachment is meant one that stems from the
> "givens"—or . . . as culture is inevitably involved, the assumed
> "givens"—of social existence: immediate contiguity and kin
> connection mainly, but beyond them the giveness that stems
> from being born into a particular religious community, speaking
> a particular language . . . and following particular social cus-
> toms. These congruities of blood, speech, custom, and so on,
> are seen to have an ineffable, and at times overpowering, coer-
> civeness in and of themselves. . . . [Such a tie exhibits] some
> unaccountable absolute import attributed to the very tie itself.

Both Shils and Geertz note that attachments to civil as well as
primordial clusters can differ from person to person and from
society to society. Geertz, however, is clear in arguing that one

may characterize societies along a sort of continuum of differential investments that are made on one cluster over the other. What I wish to begin to make clear is that one may characterize persons in exactly the same way.

In contemporary America, few persons have investments in civil ties to the exclusion of primordial ones, and vice-versa. It is reasonable, therefore, to postulate the absence of serious conflict, for any given person, between investments in one cluster and the other. Most Americans feel little, if any, conflict between being an American and a Catholic; between being a chemist and a Jew; between being a mother or a father—with certain perceived and felt responsibilities with regard to the moral upbringing of one's children—and a citizen and resident of the United States. Few persons feel these sorts of conflicts; but some do.

In the preceding section of this chapter, working from a holistic notion of social identity, I described a kind of hyperinvestment in ethnic identifications over others (occupational, civil, political, etc.). I described an intensification of ethnic identity—in this case Jewishness—as a result of this hyperinvestment, and a movement towards maximization of ethnic identity—in this case, the point at which Jewishness overrides, or subordinates to it, other identities. Now note that an investment in ethnicity, Jewishness, is an investment in primordial, not civil, ties, loyalties, and attachments. It is an investment in attachments to Judaism as religion (a system of ultimate and sacred truths); to a transcendent conception of the Jewish people or nation (the attributes of which are raised to "ultimate" and sacred values [cf. J. Katz 1973:3]); to Hebrew as *lashon ha-kodesh* ("the sacred tongue"); to Israel as *Eretz Yisrael* ("the sacred land"). An investment in ethnic identity is an investment in primordial ties over civil ties. A hyperinvestment in ethnic identity, leading to the intensification of this identity in relation to a total social identity, can thus be described as the primordialization of a social identity.

The olim I studied are persons who, in America, by investing heavily or increasingly in their Jewishness, effected a primordialization of their social identities. One consequence of this structural transformation of social identities is the appearance of the very conflict between civil and primordial clusters— "chemist/Jew"—that most Americans avoid. Another consequence of primordialization is aliya. To explicate this, I shall have to examine in more detail the conflict between the clusters. And

to do this I shall return to the vital relationship that olim postulate
between conceptions of "personhood" and those of "society."

With respect to aliya, the argument must go further than the
intensification of Jewishness and the resultant primordialization
of social identity. These occurred in America, and, in the last
analysis, an individual may primordialize his or her social identity
and remain in America, albeit uncomfortably and in a state of
some conflict. We must return, in effect, to one of the questions
that began this chapter—not, Why migrate? but, Why Israel? We
should recall the partial response of one unhappy oleh: "If there
was another Jewish state, I'd live there."

A more complete response already has been hinted at. In the
preceding section, when social identity dynamics were discussed
in terms of their psychodynamic correlates, I spoke of the identity
conflict that ensues when a person's internalized hierarchy of
identities fails to achieve consonance, complementarity, or consensus with the hierarchies of others. Such identity conflict at a
certain level of intensity is assumed to be painful for the person;
he will attempt to regain equilibrium by resolving the conflict. In
doing this he has two basic options: he can attempt to restructure
his hierarchy to regain consensus within his existing community
of others; or he can seek a community of others where—he believes—his hierarchy is part of the consensus. American olim, I
argued, are individuals who, unable or unwilling to attempt the
former, make aliya in attempting the latter. Now it should be clear
that the person might seek a community of others that exists as a
subcommunity within the larger society. In that case, such a person would associate himself with Jewish communities, and their
affairs, as they are to be found in cities all over the United States.
American olim, however, do not or cannot accept this solution; in
part because their dissatisfactions are focused upon the larger
American society, the solution they seek transcends "communities" to deal with "society." They conceive of Israel as a
certain kind of society, a "Jewish society," and they decide that
only in such a society can they truly belong and live|fully as Jews.

But can we say anything more about their conception of Israeli
society, other than that it is a Jewish society? I believe we can.
Recall the remarks of Yehuda—an immigrant of the nationalist
type—cited earlier. "I'm here," he said, and "loyal" to Israel,
"because it's my family." I wrote that his identification with

Israel is felt to be something more than identification with an Israeli national community. By that I meant that Yehuda—and many like him—identified with Israel as a moral community (cf. Bailey 1971). For it was not the quality of community life, per se, that they rejected in America; rather it was the quality of the Jewish community as it was seen to exist, as a part of America. The solution they sought dealt with society, but it is a society of a certain kind: a society conceived, in toto, as one moral community. The basic, root metaphor used by the olim in speaking about this society was that of the family. The way they expressed this metaphor most often was as follows: "Kol Yehudim mishpaha ahad" ("All Jews constitute a single family"). In my interviews, I found this particular expression to predominate over others: "Kol Yehudim haverim" ("All Jews are 'comrades'"), or "Kol Yehudim 'am ahad" ("All Jews constitute a single people"). The expression that uses the image of family has one clear implication that the latter two lack, or possess weakly. The implication is that we (and they) are dealing somehow with ties of blood. What can we say about an image of (Jewish/Israeli) society at whose center is the metaphor of a "family," united by ties of "blood"?

Let us return momentarily to Geertz's discussion of primordial and civil attachments. He wrote that it is possible to characterize different societies by the differential investments their members make in one cluster of attachments over another. I argued that it is possible to characterize persons in the same way: thus, one can speak of the primordialization of social identities. But if we look at the formula more closely, we see that societies characterized by members' investments in primordial over civil ties are of a certain sort. They are those societies anthropologists, and others, have called traditional (cf. Black 1967:9ff). The traditional society is one where ties to kin, language, religion, and other particularistic, often ascriptive, groupings and identities predominate over—or preclude—ties to such universalistic, achieved identities as union member, party member, or citizen.

The sentiments, attachments, and loyalties that characterize a traditional society are those which Geertz called primordial. At the core of an ethnic identity are identifications with those same sentiments, attachments, and loyalties: to some special language; to religion; to kin; to the givens of social existence; to bonds mediated, ineffably, by blood. An investment in an ethnic identity is an investment in some or all of these ties. I have argued already that a hyperinvestment can be characterized as a primordialization of a social identity: this is what happened with the olim. But now note that these olim had invested, in America, in something more than their ethnic identity, or Jewishness. They had invested, in fact, in an image of a society where that identity would find consensus, consonance, or complementarity. If, as I wrote earlier, their objective critique of American society is also a critique of modernity, I argue now that their investment in Israel is an investment in their image of tradition.

It is not that the olim's investment in primordial sentiments at the core of their ethnic identity makes an investment in tradition inevitable: it need not. It is, however, that these olim invested in an image of a certain kind of society. This is a society whose template is *mishpaha* ("the family"). It is a society where, as we shall see, they believed relations among Jews (i.e., between themselves and others) would be, as in a family, warm, intense, face-to-face, diffuse, multiplex, and moral. The image of the society in which they invested is that of a gemeinschaft, not a gesellschaft. Members of this society are expected to relate to one another as something more than *haverim* ("comrades").

The American Jew who has invested in, and maximized, his Jewishness in relation to his total social identity has primordialized that social identity. He may well remain in America. But the American Jew who goes further—who invests also in an image of a primordial society where that identity fits in, is at home, or belongs—has done more than effect the primordialization of his social identity. For this American Jew makes aliya, and in his doing so we witness, I believe, the traditionalization of a social identity.

In the preceding section of this chapter, when I focused on such social-identity dynamics as "polarization" (Zavalloni 1973:86), "degrees of centrality" (Miller 1961:282–83), and "hypercathexis" (Devereux 1975:65ff), I was concerned mainly with their psychodynamic correlates. In this present section I have focused upon, along with primordializing and traditionalizing, what may be called the sociodynamic correlates of social identity dynamics.

Wallace and Fogelson (1965) have written of identity in terms of "ideal," "claimed," "real," and "feared" images of self. The

person, they argue, will usually move, in interpersonal communications, to "reduce the dissonance" between real and ideal
identity, and to "maximize the dissonance" between feared and
real identity. I argue, in effect, that individuals fashion for themselves, and internalize, "ideal," "claimed," "real," and
"feared" images of society or societies. Such images are interdependent with images of self. The olim (in this scheme) are
persons who, in minimizing the dissonance between their ideal
self (the religious Jew) and their real self (themselves as practicing
religious Jews), end up by maximizing the dissonance between
their real society (twentieth-century American) and their ideal
society (Israeli/Jewish). Increasingly, in fact, their real society
becomes congruent with their image of a feared society
(twentieth-century American/gesellschaft). And they move, quite
literally, to obliterate this congruence; to substitute for it a congruence between ideal (Israeli/Jewish/gemeinschaft) and real
(themselves as members of Israeli/Jewish/gemeinschaft) society.

I do not believe that the notions of primordializing or traditionalizing identities are radical ones. There has long been among
certain students of modernization a basic commitment to the social psychology of persons in modernizing societies. Such a
commitment was basic to Weber's articulation of the relationship
between the "Protestant ethic" and the "spirit of capitalism."
More recently, Daniel Lerner (1958) wrote of the "personality
matrix" upon which, in part, successful modernization depends.
Alex Inkeles and co-workers have written of the "modernizing
personality" from a cross-cultural perspective (see Inkeles and
Smith 1974; Inkeles 1975). Still others have pursued their interest
in the "measurement of modernism" among individuals (see Kahl
1968). In part, then, my description of American olim as possessing "traditionalizing social identities" is meant to be a contribution to the above works and their concerns.[11] I am writing,
however, of individuals who themselves stand in a different perspective. They lived in the midst of modernity; were alienated
from it; apparently rejected it; and sought at last a different kind
of society. It is a society where, they believed, their particular
personality matrix would find consonance in a community of
like-minded others.

In another sense, however, I offer the notions of primordializing and traditionalizing because of their direct relevance for the

study at hand. This will become clearer in the following chapters, as I consider some of the dynamics of these Americans' absorption into Israeli society—*not* their ideal image of it—and some aspects of Israeli sociological models that have dealt with immigrants' absorption.

Finally, I offer these notions to bring closure to an argument begun in Chapter 2. There, while tracing Zionism in its historical development, I followed Halpern (1961) in tracing also the rapprochement of Zionism with traditionalism at the expense of modernism. For it was traditionalism that provided the only conception of Jews upon which Zionism might base itself. After Enlightenment, Emancipation, Reform, and *embourgeoisement,* this was a conception of Jews as an ethnic entity (cf. Halpern 1961:81). By the time I traced Jewry and Zionism to the shores of America, the problem of rapprochement had to be faced again. This time the issue was the crucial lack of centrality of aliya to American Zionism. It was claimed, after all, that "America was different," and the question became, How was it different?

America was different, I wrote, insofar as it was not perceived, by the great majority of American Jews, to be "exile." Without a conception of "exile," what is the necessity for redemption in "Zion"? American Zionism was different, I wrote, insofar as it failed to connect with the only conception of a Jewish entity that, earlier and elsewhere, as in the congresses at Basel, had made Zionism meaningful and possible. In the face of the corrosive and potent "superidentity" of American modernity (cf. Erikson 1963:282), this was a conception of a Jewish entity as an ethnic entity. It is those American Jews who hold or come to hold to this conception that this study takes as its focus. In this chapter, then, I have tried to explicate what it means, psycho- and sociodynamically, to hold or come to hold to this ethnic conception. What I have argued, ultimately, is that, as with the movement of Zionism itself, the fundamental movement of these persons, the olim, emotionally even more than intellectually, is back toward tradition (cf. Halpern 1961:103).[12]

Aliya and Change
Traditionalizing

[There is] . . . a basic fact about Israeli life, without which nothing here can be understood, that Israel is at base a community of faith: It is a *mishpoche,* not a state. You love it even as you hate it, and you tie your fate to it, in a kind of fury, against all conventional logic, and even as you leave it to drive a taxi in New York City, you miss it very badly.
Amos Elon, in *New York Times Book Review*

The Absorption of Immigrants

For many years Israel sociology (and the sociology of Israel) took as its most studied topic the dynamics of "the absorption of immigrants." Much of this literature has concerned itself with the traumatic early period surrounding the formation of the state or with the special problems of Oriental, Afro-Asian Jews. Orientations have been broadly based, in one sense. They have ranged from sociological (Eisenstadt 1954; Matras 1965), to social-psychological (Shuval 1963), to psychiatric (Weinberg 1961), to anthropological (Weingrod 1966). In another sense, however, almost all the literature reflects a common concern with the relationship between immigration, absorption, and social change. Such a concern is eminently reasonable in any case, and no special defense is necessary of it here. Quite to the contrary, the special circumstances that surrounded the establishment of the Yishuv, its transformation after statehood, and the extreme cultural diversity of Jewish immigrants make the study of immigration and absorption in the context of social change a vital and necessary, as well as reasonable, focus for Israeli social science. The point that must interest us here, however, particularly with respect to Oriental immigrants, is the framework of social change that was postulated as the context for absorption.

123

Between 1948 and 1952 Afro-Asian Jewish immigration accounted for more than half of the total aliya (see table A4). The Israeli society into which the Oriental Jews entered, however, was created and dominated (and still is dominated) by Jews from Europe, in the main from Russia and Poland. The Orientals entered a society created by students, intellectuals, socialists of every hue, some small merchants, and utopian visionaries. They entered a society created by Jews who had experienced—even if from the shtetl and belatedly—the general traumas of a modernization that all Europe was passing through. As a nationalism, Zionism was a relative latecomer on the European scene; but as a nationalism it bore a European, as well as its Jewish, stamp. Although the waves of Oriental immigrants have diminished since the late 1950s, a higher birth rate in Oriental communities has resulted in the fact that more than half of the Jewish population of Israel consists of Jews from African, Middle Eastern, or Asian countries.[1]

It was expected, of these Oriental Jewish immigrants, that they would adapt to the prevailing ethos of an Eastern European Israeli society, and not that the society ought to undergo radical structural changes to adapt to them—hence, I suspect, the very metaphor "absorption." Absorption was conceived within a framework of social change; but it was change of a special sort. S. N. Eisenstadt, who was one of the earliest and remains, in some ways, the most influential student of immigrant absorption, made something called the "predisposition to change" a key variable in his various analyses (1952; 1954; 1967). He related degrees of "predisposition to change" to different family structures as they were found in different communities of the Diaspora (see, e.g., 1954:143–68). The communities were placed along a continuum that ranged from tradition towards modernity.[2] Eisenstadt left no doubts about the position on the continuum where the immigrants' destination, the Israeli community, was to be found: it was, so far as the Orientals were concerned, towards modernity.

A few excerpts from Eisenstadt's basic work will suffice to illustrate this point. In speaking of the small proportion of Oriental Jews in the population of the pre-state Jewish community of Palestine (i.e., the Yishuv), he wrote that the "impact of modern conditions" on them—those conditions imported and instituted by the European Zionist pioneers—could be "compared in some ways with any situation of culture contact between a modern, advanced economy and 'backward' people (peasants, etc.)" (1954:95). Later, when he turned to discuss the absorption of Oriental immigrants who arrived after the establishment of the state, he wrote of the development of a "crisis" among the Orientals,

> owing to the impact of the absorbing society [i.e., Israel] on the traditional pattern [of the immigrants], that gives rise to the various dynamic processes of adaptation among the immigrants. . . . In general it may be said that in cases of negative outcome of the crisis [i.e., maladaptation, "poor absorption"], the immigrants tend to perpetuate many aspects of their traditional structures . . . without changing them in accordance with some of the universal role-demands of the absorbing society. (1954:154, 156)

It should begin to be clear what sort of social change was linked to absorption. Absorption was conceived within the general framework of the transition, for the Oriental immigrants, from their traditional societies of origin to modern Israel. Absorption into Israeli society presupposed a special sort of acculturation, that is, the willingness or the ability, on the part of the Oriental Jews, to modernize in harmony with their new home.[3]

Following Eisenstadt's influential work, came a series of anthropological studies on one of the major forms of Oriental immigrant absorption, the *moshav-olim* ("the immigrants' moshav"). Each moshav, at least initially, was conceived as an "administered community" that was to undergo "directed" social change under the guidance of Israeli advisers. These advisers were external to the community and followed a national development program (see Willner 1969). A major focus of these studies became, naturally enough, the sorts of relations each moshav and its members formed with these outside agents of change. Research was carried out in a number of different moshavim, composed of immigrant groups from Morocco (Weingrod 1966; Shokeid 1971), the Tunisian island of Djerba (Deshen 1966), Tripolitania (Goldberg 1972), and Cochin, in India (Kushner 1973). In some cases the moshav members adopted a very passive stance with agents of Israeli bureaucracies—for example, transforming the agents into all-powerful "sheikhs" as they had existed in their lands of origin; in other cases the agents were actively related to, and used as resources, in factional fights that often predated the community's settlement in Israel.

In general the anthropologists, on the basis of community studies, developed a more flexible conception of tradition and modernity. It was demonstrated, for example, that the cultural continuities some communities exhibited with their pre-aliya past were occasionally utilized by members to effect a good absorption into Israeli society (see Deshen and Shokeid 1974). In these cases, *contra* Eisenstadt, the retention of "tradition"—or some elements of it—did not inevitably augur negative outcomes. Indeed, in a more recent statement, Eisenstadt refers to some of these works, and notes that

> There has been a growing recognition that traditional forms do more than merely "persist" in, or influence the degree to which different groups adjust to, new, modern settings. Instead, it is increasingly recognized that these forces may also shape or influence the contours of the emerging modern settings. (1974:15–16)

This notion that traditional (Oriental) forms may shape the contours of the emerging modern (Israeli) settings is an important one; it gives some clue about the nature of the society into which American immigrants are expected to be absorbed. I shall return to it shortly, as some of the questions that are to guide this and the following chapter are formulated.

Despite the flexibility of "tradition" and "modernity," the two terms have remained central to most discussions of absorption. In a recent review Weller (1974:40–41) summarized some of the "fundamental changes" the Oriental, "tradition-oriented" immigrants had to make in their adaptation to moshav life:

> The importance of the extended family became attenuated as the nuclear family was the unit of activity in the moshav. The work required ... a knowledge of the scientific basis of agricultural procedures. ... This was easier for the immigrants ... from Western countries to achieve, as they had a tradition of scientific learning. ... The Eastern immigrants also required a redefinition of sexual roles. ... the Eastern immi-

grants had now to learn how to organize their work with the future in mind.... They also had to learn a new governing system with a democratic base.... [and to] negotiate with a bureaucratic system.

From the attenuation of extended kin ties, the acceptance of rational, scientific learning, the redefinition of sexual roles, the achievement of a future orientation, the learning of new roles in a participatory democracy with a bureaucratic base, these "fundamental changes" necessary for successful absorption read like a textbook description of modernization (cf. Black 1967: chap. 1; Peacock and Kirsch 1970: chap. 2).

As the immigrant groups of the 1950s became the Israeli ethnic groups of today, a new perception was brought to problems of absorption. Today, more than a quarter-century after the formation of the state, a body of Israeli sociology that is attempting to account for social, economic, and political inequalities based on the major "Ashkenazi-Sephardi" cleavage will often point to overly rapid attempts at modernizing the Oriental immigrants. The Orientals lost their traditional values and ties (e.g., to the patriarchal, extended family and kin, to prestige models based on "Torah learning"), while at the same time they failed to gain access to the kinds of prizes (political office, university degrees, white-collar positions in industry or the bureaucracies) as they are defined in a universalistic, secular, achievement-oriented modern nation-state (cf. Lissak 1969; Weingrod 1971; Heller 1973, 1975). In this regard, it is interesting to consider a critique put forward by a young sociologist, himself of Oriental background. Sammy Smooha (1972) has observed that, in general, Ashkenazim are willing to recognize the existence of "two Israels" only when the problem is described in class, not ethnic, terms; described, that is, in terms befitting a thoroughly modern society.

With respect to the Orientals, the linking of absorption with modernization is a pervasive one. It has influenced both practical programs and theoretical thinking about aliya and klita. The linking has much to recommend it. The Jewish immigrant from Yemen or the Atlas Mountains of Morocco, borne suddenly—and as if by magic carpet—to a new home in urbanized and industrializing Israel, did confront a series of dislocations that correspond to aspects of our notion of modernization. That the linking also

provides some insight into a kind of Israeli hubris is beyond that
which directly concerns us here. For here, the linking raises some
interesting questions. If Oriental immigrants can be said to modernize as they are absorbed, what can be said about American
immigrants? At the risk of substituting one hubris for another:
What happens when a group of immigrants from a modern society
(the U.S.) attempts to settle in a relatively less modern society
(Israel)? And, most crucially: How is the Americans' absorption
affected by the very dynamics—the traditionalization of their social identities—that brought them to make aliya?

These are some of the questions that will guide us through this
and the following chapter. What I wish to demonstrate is this: that
having invested in an image of a traditional society, these American olim find themselves confronting a society that in fact is—in
some ways and compared to the U.S.—a traditional society. They
must learn certain new skills in order to cope; they suffer certain
dislocations as wrenching as those suffered by the Orientals; and,
as we shall see in Chapter 7, they react, often, in typically American (and modern) ways.

Traditionalizing and the Style of Social Relationships

There are problems in working with such dichotomies as traditional and modern, and not the least of these has to do with
referents. If one draws up a list of attributes (industrial development, political participation, consumption patterns, and so on) by
which one would call Israel traditional and the U.S. modern, then
clearly, by these same criteria, Israel would appear modern in
contrast to its immediate neighbors and, indeed, to most of the
Third World. In terms of economic criteria it would not be difficult to show that, compared to the U.S., Israel is a developing
nation and that much of the dislocation olim report is a result of
the move from a developed to a developing economy. However,
there is some evidence to show that part of Israel's attraction to
the olim is based precisely on the country's "under-developed"
character compared to that of the U.S. Here the olim speak often
of the "contributions" they feel able to make to Israel—given its
stage of development and the skills (educational, professional,
etc.) they bring with them from America. This is an important

claim, and I shall examine it in some detail in Chapter 7. For the present, however, it is sufficient to argue that not all the dislocation olim report is to be explained by their move from developed to developing economies: and that the conception of tradition I want to employ need not rest squarely on an econometrician's graph.

In this chapter I am concerned with some of the major sources of dislocation that olim report; I deal, that is, with certain aspects of the absorption of American immigrants. My essential proposition about the Israeli society into which they are absorbed follows Eisenstadt's remarks (1974:15–16) quoted earlier: it is a society shaped by some of the traditional forms and forces of its immediate history. Whether it ever represented modernity to the Oriental immigrants, it does not do so to the American. If the Orientals, however, can be said to have modernized in concert with their absorption, then for the Americans I claim a different sort of process. They must traditionalize—with respect to certain aspects of Israeli society—if they are to be absorbed. If this is so, an important question is raised: What is the relationship, if any, between the traditionalizing that they effect in Israel, with absorption, and the traditionalizing, already described, that they effected with aliya?

Upon what framework, if not the economic one of development, do I base this notion of traditionalizing? Earlier I argued that the distinction between traditional and modern societies has implications of a sociodynamic nature: implications for the kinds of statuses, groupings, and sodalities which predominate, and to which individuals' ties and loyalties are directed. Here the focus becomes the stuff of social relationships: the sets of moral postulates by which they are defined, the rules by which they operate—their "style." In fact, here too social theory has presented us a language of dichotomies. Relationships can be based on mechanical or organic solidarities; they can be of gemeinschaft or gesellschaft; they can be based on status or contract, on particularism or universalism; they can be multiplex or single-stranded.

The point is not to multiply these dichotomies. Their virtue lies in allowing one to put aside for the moment the omnibus distinction between tradition and modernity, while one realigns the distinction to focus on the substance of social relationships, their articulation and style. The omnibus proposition is that American olim move from a modern to a "not-so-modern" society. Let me borrow one of the dichotomies, Henry Maine's, and rephrase this: American olim move from a society in which certain sets of relations are defined by contract, to a society in which these same sets are defined, and articulated, in terms of status. Two such major sets are those of bureaucratic and business relations. Both will be discussed in this chapter; the problems of doing business—and some solutions—will appear again in Chapter 7. First, however, we need to consider one essential transition the oleh makes in his move from American to Israeli society. This is a question of scale.

Societal Scale

American olim move from a large-scale to a small-scale society. Most find this, in the abstract, an attractive proposition. A typical remark is: "In America I felt like a cog in a giant machine. I felt anonymous. I couldn't see how the work I was doing [electrical engineering] made any sort of contribution. Israel is a small country. The individual, and what he does, counts for more, here." Those olim who settled initially on a kibbutz or moshav often spoke of attractions having to do with scale: "I had thought, with its size as well as ideology, that on a kibbutz I could not only live a different sort of life in relation to the land but also in relation to other people, my *haverim* ["comrades": fellow kibbutz-members]."[4]

Scale depends, of course, on such grossly measurable attributes as population size, density, and so on. According to these criteria, Israel is, compared to the United States, a small-scale society. But smallness of scale does not depend solely on smallness of population; although the latter may be necessary, it is not sufficient. In Israel, smallness of scale is effected also by a lack of significant regional differences—cultural, linguistic, etc.—within the country,[5] and by a host of other, less tangible, factors. I am tempted to gloss them as a "shared sense of purpose." It is not a very good gloss. A sense of "everyone being plugged in to the same central nervous system," as one oleh put it, is more evocative. He added:

You know how Israelis are compulsive [radio] listeners to news. Especially during wartime, but even during peace. I sit on buses and every hour, when the news comes on, the driver turns up his set and conversation in the bus stops. It stops at least as long as the headlines are read. Everyone listens, and if everything is more or less *be-seder* ["in order"; "O.K."], conservation continues. In those moments I feel like three million of us are plugged into the same place. We are one organism.

Scale involves degrees of sharing—sharing of understandings, values, and so on—that are difficult to quantify. Smallness of scale has implications for generational differences, for example, as these remarks by a sabra, a former aliya emissary, indicate:

There are so many differences between Israelis and Americans, klita is difficult. . . . Israelis say "We," Americans "I." In Israel, the personal history of a forty-year-old and a twenty-year-old, in terms of Army, wars, and *hevra* ["group," "gang," "clique"], are really very similar. In America the difference in personal history between a forty- and a twenty-year-old is enormous.

Smallness of scale is often associated with gemeinschaft. One oleh told me of a young American relative who had come to look him up on a visit to Jerusalem. He possessed only the oleh's name, and the name of the neighborhood (Ramat Eshkol) in which he lived. The young man spoke no Hebrew.

He walked around for a while, looking for someone who spoke English. He found people who did, but none knew me. So someone took B. home, gave him some coffee, and rounded up all the available kids to canvass Ramat Eshkol and find us. There are—how many?—2,500 families in Ramat Eshkol? Within an hour some kids found us, and we picked B. up.

Another spoke of his first weeks in the country:

When I first came to Jerusalem—you walk in the streets, let's say a guy gives you an address of Moshe Pipik ["John Doe"—almost] in Rehavia. O.K., Rehavia—twenty, thirty streets. You walk to Rehavia and you stop three Jews for directions. By the time you've stopped the third, he'll *take* you there. I remember once I walked with a little *petek* ["note"] in my hand, looking for an address. You know, it takes you a while to learn Hebrew, and I couldn't read this guy's handwriting. So I stopped this guy to ask him where the address was. I showed him the petek, and he looked at it and said: *"Him?* What do you want to go *there* for?" And I said: "I was invited for tea." He said: "Why do you want to go there for tea? Come to my house, I'll give you better tea!"

That's Israel. It's like everyone says: We're all one mish-paha; we're all responsible for one another.

A woman spoke of the time when she learned her husband had been wounded in the Sinai:

When David was wounded, this place was always filled. People would call, complete strangers, asking if they could do anything to help me. The phone started ringing at seven in the morning and didn't stop until eleven at night; it got so I had to take it off the hook, just so I could take care of my children. Literally, *strangers* called. People called because they heard David was wounded and I was alone with the kids.

David added:

I think this is a very Jewish thing, the kind of thing that happened in the shtetl, where people were very concerned with one another—as opposed to America, where you don't know who your neighbor is.

In all of these examples, smallness of scale is seen by immigrants to be a virtue; social relations in a small-scale society are characterized, immigrants assert, by their special warmth or ease of access. In this way scale is related to the positive attributes of gemeinschaft. At the same time, however, scale has other implications for social structure. In large-scale social systems many (if not most) of the relations between individuals are role-specific, single-stranded, or "simplex." In a large American city, the passenger on a bus and its driver are likely to interact entirely within the limits of their respective roles as "passenger" and "driver"; months may elapse before the passenger on a particular route and a driver on that route begin to exchange even the most casual greetings. As scale decreases, the possibilities for many-stranded, "multiplex," relations with individuals increase (imagine a passenger taking the same taxi, daily, between place of work and home). This point has important consequences for immigrant absorption.

Pearl Katz (1974) has examined the social networks of American olim and noted that well-acculturated individuals have networks which include many Israelis and which are able to expand and ramify, adding further links to other Israelis. What is equally important, however, is that these added links are eventually made into many-stranded links. While initially, newly formed relations may be "simplex," in Israel as in other small-scale societies, especially Mediterranean ones, the goal of the individual is to maximize multiplexity (cf. Barnes 1968:126–28). This means he aims to have as many multistranded links with as many other people as he can; and they with him.

It should begin to be clear that there are implications for the style of social relations in small-scale social systems, other than that they are suffused with gemütlichkeit. For in making the transition from large to small scale the immigrant must learn (among many other things) how to nurture, invoke, and utilize multiplexity in relations formerly characterized by their single-strandedness. In many cases this involves, to use Maine's terms, the transformation of contract-based links into status-based ones. In short, negotiating relations in a small-scale social system must be learned. Negotiating a gemeinschaft is an acquired skill. And if acquisition does not proceed smoothly, the image of a gemeinschaft that the immigrant had internalized, in Chicago, may exhibit great dissonance with its reality, in a customs-shed in Lod.

Bureaucratic Encounters: Socialization to Tradition

In Chapter 4, I tried to give some idea of the growing bureaucratization of institutional support and apparatus for the absorption of immigrants. Such bureaucratization, in fact, affected most sectors of Israeli society. For Israeli sociology, however, the study of encounters between new immigrants, especially Orientals, and bureaucracy has held a special place. It was, that is, central to the equivalence that was drawn between absorption and modernization. The basic assumptions were as follows: first, that the complex, formal, and rational (Israeli) bureaucracy was a manifestation of Israeli modernity; second, that the Oriental immigrants

> had come from traditional societies, innocent of the norms and structures which apply to the peculiar kinds of relationships characterizing formal organizations. And, indeed, in those days [early 1950s] . . . it was not at all unusual to observe a new immigrant from, say, Yemen, bargaining with the bus driver over the fare, or asking to be let off in front of his home rather than at the bus stop. The outbreak of arguments . . . was a common sight. (E. Katz and Danet 1973:14)

With these assumptions—or postulates—bureaucracy and absorption were connected to modernity, or modernization. This was the approach adopted by Eisenstadt in his seminal work (1954) on immigrant absorption, and it became the orientation of a series of studies in the late 1950s. Two approaches characterized these latter works. The first dealt with the bureaucratic socialization of the client, that is,

> with the adaptation of new-comers from traditional familistic backgrounds to new role expectations such as those implicit in becoming a factory worker, a hospital patient, a client of a social welfare worker, or even a bus passenger. (E. Katz and Eisenstadt 1960:73)

This approach is still evident in recent research: "Bureaucratic socialization," wrote Danet and Hartman (1972a:10), with reference to Israel, "is part of the wider process of psychological modernization."

While the first approach dealt with the effects of Israeli bureaucracy on the new immigrants, a second approach—thus far less pervasive—had dealt with the effects of the traditional Orientals on Israeli bureaucracy. Because the Israeli bureaucrat was also a socializing agent—socializing for modernity—he often found himself, in his role as teacher, stepping out of his role as bureaucrat. "The bureaucrat," wrote Katz and Eisenstadt (1960:79), "teaches the client how to be a client so that he (the bureaucrat) can go on being a bureaucrat." In doing this, the bureaucrat more than occasionally had to give up some of the attributes of bureaucratic modernity: role specificity (single-strandedness), universalism (equality of service), and affective neutrality. For these reasons—and for some others rooted in the historical structure of the Yishuv—"what came into being was not a pure, Weberian type of neutral bureaucracy" (Eisenstadt 1954:130). In their roles as agents of socialization, as teachers, exemplars, or (on occasion) advocates, many Israeli bureaucrats found themselves peronalizing their offices and authority. This had the effect of leading to a "debureaucratization" of Israel bureaucracy (cf. Eisenstadt 1970; 1974:15–16).

Even if they accept the notion of debureaucratization, most recent studies are based still on the orientation of the first approach: to absorb one must deal effectively with bureaucracy; to deal bureaucratically is, for those from traditional cultures, to modernize. The variable of bureaucratic socialization has been refined to specify "bureaucratic competence" and the bureaucratic strategies and attitudes of different ethnic groups. A series of studies by Brenda Danet (1970; 1971; 1973) and co-workers (Danet and Hartman 1972a; 1972b; E. Katz and Danet 1966; E. Katz et al. 1969; Danet and Gurevitch 1972) exemplifies this approach. With the caveat that, in Israeli bureaucracy, "modern and traditional means of obtaining goals are institutionalized side by side" (Danet and Hartman 1972a:20), and with the addition, to ethnicity, of such background variables as education and occupation, these studies demonstrate in a variety of settings that Oriental Jews are generally less bureaucratically competent than Jews from the West; that they, the Orientals, approach bureaucrats in a diffuse fashion (i.e., seeking multiplexity); and that they believe in the efficacy of "personal influence" (*proteksia*), for the attainment of goals, more so than do Westerners. In one study (Danet and Gurevitch 1972), with respect to the variable "role specificity" in approaching bureaucrats, the "predicted order of immigrant groups, from most role-specific to most diffuse, was: Western Europe [includes English-speakers], Eastern Europe, and Middle Eastern." This order was statistically confirmed.

As a whole, this literature lends strong support to the absorption-as-modernization model. But there are a few surprises. While investigating the kinds of appeals that "moderns" versus "traditionals" direct to bureaucracy, Katz and Danet

(1966) hypothesized that, among other things, the "moderns" will offer appeals based upon bureaucratically normative principles, while the "traditionals" will appeal to "altruism." The latter kind of appeal is, of course, nonbureaucratic. This hypothesis was confirmed. But when the sample was further stratified by "newcomer" and "old-timer" a problem arose. Because Israeli bureaucracy was conceived to be essentially modern, it was expected that, as Oriental newcomers become old-timers in Israel, they would undergo bureaucratic socialization and would become, as a group, more bureaucratic. While differences would still exist between Orientals and Westerners, as groups, the greatest *change* in bureaucratic behavior was expected to take place between Oriental newcomers and old-timers. Because newcomer Westerners were already bureaucratic (modern), they would exhibit as a group little change in bureaucratic behavior: they had no need for bureaucratic socialization to modernity.

This hypothesis was not confirmed; what surprised Katz and Danet, in fact, was the "finding that it is respondents of Western origin who change most as a result of experience [with the bureaucracy], rather than the Easterners." It seems, that is, that rather than the "socialization of the Easterners to bureaucratic ways," what occurred was "the *debureaucratization* of the Western group" (1966:185). The data of Katz and Danet supported the "idea that clients learn through experience that it pays to ask for a favor" (1966:188). It appears that Western clients *learn* to appeal to altruism.

Katz and Danet have difficulty in resolving this apparent paradox. And they should: for if Israeli bureaucracy is stamped as *modern,* it must follow logically that it is the traditionals who are socialized to it, as they are absorbed. Their explanation, therefore, invokes debureaucratization. It is clear, however, that the Western new immigrants, or newcomers, are also undergoing bureaucratic socialization in Israel. But as they learn that "it pays to ask for a favor," that it pays to appeal to "altruism," they are not being socialized for modernity. Rather, the Westerners learn to deal with an Israeli bureaucracy in which client-bureaucrat relationships are more diffuse, more particularistic, and less affectively neutral than those they knew in the West. If we follow, therefore, the sociological logic that connected bureaucratic socialization to modernization, we must ask what the implications

of debureaucratization—as Katz and Danet put it—are. If the
Orientals were said to have modernized as they were bureaucratized, what can we say about the Westerners who are *debu*-
reaucratized? If we do away with the proposition that Israeli bureaucracy presents an equally modern face to all its clients, the
implications of debureaucratization are clear. The Westerners are
socialized to Israeli bureaucracy, but this socialization is not
modernization. It is something different. The Westerners—our
Americans, in particular—learn to do something else as they are
absorbed. In this case, with respect to bureaucracy, they debu-
reaucratize. They traditionalize.

American olim experience great difficulties with Israeli bureaucracy. "The American," writes Weller (1974:32), "accustomed
to a relatively efficient bureaucracy, built on the concept of service, found the confusion and his new role as a client almost
incomprehensible and even frightening." David Katz and Aaron
Antonovsky (1973) presented 553 North American olim (arrived
1957–66) with eighty-five "problem issues" in adjustment to Israel. Four of these dealt directly with bureaucracy. By percentages, the four bureaucratic items ranked among the top five
problem issues. Jubas (1974:189ff) presented his sample of post-
1967 olim with a list of twenty-one "hypothetical factors for a
decision to leave Israel." The factor of "red-tape and bureaucracy" ranked first, in both "very important" and "combined
importance" categories. In my own survey, conducted in
Jerusalem, 97 percent of the respondents found that Israeli bureaucracy was "more difficult to deal with" than American bureaucracy. One percent found the two bureaucracies "equally
difficult"; 2 percent had more difficulty in America.
  Two important points should be noted. First, Israeli society is
in general more bureaucratic than is American society, and many
olim complain of this. Second, as new immigrants, the Americans
must deal with some bureaucracies—the Jewish Agency, etc.—
that Israelis need not. The combination of high bureaucratization
and new-immigrant status means that the *oleh hadash* often deals
with as much bureaucracy in his first three years in Israel as the
native-born Israeli does in his first eighteen. Undoubtedly, some
of the problems Americans encounter are based on simple frequency of bureaucratic contact. Katz and Antonovsky's data

(1973:251) support the view that bureaucratic contacts are perceived to be somewhat less problematic as a function of length of residence in Israel.

Nevertheless, frequency of contact cannot account for all the problems. To attempt to control for frequency—at least with respect to attitudes towards relative difficulty—I presented the Jerusalem respondents with two options for the attitude "Israeli bureaucracy is more difficult to deal with than American." The first option allowed the respondent to answer affirmatively, but added: "(Israeli bureaucracy is more difficult)...but *only* because I have to deal with bureaucracy more here than I did in the U.S." The second option read: "Even taking into account that I deal with bureaucracy more here than I did in the U.S., it is still the case that Israeli bureaucracy is more difficult to deal with." Of the 97 percent who perceived the Israeli bureaucracy to be more difficult to deal with than the American, 28 percent chose the first statement (the frequency function), while 69 percent chose the second. Moreover, as Weller's remarks indicate, the roots of the bureaucratic problem for Americans lie in such issues as "efficiency," the "concept of service," and the demands of the client-role—not in simple frequency of contact. In other words, for the Orientals it was expected that socialization to bureaucratic norms—affective neutrality, universalism, and so on—would be problematic. American immigrants, on the other hand, "describe their contact with bureaucracy as problematic in terms of deviations from bureaucratic norms, rather than in terms of bureaucratic norms *per se*" (Katz and Antonovsky 1973:256). When asked to choose the single most "bothersome" aspect of dealing with Israeli bureaucracy, the modal response of the Jerusalem sample (at 38 percent) was the following: "It doesn't seem to me that the same rules apply to everyone equally." This is a complaint against a deviation from the bureaucratic norm of universalism.[6]

There is another explanation for why bureaucracy is perceived to be relatively less problematic as a function of length of residence. This is that the immigrant is socialized not to the bureaucratic norms but to the deviations from these norms. However "incomprehensible and even frightening" the role of client appears at first, it is a role and it can be learned. In the following pages I shall examine the kinds of skills that are deemed necessary to play the client role in Israel. We go, to paraphrase Goffman, backstage.

"Seven years ago, when I first came to Israel," said Aaron,

I was surprised by how much life here was permeated with the need for licenses and stamps on official forms. But you can get used to that. What I really had to learn was the system. In the U.S., when you go to a government office, the clerk is there to help you. He'll tell you the rules, and he'll help you follow the rules, and *within* the rules he might even help you to get around the rules. Not here. The rules don't apply to everyone equally, so if the *pakid* ["clerk," "bureaucrat"] doesn't know you, or God forbid doesn't like you, you're dead. This is really part of a whole Israeli complex. Take income tax. The U.S. government doesn't want you to pay the highest possible tax; they want you to pay the taxes, and they give you choices—long-form, short-form, joint returns, and so on—and they tell you: Pick the way that's best for you. Here the mentality is different: If the pakid knows you, he'll bend the rules—he'll call an "X" a "Y" to get a deduction. But in general, the mentality is to force the guy to pay the highest tax. They call this socialism, but it's really Oriental despotism.

So gradually I began to learn the system. The first thing you learn is to relate to the pakid differently. You don't relate to him as a clerk but as a whole person—"How's the family?" and so on. Therefore, I learned, it's better if you actually *know* the pakid, so you can not only ask him "How's the family?" but also "Is your daughter Rivka married yet?" Now obviously you can't know every clerk in the country. So let's say you have to go to the Ministry of Commerce and Industry on Tuesday. So you ask all your friends, acquaintances, and relatives if they know a pakid in that ministry. And if they do, you go to him. You say, "Shmuel sent me." This is having *proteksia* ["personal influence"]. And it works. Let me give you an example.

Some kids were playing ball and broke the windshield of my car. I couldn't get a replacement in the country. So I go to *mekhes* ["customs"] to find out about importing one. But the guy I go to is the brother of a neighbor. I know, because I asked around of all my neighbors. So we talk, and talk, and then get to my problem—you can't rush, because, from *his* point of view, maybe you have a son who will marry Rivka! So we get to my problem. Now the import tax on a new windshield would have

cost me around 1000 IL—under *one* import category, "glass,"
or something. So we talk some more. Then he tells me if I *let*
him—got it?—let him import under *another* category—car
parts—the tax would be about 600 IL. So we talk. And I tell
him how I'm going to *miluim* [military reserve duty] next
month. Now we have a real *kesher* ["connection"], because
every Israeli does that. So he says: "Look, your windshield is
tinted glass, right?" I say, "Sure but what's that got to do with
it?" "Well," he says, "why don't we import it under *medical*
glass? As medical equipment." Because then the tax is next to
nothing. "Can you do that?" I ask. He says: *Betah, 'ain baya!*
["Sure, no problem!"].

Now imagine that—importing a car windshield as medical
equipment! But it could have gone the other way. If he didn't
know me, and if I couldn't establish a *kesher* with him, or,
worse, if he didn't like me—imagine what category he could
have imported the windshield under! This is what happens to
many new olim. They have to learn the system. They have to
learn this is the Middle East, you have to have someone to
intercede on your behalf."

Another oleh, Jonathan, has lived in Israel for five years. In the
United States he had worked for a municipal bureaucracy; in
Israel he is an educational administrator. His remarks provide a
sort of controlled comparison between American and Israeli bureaucracies.

Look, in the States things weren't always so rational either.
But at least we had the sense of being "public servants." I
mean, we may have screwed over some clients in the U.S., but
we felt guilty about it—we really did think we ought to be doing
something called public service. There's none of that here.

Basically, in the States they go more or less by the rules,
especially in the federal agencies we dealt with. They may have
carried out the regulations to the letter, to your disadvantage,
but they went by the regulations. Here there are regulations
too, but they can be bent by persons. Let's say I'm having
trouble getting a driver's license because of my disability [a war
wound]. Now in the U.S., even if I know some bigshot in the
motor vehicle bureau, if it's a technical thing, like my disability, the odds are he won't be able to do anything for me—
short of the state legislature amending the law—even if he likes
me or I'm his brother. In Israel it doesn't work that way. Even

if there's a technical reason, a regulation, why I shouldn't get a license, there's always some guy, if you know the right one to go to, who can get you a license. And I'm not talking about bribery. The system works on proteksia, not on money changing hands. Proteksia is based on reciprocity; on trading favors; on personal contacts. In a way it's more primitive than bribery. We're not talking about cash credit but about social credit.
Proteksia is to bribery what barter is to cash.

Both Aaron and Jonathan are individuals who have adapted—with considerable insight—to certain deviations from bureaucratic norms. Rules, they have realized, are not necessarily applied on universalistic principles; in the bureaucrat-client relationship, role specificity, or single-strandedness, is not necessarily maintained; and neither is affective neutrality. They have learned something else: that by adapting to the normative deviations, by invoking particularism through proteksia, by seeking multiplexity and affective valence, they can manipulate the system to their advantage. In doing these things, however, Aaron and Jonathan recognize that the deviations are deviations from some set of bureaucratic norms. "This is the Middle East," they say. They approach the system pragmatically; they know—from a previous bureaucratic socialization in America—how the game ought to be played. They recognize the existence of normative rules. They recognize also, however, that there are rules that specify how to win. These are pragmatic rules (cf. Bailey 1969). In part, these rules have been described in their transcripts.

It is not surprising that both Aaron and Jonathan served in the Israeli army. For, among other things, service in the army provides the opportunity to enlarge one's social network, adding links with Israelis, and to invoke multiplexity for existing links—for example, by sharing the problems of reservist duties. Many Americans, however, do not serve in the army; many learn only slowly how to play the bureaucratic game to win; and some seem to learn not at all. In these cases interviews are filled with horror stories of bureaucratic encounters gone wrong. "I hate having to go to any office," said Martin, an oleh of 1972.

I work myself into a state of rage before I even get there. I know I'm going to get screwed. In Israel there are no rules. The pakid has all the discretion. If he likes you, he gives you more, and if he doesn't like you, he gives you nothing. You really have the feeling that the pakid, in his office, is actually dispensing whatever it is—licenses, mortgages, loans—by grace; by his own personal power. In the States no bureaucrat acts by grace. His authority comes from his position—the power of the position isn't his own. Every postal pakid in Israel, behind his cage, thinks he's a Jewish Cardinal Spellman.

Martin's use of "grace," "dispensation," "authority," and so on, makes almost superfluous a point-by-point comparison of Israel's bureaucracy with Weber's ideal-typic one (but cf. Gerth and Mills 1958:196–244). My aim here, however, is not merely to assert that Israeli bureaucracy deviates in important ways from the modern, rational, Western model. Eisenstadt, and Danet and Hartman, among others, have already demonstrated that in Israel traditional and modern elements are "institutionalized side by side." I am interested, rather, in demonstrating that it is the traditional elements that must be mastered by Americans if they are to succeed in bureaucratic encounters. Danet et al. speak of "bureaucratic competence" as an attribute of modernity and "moderns," and they find that Oriental Jews lack it. My focus is wider; for, to paraphrase Chomsky, I am interested also in bureaucratic performance, and in Israel this is very much an attribute of tradition and "traditionals."

The socialization of American immigrants to bureaucratic performance is not an easy one. In part, socialization demands the acquisition of new skills: and all socialization incurs unseemly accidents along the way.

"Let me tell you this story," said Ephraim, resident six years.

It happened to friends of ours who arrived after us. They were at a *merkaz klita* ["absorption center"] in Beersheva, and for a year they went through the usual *balagan* ["confusion"] to get a mortgage to buy an apartment. Finally, one day my friend went into the ministry office to sign some forms. And he was told that all they needed was to bring three co-signers the next day. Now, "co-signers" in Hebrew is *areivim* [literally: "guarantors"], and "Arabs" is 'aravim.' The guy's Hebrew wasn't perfect, and he said to the pakid: 'Wait, you want me to bring three *aravim* tomorrow for a loan?' and the pakid said: "I just told you: three *areivim*."

My friend went home to his wife and said: "All we need to do is bring three Arabs with us tomorrow." And she said: "*Arabs? Why Arabs? Where will we get them?*" He said: "Who knows why Arabs? If they want Arabs they'll get Arabs. I'll go to the *shuk* ["market"] tomorrow morning and bring in the first three Arabs I find."

The next day he goes to the shuk, gives ten *lirot* each to three Bedouin, and they all march to the ministry. You're laughing? [I was]. All right. It's a funny story, yes? But it just shows that people become so used to absolutely incredible things that are asked of them, that they don't even question them rationally any more. The pakid wanted three *aravim*? Fine. We'll bring him three *aravim*! Without asking, "Why would you want three Arabs for an apartment mortgage?" Without thinking logically. But where *is* the logic here?

In negotiating the bureaucratic encounter, Americans learn that what was, in the United States, a bureaucrat-client relationship based upon contract is, in Israel, a relationship based largely on status. Said Dennis, who himself works in the Jewish Agency:

The system can be worked with, but you have to be nice to everyone in it. You have to be very personal. You have to go to see people a number of times, and shake their hands, and drink coffee with them; you have to develop a *trust* here, with people. Trust is very important. If you are a bureaucrat like I am—I'm almost ashamed to say it, but that's what I am, a pakid—you have to be willing to move and be flexible, to bend or break rules for or against *persons,* to make the system work.

Dennis's statement is remarkable in several ways, for example, in its clarity. It also illustrates the socialization of a bureaucrat to Israeli bureaucracy. Yet one cannot quite call it bureaucratic socialization. It appears to be, in fact, an instance of *de*bureaucratic socialization.

Interview transcripts were filled with examples of favored bureaucratic strategies. But aside from the almost universal dictum, "Seek thee proteksia," the strategies were characterized by their diversity. Some said: "Speak only Hebrew in offices, no matter how poorly." Others, "Speak only English." Still others, "Find a pakid who speaks Yiddish, and establish a kesher that way." Some said, "Scream and holler." Others, "*Never* raise your voice." Women have different strategies: "Act tough: Israelis don't expect it." "Cry—out will come the tea." "Flirt." "Bring your kids and instruct them to climb all over the place and to ignore you when you tell them to stop. The pakidim then will want to get you out as soon as possible." The diversity of strategies is due partly to differences in personal styles and to the varying exigencies of particular bureaucratic encounters; but partly, I suspect, it is due also to a general lack of agreement about which strategies will work. With respect to the learning of pragmatic rules, relatively few olim are comfortable in their roles as clients; I shall return to this point in the chapter's final section.

Nevertheless, the almost universal idiom for insuring bureaucratic success, in the eyes of olim, is the possession and use of proteksia. Eighty-two percent of the Jerusalem sample attached at least "fair" importance to it—of whom half thought it was "very important." Only 3 percent believed proteksia was "not at all important." Close to three-fourths of the sample said they have used proteksia at least once; 15 percent said they use it often; 26 percent said they have never used proteksia. Interestingly, several olim interpreted the "real" function of the Jewish Agency and Ministry of Immigrant Absorption to be that of possessing institutional proteksia for the newcomer, who possesses none. One oleh said: "If it really worked that way, everything would be fine. But unfortunately it just ends up that you need proteksia to approach the very organizations that ought to be your proteksia." Finally, 65 percent of the Jerusalem sample thought proteksia was important but "a bad thing, morally wrong." Of that proportion, 14 percent said that because it was wrong they would not invoke it; 51 percent said they invoke it when "they have to," in spite of its being morally wrong. Close to one-third said they use it "whenever they have to, without thinking about it too much."

Olim talk about proteksia a lot: how to get it ("build up your network"); how to use it ("along with regular channels"); why they don't have it ("I'm just a greenhorn here," or, "I don't look for it"). It seems to them to be, as one put it, "Such a concrete thing in Israel, I feel I can reach out in offices and touch it. Maybe that's why Israelis call it 'Vitamin P'." Proteksia, that is, comes to stand for the essence of Israeli bureaucratic encounters: do not expect universalism; do not expect role specificity; do not expect affective neutrality. Some olim view proteksia, symbolically, as a pragmatic guide: utilize particularism; maximize multiplexity; encourage affective valence. The majority, however, do not see it as an ethical guide. They think it is a bad thing.

I want to close this section by citing a semiofficial guide to bureaucracy in Israel. On a regular basis, the Ministry of Immigrant Absorption communicates articles to the *Jerusalem Post* that are aimed at the English-speaking new immigrant. In the past, pieces have dealt with technical visa questions, housing in Israel, military responsibilities, and so on. Recently, a Ministry article took up the problem of *bureaucratia*.[7] In a straightforward way, the writer of the piece admitted there were some difficulties to be overcome and then, under the subheading "How to overcome it all," he advised the following:

> Once he does arrive in Israel, the new immigrant needs to remember two important words: *sechel* and *savlanut* (intelligence and patience). Patience because everything—even when it is working properly—takes a long time in Israel, and intelligence because it immediately becomes necessary to find faster ways through the paperwork and officialdom. A keen eye helps: watch how the native gets things done, which tactics work to get a clerk's attention, and which excuses get you to the head of a long line of waiting, suffering citizens.
>
> Another vital ingredient is "Vitamin P"—*protectzia*. To an American this term smacks of the Mafia and secret payoffs, but in Israel it most often means simply "knowing someone who knows someone who knows someone" who can help get the right person to help you with your problem.

The writer next adds an insight that relates societal scale to, among other things, multiplexity and a peculiarly Mediterranean sense of social relations:

> It is probably for this reason—more than for any other—that, despite all the shouting and arguing that goes on in clerk vs. citizen confrontations, the two sides rarely part on totally unfriendly terms: in a country as small as Israel, the two may meet again and the situation could well be reversed.[8]

He then admits that there are other options—bureaucratic ones:

> When all else fails in dealing with Israeli bureaucracy, the old "let me speak to your boss" line still pulls some weight. That, plus letters to government ministers. . . . These are the classic tools of the frustrated citizen and often produce results.

I am impressed by the quaintness with which classicism is here imbued. Finally, however, the ministry writer turns to the rewards of successful "bureaucratic" socialization.

> Eventually the hardiest immigrants survive the ordeal and go on to become good Israeli citizens themselves. Some even end up working in the government, hopefully bringing to their jobs a compassion and understanding for those still to come.

As the hardiest survive, the sociology of absorption becomes the sociobiology of absorption. More to the point: the new immigrant becomes a good Israeli—getting to the head of long lines of waiting, suffering citizens manqués; and some even become pakidim themselves, bringing compassion and understanding, among other things, to their bureaucratic roles, in place of, perhaps, standards of universalism, specificity, and affective neutrality.

If one takes this piece as a guide, the new immigrant is not only expected by the Ministry of Immigrant Absorption to traditionalize in order to absorb: he is being forthrightly encouraged to do so.

"Doing Business"

When the Jerusalem sample was asked the following, "Some people think that 'doing business' in Israel is something very different from doing business in the U.S., while other people think it's not different. With which opinion do you agree?" close to 90 percent of the respondents replied that "doing business" in Israel was "very different." Those who answered affirmatively were then asked to name two ways in which doing business in Israel differed from doing it in the U.S. Broadly, these responses can be grouped in three clusters. One can be represented by the remarks, "too much government interference," or "too much bureaucracy." The second cluster grouped what may be called macro-level differences, among them: market scale, the problems of an economy always geared to war and defense, "the higher tax rates in a welfare state," and so on. The third cluster grouped a series of observations on business relations in Israel. This was the largest cluster. Responses here included: "Attitudes towards consumers are unenlightened"; "Businessmen lie and deceive"; "Manufacturers don't take responsibilities, therefore they cannot innovate"; and, simply, "the Levantine mentality and morality."

The second cluster, though important, will not concern us here. The first cluster entails certain problems in negotiating social relations that were discussed in the previous section. Because the businessman is operating in a highly bureaucratized environment, he, especially, requires the skills necessary for negotiating successful bureaucratic encounters. Take Aaron, on the subject of proteksia:

> In this country it's very difficult to do something without someone. For example, when I started my own business, I needed an import license and just couldn't get one—all kinds of government regulations, and a pakid who told me, "You don't need an import license, you never had one before. Why now?" Do you believe this? The *clerk* judged that I didn't need one!
>
> So in this case proteksia meant that I found a friend who knew the director-general of the Ministry of Commerce and Industry. And my friend took me in—I'd been trying for six months on my own! The director was an Englishman, and my friend introduced me to him. The Englishman calls up the pakid and says: "Give this man an import license." And I went downstairs and picked it up.

Later in the interview Aaron returned to this story and the subject of proteksia:

> When I first tried to get the license, by the way, and before I found my contact for the director-general, I made the big mistake of trying to offer that pakid some money—to bribe him. Boy, did I land on my ass! I thought he'd call the Marines in! In the States, a little cash to grease the wheels always worked, but I learned then and there you can't do that, by and large, in

Israel. In fact, I think that because I tried to bribe him, the pakid really had it in for me. What did I learn? I learned *people* grease the wheels here, not just money.

There is another way to articulate what Aaron had learned. In its purest form, the bribe is an expression of a contract relationship. It is payment given for services rendered. Although proteksia, too, is based on a form of reciprocity, the basis of the relationship is different; the basis is status, not contract. Another oleh put it this way: "You can bribe someone for fifteen years and make him rich, and he still owes you nothing you haven't paid for in advance. But each time you use proteksia, or give it, you make—in a funny way—your total relationship with that guy stronger."

Almost by definition, the successful businessman acquires traditionalizing skills to negotiate Israeli *bureaucratia*. There are important ways in which these skills are harnessed in the service of something other than traditionalizing; they are to be discussed in Chapter 7. For the present, however, I want to leave the first cluster—the problems of "government interference" and bureaucracy—and focus on the third, the one concerned broadly with business relations. It is not surprising that this cluster of responses was the largest, for the style of business relations affects the consumer (a category that includes the majority of American olim) as well as the businessman (one that includes a minority, between 10 and 15 percent).

In general, the responses on how doing business in Israel differs from doing business in the U.S. deal with the problems of "business ethics," such as "honesty," "accountability," and the "worth of a written contract" or "someone's word." Some of the other and related responses to this query were as follows:

> (Israeli) business is not oriented to customer service.
> It is not competitive.
> Lack of standards of excellence.
> The customer is always wrong.
> No "go-getter" attitude.
> No rational planning possible.
> Americans get taken.

> No one honors their word.
> Too much bargaining . . . the price always depends
> on *who* you are.
> Mediterranean mentality.
> Businesses are not businesslike.
> Lack of what we call "WASP know-how and
> efficiency."

It is clear that the overarching standard of comparison for the "Mediterranean"—or more often "Levantine"—business mentality is the American or, as one respondent put it, the "WASP." Honesty, efficiency, and rationality are extolled; their apparent absence, in Israel, bemoaned. As in the case of bureaucracy, the best informants on doing business in Israel are the businessmen themselves. The best examples, here, are not among those doing business in sophisticated areas—electronics or information processing, for example—although here, too, informants complain of the absence of rationality. Rather, it is often on the level of the most basic buying and selling that the frustrations are the greatest.

"Look," said Natan, a resident of six years,

> I run a small *makolet* ["grocery store"], one hundred square meters. But the answers I get, in dealing with suppliers—if American Jews would hear this they wouldn't believe it. I mean, you've been raised in America, try to imagine this. You have a market, and there's a particular challah that sells well. I know the man who runs the bakery; he comes from Eastern Europe. And I say to him: "Eliezer, I took the first week fifty challahs, and second week one hundred, I get now up to three hundred challahs—cash." Ordinarily I never pay cash, but if there's a product I want, like a challah, because it brings people into the store, I'm willing to pay cash, even if I don't make much profit on the product. "Eliezer," I say, "Send the challahs by truck out to my store in G—— [a suburb of Jerusalem]." He says: "No." He'll only send them to my house. So first I have to load the challahs in my car, then I have to bring them out to G—— myself. I say, "Eliezer, *send* me the challahs. I'm paying you cash, no checks." And he knows me—because Jerusalem is a small town and within days everyone knows everyone else—and he knows I'm doing well. I say: "Send them out, you've got a truck—and you'll get cash." He

says: "No! You people come from America and you want to
ein-reisin di weldt!" [Yiddish: "Tear up the world"].

So I got very angry and went down to his *ma'afiya* ["bakery"] and—without exaggeration—maybe the whole bakery is
three times as big as my car. And I say: "Eliezer, why don't
you put in another machine, buy another truck, and bring chal-
lahs to whoever wants them?"

He says: "What do I need it for? I don't even go to all of
Jerusalem, so I'm going to go to the suburbs? I don't want to
keep books, this is enough. You Americans come here like
Cossacks with your business-this, business-that. *Genug!*
["Enough"].

Now I can multiply this by a hundred examples. And if I told
these stories to an American Jew he'd call me an anti-Semite.
Look, there are a lot of *Gruzenim* [Jews from Soviet Georgia]
near my store, and I find out they like a certain kind of vodka
called "Red Vodka." So I track down the producer of such a
vodka in Jerusalem. You should see their plant—to an American it looks like something out of the Smithsonian Institution.
So I call up Moshe, and according to his Hebrew I see right
away he speaks Yiddish, so I figure I'll speak Yiddish to him,
and I say [in Yiddish]: "Moshe, I want to order thirty cases of
Red Vodka, and your man will receive cash, not a check, as
soon as he comes." You know what his answer was? "I'll have
to speak to my brother-in-law." I ask: "Moshe, are you the
owner?" He says yes. "Are you partners with your brother-
in-law?" He says no, his brother-in-law works for him. So I
say: "Then why speak to your brother-in-law? I'm ordering
thirty cases of vodka! Now it's true you never dealt with me
before, but as soon as your man comes he'll get cash."

He says: "No, I must talk to my brother-in-law."

I say: "God in heaven! Do you own a distillery?" He says
yes. "Do you make vodka?" He says yes. "So *send* me
vodka!" No.

Two days later I talk to Moshe's brother-in-law. He agrees
to let Moshe send me thirty cases of Red Vodka. But he adds:
"If it's raining, my man won't come out."

Can you believe this mentality? Can you imagine calling up a
supplier, in America, a guy who has whiskey, and you say,
"Bring out thirty cases and you'll get money on the spot." I
mean, is he going to tell you that if it rains he's not coming? It's
inconceivable. Here it's a daily thing. And this is something I
really didn't *see*—as well as I thought I knew Israel—until I
opened my own business.

I finally got the vodka, by the way. Even though it was as if I was asking for Moshe's daughter's hand in marriage.

In talking about business relations, as compared to bureaucratic ones, it is less easy to specify exact points in encounters where, for example, multiplexity is (or ought to be) sought, and so on. Proteksia is important in the world of doing business, to be sure, but its clearest expression yet remains in the context of *bureaucratia*. When they speak about—or rail against—business in Israel, the Americans rely on a set of standards—"principles"—of honesty, efficiency, rationality, to which doing business in Israel is compared and found lacking. More importantly, there is a crucial difference in the way Americans perceive bureaucratic encounters and business encounters. In the former, they feel forced to enter and play the game like an Israeli, as they best they can, in order to win. Statements against, for example, proteksia, are invariably moral or normative ones ("It's not right"), rather than pragmatic ("It doesn't work"—although olim do say, "It doesn't work for *me*"). For business affairs, especially among those olim who are in business, the perception is clear that certain changes—in the direction of honesty, efficiency, and rationality—ought to take place. Traditionalizing skills are less willingly acquired in the business world that in the world of bureaucracy. This fact has important implications that I shall take up in the next chapter; for now, consider the remarks of Bernard, who has a small but growing business:

> The bureaucracy? I've learned not to fight it but to work with it. I've learned there are different rules for dealing with this bureaucracy, different than in the States, and I've tried to learn these rules and work with them. Like proteksia; like how to avoid lines; like how not to take "No" for an answer; like learning who is the guy on a higher level who can help you, and avoiding the lowly pakid altogether and going to *that* guy.
>
> It didn't just happen: I had to learn the ropes. But I accept the ropes—at least of the bureaucracy. My business is a different thing. *It* is my own, and I try to run it like an American business, with service and efficiency and responsibility. It would be even better than it is, but the bureaucracy is so much a part of everyday life here that you go up against it all the time, and that means you can never get too rational.
>
> I may sound like a right-wing fanatic, but the truth is I was a

Leftie in the States, marched against the Vietnam War and all that—but living in Israel has made me appreciate the capitalistic system and free enterprise.

This newfound appreciation for "capitalism" and "free enterprise," as well as the perception of what another oleh called the "lack of WASP know-how and efficiency," in Israel, will appear again. For the present, however, we need to return to some of the questions that began this chapter. With respect to bureaucratic and business relations, at least, how is the Americans' absorption affected by the very dynamics—the traditionalization of social identities—that brought them to make aliya? What is the relationship between the kind of traditionalizing they effect in Israel with absorption, and the traditionalizing they effected with aliya?

Traditionalizing: Expressive and Instrumental

In Chapter 5, I described a process whereby certain American Jews make a hyperinvestment in their ethnic identity, their Jewishness, over other parts of their total social identity. They have invested in a particular image of self. Some of these individuals make another investment, in a particular image of society. It is a society where, they believe, their self can attain or regain a measure of consensus, consonance, or complementarity. The two images are interdependent. The primordial ties, loyalties, and sentiments that are at the core of an ethnic identity are, in a sense, projected to form an image of a primordial society where consensus and the rest can be reached. It is a society whose template in *mishpaha,* the family. The image of the society in which the olim (in America) invest is a gemeinschaft, not a gesellschaft. As they reject aspects of America's modernity, they embrace in Israel an image of tradition.

In the present chapter I have "followed" these individuals to Israel, and to their confrontations with something other than their ideal image of Israeli society. My discussion was framed by a consideration of the sociology of absorption. This sociology was built to account for problems in the adjustment and adaptation to Israel of Oriental Jews. An equivalence was drawn between absorption and modernization. Throughout this chapter, I have argued that, so far as American olim are concerned, the equivalence must be stood on its head. For the American oleh, the significant process in his absorption to Israel is not his modernization but his traditionalization. But there is a tension between the traditionalizing that brought the olim to Israel and the traditionalizing they face once in Israel: the two are not the same. In America, they had invested in an image of gemeinschaft; in Israel they must acquire skills that enable them to function in a gemeinschaft.

The view of adjustment as the acquisition of new skills, new roles, or as education in a new style of social relationships, is not a radical one for studies of acculturation or the resocialization of adults. But we must attend very carefully to the nature of the skills, the substance of the roles, and the ethos that imbues the style of social relationships. In bureaucratic encounters the oleh learns, among many other things, to replace cash credits with social credits. As a client, he learns that what was a contract or simplex relationship in America is best approached (in terms of his success in the encounter), in Israel through status or multiplex terms. In business relations he learns, with even less equanimity, to expect the absence of contract in the literal meaning of the term. The problems here are with "honesty," "efficiency," or "business ethics"; at root, doing business is felt to lack the basis of rationality it had in America. "There is too much bargaining," as one oleh put it. "The price always depends on who you are." And, indeed, this is what we might expect, for the question of who one is, is always a paramount one—in gemeinschaften and in moral communities.

I have argued that in learning these new skills and roles the immigrant traditionalizes. The argument does not posit tradition (Israel) and modernity (the U.S.) as polar opposites on some cosmic continuum. The argument concerns processes. One, modernization, has received much scholarly attention; the other, traditionalization, less.

In Israel both processes occur within the same locus of activities, within the same institutions. They are distinguishable by reference to the actors involved. An oleh from Yemen or Morocco is taught that goods or services—for example a business license—formerly procured through influential kinsmen are now to be got from a universalistic, simplex, affectively neutral (Israeli, modern) bureaucracy. The language of absorption tells us he is being modernized. An American oleh, already socialized to such a bureaucracy, and perhaps the holder of a similar license in the United States, learns that his chances of getting the license in Israel increase dramatically if a neighbor calls his brother-in-law whose Army friend works in the appropriate office (or in a nearly appropriate office!). He learns, that is, to manipulate a system which is more particularistic, multiplex, and affectively valenced than the one he knew in the United States. My question is simple: Is there a language of absorption able to specify, *here is an individual who is being traditionalized*?

It is important, however, to separate the two senses of traditionalizing that I have talked about. A person who invests in an ethnic identity and maximizes the investment, contextualizing the identity in a particular image of society, has traditionalized his social identity in an expressive mode. He has made certain ties, loyalties, and values primary or ultimate ones. The person who knows that the first step in procuring a business license is the activation of proteksia, of kin or *hevra* ("group") contacts in his personal network, leading to face-to-face work with the appropriate pakid, is also traditionalizing, but in an instrumental mode. If this person is an American, he is probably uncomfortable with this second form of traditionalizing, ill at ease when what ought to be an affectively neutral bureaucratic encounter becomes affectively charged.

The first traditionalizing of identity brings him from America to Israel. At root this is an expressive transformation, concerned chiefly with values. To be sure, there is an instrumental component too: a heightened self-identification as a Jew most often occurs in conjunction with Zionist, religious, or culturalist involvements, in the contexts of synagogue or community. Aliya itself can be viewed as an instrumental outcome of this process.

The second form of traditionalizing takes place in Israel. At root it is instrumental; it occurs in the context of goal-oriented behavior and concerns learning new skills, strategies, and tactics that are deemed necessary and central for attaining the goal. Here, however, there is an expressive component involving the extent to which the oleh feels himself "becoming an Israeli." Olim would begin a story of a successful bureaucratic encounter with: "I knew I was an Israeli when ... " or would conclude one with: "After that I knew I was becoming an Israeli." One oleh, resident since 1968, added: "By now my wife and I are good enough Israelis to be proteksia for our friends, for people who came after us."

For all this, however, I think it is important not to over-emphasize this emergent expressive component. In the first place, the above remarks by olim were often spoken with 'less ingenuousness and more cynicism ("good *enough* Israelis ...") than may be apparent in a transcript. To say one has learned and utilizes new skills to pursue certain goals in certain kinds of en-counters, is to say one has learned to play a new role—let us say a new client role in the client-bureaucrat pair. But there is a great difference between merely learning a new role, adding it to one's behavioral repertoire and playing it in appropriate situations more or less convincingly (instrumental role-playing), and internalizing the role: believing, in a particular situation, that this is the "only," "right," or "natural" role to be played (here the role has become expressive). Clearly, as their remarks indicate, these olim feel that playing a certain type of client role is to take on the identity of "Israeli" ("I felt like an Israeli when ..."). But this Israeli identity is worn like an ill-fitting mantle: cynically, re-signedly, or in plain discomfort. So long as roles are played, in the main, instrumentally, the olim play them "like Israelis"—but re-tain their identity as "Americans." It is when a role is inter-nalized that it becomes expressive: it is expressive of what is "right" and of how things "ought" to be. Such roles become significant—heavily loaded—constituents of social identity.

The first traditionalizing—with its investment in the identity Jew, in America—has implications for a structural transformation of social identity. It is unlikely that the second traditionalizing—playing certain roles "like an Israeli" without making them also expressive—carries with it the same identity-transforming po-tency. The olim are uncomfortable playing the roles of in-strumental traditionalization.

Let me be a little more specific about the Americans' dis-comfort. In my discussion of proteksia I noted that the majority believed it to be "morally wrong, a bad thing." At that point I spoke, in Bailey's (1969) sense, of the difference between norma-tive and pragmatic rules. Even when they know how the game is played to win, they still retain the sense of how it really *ought* to be played. The difference between the normative and the prag-

matic is equivalent, in this case, to the difference between the
expressive and the instrumental. So long as the olim accept only
the pragmatic rules of the Israeli game, while retaining their own
conception of the normative rules, they continue to play,
essentially, like Americans.

The moral stance against proteksia cannot be explained, simply, as a function of the proteksia Americans don't have. On the
contrary, as an Ashkenazi, professional, English-speaking group
they possess, in general, considerably more inherent proteksia
than other new-immigrant (e.g., Russian), or even veteran (e.g.,
Moroccan) groups. Moreover, their discomfort with other bureaucratic role-playing that is not specifically related to proteksia
does in fact block their learning the skills, and thus achieving a
convincing performance in the role. There is, for instance, a
strategy that dictates one must perforce approach a pakid
aggressively—truly in affectively charged terms!—with cajoling,
begging, and even threats of physical violence. A sabra with three
years' experience as an aliya emissary in the U.S. summed up the
Americans' considerable trouble with Israeli bureaucracy in
these words:

> Americans are taught to follow rules. If you follow rules then
> things will get done; if you deviate from the rules you are a
> nonconformist and a problem. This is how they expect the Is-
> raeli bureaucracy to work, according to *rules*. But here, if you
> don't deviate from the rules you are a *nobody*. If you wait in
> line quietly for two hours you can wait for another three.
>   The Israeli knows how to break the rules—to scream and
> make a nuisance of himself. The American is turned off by this,
> but *this* is what he must learn to do to make the bureaucracy
> work for him.

According to her, then, the American must simply cease being
"turned off" by this behavior, and learn how to behave in this
way himself. But there is more to it than just learning the appropriate behavior. If the behavior remains merely instrumental, if it
remains on the level of pragmatics only, the ego (the client) remains expressively an American; and alter (the bureaucrat) perceives this quickly. One oleh, resident in Israel five years and the
owner of a small electronics company, noted some of the difficulties in following the sabra's advice, even if one wants to:

I know people say you have to holler and scream and turn the pakid's desk over on him. But the problem with hollering and screaming and reaching for the desk is that, in the end, you really have to be prepared to turn the damn thing over. I'm not, and when they hear my [American] Hebrew accent they *know* I'm not.

I keep thinking: I know what the rules say, and by the rules I'm entitled to this mortgage; besides—how can a damned clerk stop you from getting a mortgage?

["Can he?" someone asked.]

Oh, every time.

The tension between the two forms of traditionalizing, expressive and instrumental, has manifested itself in areas other than bureaucratic and business encounters. It has been present in the basic way the State of Israel desired to relate to Diaspora Jews, and in the way Jews of the American Diaspora have related back. Earlier I wrote that the olim, in America, had an image of Israeli society at whose center was *mishpaha* ["family"]. The society was conceived, in toto, as a moral community in which members would relate to one another as something more than *haverim* ["comrades"], and as something more than citizens.

It is, I think, the distance between "family member" and "citizen" that separates Henry Maine's "status" from "contract." In a nation-state citizens are bound to each other by contract, and there are routine procedures for revoking citizenship or conferring it on the non-native-born. The latter is known as "naturalization"—like "absorption," an interesting metaphor. Citizenship "by naturalization" is perhaps the ultimate expression of Maine's idea of contract. Now consider Israel. Two of its first "basic laws" are the Law of Return (1950), which grants to every Jew the right to settle in Israel, and the Nationality Law (1952), which grants to every oleh automatic Israeli citizenship. With regard to Jews, there is no such thing as naturalization in (or to) Israel. This is to say that the state relates to every Jew, in all places, on the basis of his being a Jew; relates to him by status. There is no period of probationary waiting, nor are there lessons on the Bill of Rights to be learned. The state extended the invitation to Diaspora Jews to activate this relationship of status, by making aliya. What was the reaction of those Western, and especially American, Jews who accepted the invitation?

After the Six-Day War, when Israel was trying to encourage aliya from Western democracies, it found a reluctance on the part of these olim to accept their automatic Israeli citizenship. On the advice of a consultative committee, the Minister of Interior in June 1969, instituted the special visa category called "potential oleh." Among the other things this category provides for (e.g., a military service deferment for those it applies to), there is a three-year wait-and-see period before a final decision on Israeli citizenship—or "permanent resident" status—must be made. A glance at table 6.1 shows that Western olim, in general, and American olim overwhelmingly, opted for potential oleh status. It seems, that is, that these immigrants were pushing a contract on a state ready to bestow rights (and duties) on the basis of pure status. Given the choice between oleh and potential oleh (automatic vs. deferred citizenship), olim from various countries chose as indicated in the table.[9]

Table 6.1   Olim vs. Potential Olim, by Last Country of Residence, Arrived 1969–71

Country	Potential Olim	Olim	Total	Percent Olim
U.S.	17,168	2,359	19,527	12.1
U.K.	3,663	1,066	4,729	22.5
Argentina	2,184	2,654	4,838	54.9
France	4,344	8,643	12,987	66.6
Iran	1,026	4,923	5,949	82.8
USSR	19	16,831	16,850	99.9

SOURCE: Adapted from data in *Immigration to Israel, 1948–1972*, special series no. 416, pt. 1 (Jerusalem: Israel Central Bureau of Statistics, 1973), table 4, p. 21.

Finally, the tension between the two forms of traditionalizing, expressive and instrumental, is rooted in a special sort of dissonance. It is, in Wallace and Fogelson's (1965) sense, a dissonance between the ideal image of a society the olim had internalized in the U.S. and the real society they confront in Israel. But it is *not* the difference between valuations of gesellschaft and gemeinschaft that engenders the dissonance, as was the case in America. In Israel, rather, it is a dissonance engendered by the difference between an ideal image of gemeinschaft and its reality.

Internalized images of society are interdependent with internalized images of self. In America, our olim were persons who, in minimizing the dissonance between their ideal self (e.g., the religious Jew) and their real self (themselves as a practicing religious Jew), ended up by maximizing the dissonance between their real society (American/gesellschaft) and their ideal society (Israeli-Jewish/gemeinschaft). Increasingly, their real society became congruent with their image of a feared society; they made aliya to obliterate this congruence. In Israel, however, this process is in a sense reversed. Now it is the dissonance between ideal (Israeli-Jewish/gemeinschaft) and real society (themselves as members of Israeli-Jewish/gemeinschaft) that becomes germane. Because of the dissonance, and because of the interdependence of images of self and society, questions of identity in Israel reemerge. For so long as the traditionalizing the olim effect in Israel remains only instrumental and is not made expressive, our olim are persons who, in maximizing the dissonance between ideal (Israeli) and real (Israeli) society, end up by minimizing the dissonance between ideal self (as a Jew) and what was, in the U.S., their feared self (an assimilated Jew: an American). As, increasingly, their real society (Israeli) becomes congruent with a (new) image of a feared society (called "Levantine," among other things), the congruence between ideal self (Jew) and feared self (American) becomes increasingly acute. Having come to Israel as Jews, the olim find themselves confronting it as Americans.

It is to attempts by olim to reconcile this dilemma—to come to grips with the newfound congruence between Jew and American—that I turn in the next chapter. I deal, of course, with those olim who have remained in Israel; for many, I suspect, reconcile the dilemma through emigration, yerida. The paths to reconciliation are varied but most involve a reevaluation by the olim of the meaning of aliya. For many, from their vantage point in Israel, aliya comes to be seen not only as the move to a Jewish state serving a Jewish society. It is seen—in the most basic and evolutionary sense of traditionalizing—as a move backwards in time. In that vision lies one key to resolving the dilemma.

Aliya and Change
Modernizing

> The progress of modernity ("modernization") depends on its very sense of instability and inauthenticity. For moderns, reality and authenticity are thought to be elsewhere: in other historical periods and other cultures, in purer, simpler life-styles.
>
> Dean MacCannell, *The Tourist*

A Vision of Israel: The Encroaching Levant

Towards the end of his little book on group relations in Israel, Alex Weingrod (1965:74–80) presents three different visions of Israel's "social future." The first he calls a vision based on the model of "total assimilation," the second "Levantinization," and the third—the one most likely to be realized, he believes—"ethnic pluralism." The assimilation model is what I have discussed under the name "absorption." Assimilation, writes Weingrod, "has been the goal of the veteran Europeans: this doctrine is represented by the belief that [Oriental] immigrants would give up their previous habits and adopt the traditions of the veteran community." The sociology of absorption, I have argued, put forth a particular process of social change as the standard for the orientals' assimilation. The anthropologist Weingrod is careful to specify the adoption of "the *traditions* of the veteran community."[1] The ideology of absorption, however, as it affected both theoretical thinking and practical programs, was different: with respect to Oriental immigrants, social change was linked pervasively to, and was identified as, modernization. In the previous chapter, I followed the logic of this argument and considered some of the changes Americans undergo in the course of their absorption. Here, however, change was not identified as modernization. With respect to American olim, I argued for a different sort of process: traditionalization.

160

The second vision of Israel's future, "Levantinization,"

promises the exact opposite from assimilation. Levantinization
suggests that, in the future, the numerical superiority of Middle Easterners [Jews] will result in the dominance of a rootless,
amoral spirit. The ever-growing Middle Eastern majority (in
this view) adopts only a thin veneer of Western custom, while
beneath that veneer there remains the cynical volatile spirit of
the Levant. The ascendance of this Levantine type will finally
signal the end of great social dreams: the wish to create the
"good society" will sink under the sheer weight of Middle
Eastern numbers. And indeed, so this viewpoint concludes, the
cynicism and signs of moral decay already present in Israeli life
attest to the growing influence of this Levantine spirit.
(1965:76)

Weingrod's description of Levantinization faithfully reflects
the viewpoint of the veteran European settlers. In this context
Levantinism is viewed as a sort of pollutant. Specifically: it will
pollute the already modern structures of Israeli society. The
"great social dreams" that are endangered are those bound up,
historically, in the principles of socialist labor-Zionism.

American olim also speak about, and express great fears for,
the Levantinization of Israel. Some of these fears have already
surfaced in the previous chapter's section on doing business.
There are, however, important differences in the Americans'
conceptions of Levantinism and Levantinization, compared to
those of the veteran European settlers. In the first place, the
Americans are not so willing to accept as a first principle the
modernity of Israeli society. Rather than view Levantinism as a
pollutant of modernity brought to Israel with the mass influx of
Oriental immigrants, therefore, the Americans tend to conceive
of it as a force that will block an Israeli modernization that has
only just taken off. Secondly, and related to the first points, the
Americans often include the veteran Europeans in their condemnation of Levantinism. The notion, that is, has been ex-
panded by Americans to include not only the "amoral. . . . cynical
volatile spirit of the Levant" but also—in the words of one
oleh—the "mean, limited, and medieval spirit of the shtetl."
Thirdly, the Americans do not so much oppose Levantinism to
the "great social dreams" of labor-Zionism, as is the case with

the veteran Europeans. Recall, in Chapter 6, Aaron's comments on the Israeli tax system: "the mentality is to force the guy to pay the highest tax. They call this 'socialism,' but it's really Oriental despotism." Recall Bernard, the businessman, discussing his own transformation from "a Leftie in the States": "living in Israel has made me appreciate the capitalistic system, and free enterprise." And recall, finally, one oleh's criticism of doing business in Israel: there is, he noted, a "lack of what we call 'WASP know-how and efficiency.'" The Americans, in short, do not oppose Levantinism to the dreams of a socialist utopia; rather, they oppose it to their image of contemporary American society, right down to its "WASP" character that had so disconcerted them, as Jews, in the U.S.

Some of these American beliefs, as well as the differences between them and the veteran European's conception of Levantinism, may be seen in the following excerpts from interview transcripts:

Dave: We are not an American country here. This is an East European country with a touch of the Levantine. You have a bureaucracy that would be inconceivable in America. You have inefficiency; you have lack of foresight—the American *logic* is not here. You have a tremendous part of the population which is backward—sociologically, psychologically, economically, emotionally—because a good part of our population, Jews and non-Jews, has come from medieval backgrounds.

Sarah: Look, this is a Levantine country. We Americans come from the most advanced society, technology, in the world. Here—what are you dealing with? A populace that comes from Russia, and that's the *high* culture, the best of them!

Moshe: Basically this country is being run by Jews from Eastern Europe who came straight from the shtetl, and Jews from Oriental countries who know very little, whose ideas of efficiency are very backward. Their conceptions are limited.

Ruth: The only reason why so many [political] parties still manage to exist here is that in some way this is still part of the Ottoman Empire: feudal. They [the parties] are all baronies.

Joe: We talk about our technology here in Israel. In a few cases we've made breakthroughs, like in agriculture. But generally speaking we're way behind, we're way behind everyone else.

Running through these comments—or underlying them—is a peculiar concern with diachronics. The population is backward; American society is advanced; feudalism, the Ottoman Empire, and baronies are invoked; despite some technological break-throughs, Israel is seen to be "way behind everyone else." For the Americans, Levantinism is not merely counterposed, syn-chronically, as the pollutant of an already modern Israeli society. The Americans expand the notion to include a temporal dimen-sion. Levantinism does not merely exist as a contemporary spirit of the Levant; it is also—and more clearly when spoken of as the spirit of the shtetl—a spirit of the "historical" past. In fact, many olim view their move to Israel as a move backwards in time:

> *Dan:* This is really a baby country and there's a lot of move-ment. When I had this [job] interview here and I saw the state of professional materials for lawyers, I said to the man as I left: "I know where you're going. I know the direction you're going, but you're twenty-five years behind the kind of life we had in the States."
> Because I felt—it's as if, in Israel, I'm stepping back in time twenty-five years, so I know how they're going to develop. I said to him: "I know how you've *got to* develop. And perhaps I can help in that development."

The fear of Levantinism is more properly located in a fear of the process of ongoing or increasing Levantinism: of Levantiniza-tion. For Americans, the predominance of this process would mean Israel would move continually backwards in time: remain-ing "way behind," it would never catch up. And, as Dan's re-marks indicate, some Americans have a great commitment to Israel's catching up. They are committed to its continued "devel-opment." They feel, moreover, that, having come from advanced America to Israel, they have a special contribution to make. They possess skills necessary for development and, more important, they possess a road-map of the course of development.

The process of Levantinization that they fear is a process of—in their eyes—undesirable social change. The Americans ad-vocate change, too, but it is of a different sort: change towards a movement forward in time. Having come to Israel as Jews, these olim confront it as "twentieth-century" Americans. Much of the frustration they feel is often reported in the "typical" Israeli re-

mark: "You Americans are all the same. You come here and want
to change things overnight. You want to make this into another
America." It is mirrored by the olim in a recurrent theme: "The
Israeli establishment doesn't really want Western and American
aliya. They're afraid of it. They know it means change."

In the present chapter, I shall examine some of the dimensions
of change that American olim advocate. I am still concerned with
the responses of these immigrants to their new home, with aspects of their absorption. This, too, was the concern of the preceding chapter, but there I dealt with a particular set of responses:
how the Americans had to acquire certain traditionalizing
skills—the use of proteksia, and so on—in order to absorb. In
that chapter, then, I dealt with ways in which the olim had to
change their social and cultural styles towards consonance with
Israeli styles. In the present chapter I deal with another set of
responses; not how the Americans change in order to make their
styles consonant with the Israelis', but how they try to implement
change that will make Israeli styles consonant with their own.

The motivations among olim for the first set of responses—
adapting to Israeli styles—may appear self-evident. That is, the
olim demonstrated a commitment to be a part of Israeli society by
the very act of aliya: it should therefore not be surprising that
they would make efforts to change, efforts towards their integration into that society. The motivations behind the second set of
responses—the desire to implement change in Israeli society—
may thus appear less clear. The olim themselves explain their
advocacy of change by their fears for the deleterious effects on
Israel of Levantinization. But these fears are complex: recall
that—however self-evident the motivations for the first set of
responses—the Americans' adoption of, and adaptation to, Israeli
styles does not run a smooth course. The traditionalizing that
they effect remains instrumental. Traditionalization is not made
expressive, and the olim continue to play roles in the Israeli
game—be it a bureaucratic or, especially, a business game—like
Americans.

We are dealing with something more psychologically salient
than the mere playing of roles. The olim, so long as Israeli roles
remain instrumental and do not become also expressive, find
themselves in the dilemma of confronting Israeli society like
Americans. It is a dilemma because the identity of "American"

was, in the U.S., a feared identity. It was held to be corrosive, and even antithetical, to the hyperinvested identity of Jew. In the fear of Levantinization, in the disdain in which it is held, lies one way out of the dilemma. For Levantinism is viewed by olim as the force that makes Israel "backward," "primitive," or "Middle Eastern." Levantinization is a highly undesirable kind of social change. Note, however, that Levantinism symbolizes the same qualities that characterize what I have called "traditionalizing": a conception of social relations wherein proteksia must be sought, and so on. Traditionalizing comes to represent the encroachment upon individuals of the "amoral. . . . cynical volatile spirit of the Levant." As Levantinism comes to be invested with the very qualities of instrumental traditionalizing with which the olim felt uncomfortable, the "spirit of the Levant" comes to stand for the difference between a previously invested ideal image of Israeli society (a gemeinschaft), and the vicissitudes of having to deal with the society's quotidian reality. And if Levantinism is a "bad" thing, then the immigrant's inability to transform instrumental into expressive traditionalizing is a "good" thing: it is a sort of testimony to his inability to become a Levantine.

The disdain and fear of Levantinization by olim make possible the reconstruction and reevaluation of the American components of their social identities. In Israel, the integrity of the hyperinvested identity Jew is protected by removing it from possible conflict with the identity American. Instead, the oleh counterposes his identity as an American to the (negatively evaluated) identities of those around him: *Levantine Israelis*. In Israel, then, the oleh's identity as an American is no longer a danger to his identity as a Jew. The identity American is, in a sense, reconstructed by olim to present a danger to the negatively evaluated identities of Israelis (or—at least—of those Israelis who are Levantine). Since these Israelis are also Jews, the integrity of the oleh's own Jewish identity is further protected by splitting the Jewish from the Levantine components of Israeli identity. In this way, when the oleh speaks of the skills or contributions he can bring or make, as an American, and when he rails against Israeli Levantinism, he is using his identity as an American in the service of his identity as a Jew.

As instrumental traditionalizing fails to be transformed into expressive, traditionalization itself is identified as Levantinization, and it is rejected. As the olim rediscover (or discover for the first time) the salience of their identities as Americans, and as the American identity is removed from conflict with the identity of Jew —and it can be, so long as one remains in Israel—then the course of absorption, as the olim chart it, seems clear. They will take what is "good" in being an American—"rationality," "honesty," and "efficiency," for example—and they will attempt to impose it on Israel. If the Israelis reject this, and many olim claim they do, the olim say it is because Israelis are afraid of change: they are themselves mired in, and part of, the spirit of the encroaching Levant.

The course of social change that these olim advocate is progressive. They believe it is a change that is both antithetical and antidotal to Levantinization. They embrace, therefore, a different conception of klita.

If Americans cannot traditionalize in response to Israel, they soon transform this into a virtue. And instead, they set out to do something else: to modernize Israeli society in response to themselves. In the extreme, one oleh set it out this way: "We've got to save this country from sliding to the level of a decadent Levantine state."

The Reconstruction of Identity and the Ideology of Change

In Chapter 5, I argued that a total social identity can be seen as a configuration of subidentities, which are differentially invested in—ethnic over occupational identities, for example. In the present chapter I have begun to sketch a different mode of identity transformation. Here particular subidentities, specifically Israeli and American, are revaluated and reconstituted, so that in effect the total social identity is reconstructed.

American identity, of course, is one with which olim had to deal before aliya: aliya is a result of this. Israeli identity, on the other hand, becomes truly problematic only after aliya.

After aliya, the olim begin to reconstruct their American identity, evaluate it positively, and place it in opposition to a negatively evaluated Israeli identity. This does not mean that American identity, in its totality, is positively reconstituted, or that Israeli identity, in its totality, is negatively reconstituted. Rather,

American and Israeli identities are effectively "split" into positively and negatively valenced clusters. Throughout the discussion that follows it is important to understand that the paramount
goal of identity-splitting is to protect the integrity of the hyperinvested identity of Jew.

The splitting of Israeli identity, as already mentioned, entails
the separation of (positive) Jewishness from the negative elements, most especially Levantinism, that olim impute to the Israelis around them:

> *Baruch:* A long time ago, in the States, I thought I'd come to
> Israel and become an Israeli. What nonsense! Who in their right
> mind would want to do that? Do you know what an Israeli is?
> An Israeli is a person who has contempt for Jewish history, for
> the Jewish religion, for anything Jewish. Here's a quick de-
> scription of a perfect Israeli: blonde, tall, good-looking and
> blue-eyed! He went through the local school system in Tel
> Aviv, and he finds me "peculiar" because I wear a *kippa*
> ["skullcap"]. I asked him: "What is Judaism?" He said, quote,
> "I am Judaism. Everything I do is Judaism." This man knows
> nothing about Judaism. There's nothing Jewish about him. No
> compassion. What is an Israeli? An Israeli is a person with a
> Jewish background, on his way to being a complete goy.

In its vehemence, Baruch's hostility to Israelis is not typical of
American olim, and his remarks indicate a negative evaluation of
much more than imputed Israeli Levantinism. Such remarks,
however, are an apt response to what certain observers have
noted as an Israeli (or Zionist) hostility to Jewishness and
Judaism (cf. Kaufman 1949; Spiro 1957). Interestingly, Spiro's
work among (Ashkenazi) sabras of kibbutz origin approached the
problem of splitting from a different perspective. He argued that
the sabras also split Jewish from Israeli identities but evaluated
the former negatively. Young kibbutz sabras in the seventh grade,
wrote Spiro, went to great lengths "to distinguish between 'modern' Israelis and Oriental and orthodox Jews, and to identify
themselves exclusively with the former" (1957:109). It is more
than a little ironic that American olim, as they split Jew from
Israeli and evaluate the former positively, base their negative
evaluation of the latter on its "primitive" and "Levantine" (and
occasionally "anti-Semitic") attributes. We see here, quite

clearly, how the imputation of "modernity" or "traditionalism,"
by one group against another, has its rhetorical, evaluative, and
ideological uses.

While Baruch's vehemence is atypical, the sort of splitting he
exemplifies is not.

> *Rebekah:* In general I don't like Israelis; that upset me at
> first, because I thought I ought to. But you know what? Israel
> doesn't belong to Israelis. It doesn't belong to Zionists. It
> doesn't belong to Golda Meir or Menahem Begin. Israel be-
> longs to every Jew in the world. This is my country; Jerusalem
> is my city. Sabras confuse Israeli patriotism with Jewish
> nationalism: that's why they resent Americans. But I don't care
> much about Israeli patriotism—the Israelis can have that. I'm
> here, and staying, damn it, for a higher reason: A *Jewish* rea-
> son.
>
> *Joshua:* How does one remain in Israel despite it all? Ba-
> sically, you say: This is mine, the good and the bad. I have a
> stake here. And if there's something bad, I have to try in my
> limited way to correct it. As Americans, we Jews do have
> something to contribute; we can raise the standard of life here.

Joshua's remarks point to the second kind of splitting necessary for a reconstruction of American (and social) identity. First,
in Israel, the identities Jew and American are not perceived to be
in conflict. Thus, if American is split into negatively and positively evaluated components, those components that were most
negative in the U.S.—the ones that were perceived to endanger
Jewish identity—are in a sense neutralized. What remains salient
are the positive components. These components include such
"American" attributes as "honesty," "efficiency," "rationality," and also "activism" and a "commitment to progress."
These are opposed, by olim, to Levantinism. In America, the
negative component of American identity was its very "goyishness," which threatened Jewish identity through assimilation.

The second process of identity reconstruction involves, then,
the splitting of American into positive and negative components.
As the negative components are neutralized, the identity Jew is
free to link up with the positive attributes of Americans: thus
Joshua is able to say: "As Americans, we Jews. . . ."

But what is crucial is this: The negative components of American identity are able to remain neutralized only so long as the individual remains in Israel. For these olim with a hyperinvestment in their Jewishness, it is only in Israel that it becomes possible to bemoan the "lack of what we call 'WASP' know-how and efficiency." In Israel, "WASP" is accorded positive qualities. In America, it represented goyishness, a danger to the identity Jew.

Many olim are aware of this; some from making visits back to the United States, others from merely thinking of return:

> *Roberta:* I think if I went back to America now I'd have some sort of identity crisis. Here I have none: I'm 100 percent an American.
> *Ronald:* There are parts of Israeli culture I like a lot. I can slip into them. I feel very uncomfortable now in the States. I've been back twice; once was in the first year here. I was supposed to stay a couple of weeks. I stayed four days and left, I just couldn't take it. Then we went back for a month, and stayed just three weeks and left. I felt uncomfortable. You know why? We landed at Kennedy and I suddenly felt like a *Jew* again. I don't mean the kind of Jew I am here, I mean the kind of Jew I always felt like in America: a minority.
>
> In fact, sometimes I don't even like the American Jewish tourists I run into here. When I see the worst of them—throwing money around—I suddenly understand the problems Israelis have in relating to them. I know there are plenty of things wrong with this country, but it hurts to hear an American tourist say them, even when he's right.

When the Americans—even *in* Israel—are confronted with too potent a reminder of American identity, the old reactions return. At that point, the person is most liable to say. . . .

> *Doris:* You know when I began to feel like an Israeli? A friend, E., married an Israeli girl and they went to live in the U.S. He's doing very well and they live in a fancy apartment in Manhattan. I remember when his wife first came to the U.S., before we went on aliya; I had to tell her how to act, how to dress, how to shop. Then we came on aliya, and they stayed in New York. She came back to visit her parents awhile ago. They live in a very poor neighborhood here, and I went over to see

her. It was August, hot. And she was the super-American!
Stockings and a skirt, and there *I* was—dressed like the—
quote—"unsophisticated, simple Israeli": no makeup, jeans,
no socks, certainly no slip. I asked her how she could dress like
that in that heat, and she said haughtily: "I *always* dress like
this." Super Mrs. America. Her kid goes to the Little Red
Schoolhouse, or some such crap. And she's *proud* she's Super
Mrs. America!

And I thought how the tables had turned. How when she first
came to the U.S. she was really like an outsider. And then she
took on American characteristics to the degree that it was—
hateful.

Doris is sensitive to the fact that she and the Israeli woman
switched "outsider" roles. The Israeli, however—at least so far
as Doris perceives it—has attained some measure of "insiderness" in New York-America; Doris's defense, in this instance, is
to claim insiderness in Israel: "I began to feel like an Israeli . . ."
in the presence of E.'s wife.

The splitting of (perceived) Israeli and American identities, and
the opposition of positive American to negative Israeli, is rarely
perfectly achieved, though some (Baruch, for example) come
closer than others. There is usually interference of one sort or
another. Olim may return to the U.S. for a visit, or even con-
template a return, and the negative attributes of American identity resurface. Alternatively, olim (Ronald, for example) come to
like parts of Israeli culture, and the negative attributes of Israeli
identity are muted. There are olim for whom instrumental traditionalizing verges on becoming expressive.

> *Ronald:* Life is a lot less hectic here; the relationships you
> form with neighbors are richer. If a bill doesn't get paid, it
> doesn't get paid. Act like Israelis: put off for next week what
> you ought to do today. I like knowing who I've got to go to get
> things done, and doing favors in return.

Occasionally, a return trip to the United States enhances the
positive evaluation of Israeli identity:

> *Joe:* I went on a month's aliya mission to the States from the
> AACI. I spoke to all kinds of groups, including pro-PLO, and I

felt an enormous pride in being thought of as the "Israeli" who was born in the U.S. It's just a little ironic that I had to return to the States to get anywhere near an identification as Israeli. Here? No. I'm an immigrant from the U.S. who speaks horrible Hebrew and can't learn to push in lines. Here I'm an American and I'm proud of that, too; when I went back for a month I guess then I had the best of both worlds.

Since the splitting of Israeli and American identities, and the opposition of negative Israeli to positive American, is rarely perfectly achieved, the most characteristic stance by olim towards both identities is one of ambivalence. Often, positive and negative evaluations are situational (based on returning for a visit to the U.S.; meeting American tourists; etc.). Nevertheless, the contours of identity reconstruction and evaluation remain clear. In Israel, the negative components of American identity are largely neutralized: the assimilatory danger of "goy" is transformed into the rational efficiency of "WASP." In Israel, the negative components of Israeli identity are accentuated: the major component is Levantinism. In this way, the American oleh who continues to play roles—expressively—like an American, is able to identify strongly with part of what was, in America, a feared identity.

The olim explain their commitment to "change" Israel—what some of them even call "modernizing" it—by their fear of Levantinization. I am arguing that their advocacy of this kind of change has another, latent function. It allows them to split the agent of progress/modernizer attribute of American identity from the goy, and thus to act like Americans in Israel—and all for the good of the Jewish state.[2] Despite the troublesome presence of Israelis (in their Levantine guises, at least), the Americans come to believe that in Israel only by being better Americans can they be good Jews. In a sense they turn the early principle of American, Brandeisian Zionism on its head; for Brandeis argued, in order to legitimate Zionism in America, that only by being a "better Jew" (i.e., a Zionist) could one become a "good American."

There is little doubt that part of the reason why Israeli identity is negatively accented is that its acquisition is almost impossible to achieve, and that many olim had supposed, through aliya, they could achieve it. This is especially true in the earliest stages of absorption, when the feared image of American identity was still salient. What is perhaps more problematic for the new immigrant is that, even if he is not referred to as an "American," he is often, with other English-speakers, lumped in the category of persons—Jews—who are called by Israelis "Anglo-Saxon" (pl: *Anglo-Saxim*).

Given some of the reasons why these persons left the United States and came to Israel, there is more than a touch of irony in their being labeled "Anglo-Saxons." "For such individuals," writes Isaacs (1966:57), "to acquire finally in Israel an identity as 'Anglo-Saxons'—even simply to be labeled as such—is a paradox whose sardonic humor they could not possibly often appreciate."

The combination of early aspirations to Israeli identity and early identification by Israelis as Anglo-Saxon, makes the plight of the new immigrant a difficult one.

> *David:* Listen: I came to Israel as a Jew, and suddenly I'm an Anglo-Saxon, a descendant of William the Conqueror. It's a very tough thing at first; I was very insulted by it. You come here, from another country, to be an Israeli, and automatically you are classified as Anglo-Saxon.
>
> It was very tough to take that in the Army. When I was in the Golan, freezing and up to my ass in mud, the Moroccans, some very primitive guys, would say: "*Amerikanje,* pass me a cigaret." I'd say back: "I'm in the same goddamn mud you are: call me *Dovid.*"
>
> It took a long time for me to accept the fact that I *am* an American in Israel. It did; it took me a very, very long time. And I was often very upset—I mean, I'm easygoing and I smile and all, but I would eat my heart out and wonder when I was going to be accepted as an Israeli. And I had this in the Army all the time.
>
> Listen: The first guy who reached me when I was wounded started talking to me in English. I mean, the shell exploded, and I was lying there in gore and shock, and this Israeli comes running up and bends over me, screaming "Medic!" and whispers [in a heavy Israeli accent], "Not vorry, Dovid, not vorry." And I started cursing him, the worst profanities, in Hebrew and Arabic—I was hysterically enraged, crying like a baby—yelling in Hebrew: "Why *English!* I just paid the price to be an Israeli, you bastard!"

American identity is not reconstructed all at once; and there is no guarantee—especially if one leaves Israel—that the reconstruction is irreversible. Nevertheless, as the oleh evaluates, and accents, the positive attributes of his American identity, certain other changes take place. For one, as he sees his younger children becoming Israelis, with whatever degree of enthusiasm or trepidation, he will often insist that they learn to read, write, and speak English. In part this is because English enjoys rising prestige in Israel as the language of international communication (Nadel et al. 1977), and entry into institutes of higher education, for example, is in part dependent on the applicant's command of the language. In part, however, many olim insist on English competency because, in the words of one, "It's important for my sabra children to know something of their other heritage." The "other heritage" to which he refers is in some sense an "Anglo-Saxon" one: the reconstruction of American identity feeds positively into the identification Anglo-Saxon as well.

The most important change entailed in the positive evaluation of American identity, however, is that it allows the olim to set a disarmingly straight course for their absorption. It allows them to face Israeli society as *American* Jews: as Jews who are agents of "progress," "development," "rationality," and change.

> *Joe:* Israelis think we're crazy, but we can change things: Americans can do that. Unfortunately, a lot of olim don't. They get stopped by that old remark: "That's the way it's done here." They know better, and they know it's wrong, but they stop at the point of: "That's the way it's done here in the Middle East, in Israel." They make themselves unhappy by stopping there, and they make it harder for people who come after them.
>
> The American has so much to offer in know-how and ideas. Now of course, from an Israeli's point of view, if you've been working at a job for twenty years, and some American comes running in, right off the plane, with new ideas about how to do your job better, of course the Israeli is not going to say: "Thank you for coming here to save me, your ideas will be put into operation tomorrow." The Israelis want to know: Is this person going to stay, or is he a six-month-sabbatical wonder? That's in addition to the feelings of jealousy, and a general inertia here. So the American does get personal resistance. But I'm sure, despite that, Americans are valued here—not just for their

money—but for the standards that they bring. I think that what Americans can do is help to raise Israeli standards—help the movement and development that has to go on.

We knew an American dentist who left because after working for *Kupat Holim* ["Sick Fund"] he said it was like working in a dental stone age, in terms of equipment, techniques, and patient-care. But certainly the dentist here in Ramat Esh-kol—an American—is not in the stone age, and I've seen a dental clinic serving kibbutzim in the Beit Shean Valley that looked as modern as anything in Chicago. Now this dentist who left—this was five years ago—thought he was stepping into a primitive situation both professionally and personally. Why didn't he, as an American, stay to change things? You see, this dentist was wrong: it may have been the kind of tools he worked with twenty-five years ago, but it changed in five years. And I'd like to think it was the Americans who brought in the technology in those five years.

Ephraim: I'll tell you where American aliya must go: into the supervisory, professional, and middle-management levels of industry; the efficiency and productivity stages; to work with what's here and develop it: to work the industrial revolution that's coming to Israel.

[He was asked, "It hasn't yet come?"]

Not really. Agriculturally things work pretty well; we don't need an agricultural revolution here. But *that's* going back how many hundreds of years? Americans bring a certain level of society, a certain value system that's needed here—maybe that's why they call us Anglo-Saxons!

The American ideology of (and for) change is pervasive. One of the primary forums for the presentation of this ideology is the Association of Americans and Canadians in Israel. In 1976, the executive director of the AACI addressed delegates to the annual convention in a written report. He first noted that Ministry of Immigrant Absorption research carried out in 1973 and 1974 showed that "proportionately more North Americans returned to their country of origin than other olim." He went on:

> The statistics further . . . show that the reason for the majority of Americans returning to the United States was due to problems of work and career: not finding the right job; unable to achieve, to produce, to advance; inefficiency of people at work; lack of up-to-date methods and facilities; and especially *not being appreciated*. (Emphasis in original)

Such values as "to achieve, to produce, to advance" are strikingly American, as perhaps is the complaint of "not being appreciated." The Americans' advocacy of change does engender hostility on the part of other Israelis, especially in the occupational sphere. For AACI's executive director, however, this hostility is simply another obstacle to be overcome. The question he went on to raise was "how much" this immigrants' association should "be concerned with the various aspects of Israeli society and, hence, be an advocate for change." Note that the question is *how much*. It seems as though any serious concern with aspects of Israeli society would—*hence*—lead one to advocacy of change. On the convention's second day the newly-elected president replied to the executive director in the course of his acceptance speech:

> We must make AACI relevant to *all* aspects of Israeli life, and seek to bring about improvements, lest we be relegated to the role of just another landmannschaft.... We [must] make our mark on the whole society. It may be said these roles can be played by others. True, but it is not happening. Profound problems are not being faced.

Agents of Change: Reformers and Entrepreneurs

In the president's remarks we see the linking of the ideology of change with the rhetoric of action: if the roles are not being played by others (these olim say), "we" shall play them. Activism or citizen action are perceived to be American attributes: good ones. The Israelis, insofar as they are Levantine, lack these attributes; worse, they do not understand or appreciate them. But Israeli hostility must be overcome (or ignored), and the pursuit of change through activism enjoined, in the service of a greater good: the future welfare of the Jewish state.

This is the rhetoric of reform; and the roles these olim wish to play are ones of reformers. Many, if not quite all, of the aspects of Israeli society or life are in need of reformation. For the olim they include especially the following.

The Quality of Life. Subsumed under the heading "the quality of life" are a host of dissatisfactions with "manners and morals" in Israel. In March 1976, more than eight hundred "Anglo-Saxons" met in Tel Aviv for the first *Koah Kan* ["Strength

Here"] Conference. The conference's four workshops dealt with: road manners and safety, general manners and etiquette, consumerism, and ecology. The various Anglo-Saxon immigrants' associations were much in evidence; the conference was organized chiefly by the South Africans' association. Many of the letters by Anglo-Saxon olim published in the *Jerusalem Post* deal with "quality of life" issues. Some olim believe Anglo-Saxons already have had much positive influence on the quality of Israeli life; they point especially to the areas of ecology and, increasingly, consumerism. Other olim are less sanguine: "This Quality of Life nonsense is silly icing on a rotten cake ... it's like trying to correct a structurally bad building by painting the roof."

Political Reform. The thrust here is toward electoral reform: some modification, if not the total dismantling, of the proportional, "party-list" system of Israeli voting. The preference is for the American-type electoral system. The presence of so many political parties in Israel also disconcerts the Americans; many advocate a change to the American two-party system. Ninety-four percent of the Jerusalem sample were in favor of some sort of electoral reform, and while 6 percent expressed "no opinion" on reform, not a single respondent thought that "the present system" worked well enough to warrant no change. In the period of fieldwork (1975–77), many of the olim were active supporters of Yigael Yadin's Democratic Movement for Change party (DMC), which had electoral reform as a central plank of its platform.[3]

Some olim, however, saw the American's role in Israel's politics to be potentially larger than one of reforming the electoral system. One oleh remarked:

As a group we are more educated and aware of the whole situation. If there were enough Americans, enough Westerners, to form some sort of pressure group, it could be conceivably formed into some sort of political party. If there was enough Western immigration, we might be able to muster a voting bloc; then it might be possible to change this "list" business, in elections. The whole system would be upset. We might ask for one-man one-vote, or something like that, and who knows, I mean, God forbid, you might have a democracy here after awhile. And I think that's part of the reason they're [the Israelis] against it—that's just another change they don't want.

Despite remarks such as these, there is little likelihood of Americans or, indeed, Anglo-Saxons, entering the political arena as, minimally, an organized pressure group (or voting bloc), or, maximally, another political party. In the first place, American formal participation in Israeli politics is at quite a low level. There is a simple reason for this. Only citizens of Israel may vote in national elections or hold national offices. As a glance at table 6.1 indicates, however, the great majority of Americans come to Israel as "potential olim," deferring for three years the acceptance of Israeli citizenship; these individuals can neither vote nor hold office on the national level. Moreover, many olim hold onto their "potential immigrant" status beyond the normative three-year period, and some—through proteksia—have lived in Israel five or more years on tourist visas. There are at all times many more Americans living in Israel than there are Americans living in Israel who are qualified to vote.

There are other factors that decrease the likelihood of American pressure groups or political parties emerging in the near future. First, formal ethnic politics has been successfully discouraged on ideological grounds; alternatively—as Smooha (1972) might argue—the Russian-Polish elite has succeeded thus far in defining ethnicity in class terms and blocking the formation of enduring ethnically-based political groupings. Secondly, the Americans as a group are divided politically, principally by their religious orientation. Generally speaking, *dati* ("observant") implies right-of-center, and *lo-dati* ("nonobservant") left-of-center on the political spectrum. On the right, the observant American may well support Gush Emunim, a group devoted to ensuring permanent Jewish settlement on the West Bank. Aside from such issues as consumerism or ecology, therefore, it would be difficult for such a person to share a consistent political platform with an American supporter of the Labour party or certainly of the dovish Moked party.

Differences in religious observance separate olim in other ways. Religious orientation accounts for some residential segregation in Jerusalem, both generally and among Americans. And because parents must choose between two "trends" in public education, religious and secular, religious orientation limits the contacts children of dati olim have with children of the lo-dati, and limits social, school-related contacts among the olim parents to, largely, one trend or the other.

Religious Reform. This is a complex topic, partly because the kind of reform olim deem necessary differs between the observant and nonobservant. Both may express dissatisfaction with what they see as the politicization of the rabbinate, or the "shady, back-room dealings" of the various religious political parties. For the dati oleh, the mix of religion and politics may prove embarrassing at times. When members of the rabbinate attack one another in political language over political issues, many find the spectacle of two venerable rabbis in public battle over worldly resources to be an uncomfortable union of the sacred and the profane. For the oleh who is lo-dati, however, the dissatisfaction reaches deeper than embarrassment. Olim who were Conservative or Reform, in the U.S., are especially distressed by the lack of separation between "church" and state they find in Israel; by the disproportionate power the religious factions wield in the political arena; and by the nonrecognition of the legitimacy of Reform and Conservative Judaism. The following letters, published in the *Jerusalem Post*,[4] typify two variant American attitudes towards religious reform; the first two writers are in favor of limiting the influence of the Orthodox.

Israel is the only country in the world which selectively discriminates against some Jews. Everywhere else, either there is no discrimination against any Jews, or there is equal discrimination against all Jews. Israel alone selectively discriminates. Against whom? Among others, against the majority of American Jews [who are Reform or Conservative].

Israel's message in effect is: "Come on aliya to the Jewish State. Whereas most immigrants are second-class citizens abroad and first-class citizens in Israel, for you, we reverse the equation: You are first-class citizens in the United States; please come to Israel and be treated religiously as second-class citizens."

...The present situation is reminiscent of the Ottoman period....

The idea that there exists in Israel real religious freedom is pretence; on the contrary, Israel is a state with dangerous theocratic leanings. The coercers are forever attempting to increase their influence and silence dissenting views.

The second letter, with its reference to the "Ottoman period," provides another illustration of the American perception of having gone "backward in time" with aliya.

The last letter was written by an Orthodox (dati) oleh. In his view, any reform that would legitimize Conservative or Reform Judaism would be a dangerous and undesirable thing. Remarkably, he seems to advocate the sectarianization of Judaism in lieu of full recognition of other than Orthodox trends: a sort of "Protestant Reformation." About Reform Judaism, in particular, he writes:

> If Reform wants freedom for themselves and not freedom to impose on others, let them declare themselves and their ministrations as Reform—as a separate sect. As part of *K'lal Yisrael* ["The Whole Community of Israel"], they must be prepared to accept standards that can serve all Jews. Then they will not be impinging with their freedom upon the freedom of other Jews.

Persons who assume the roles of religious reformers can thus serve different ends. Some datiim desire the sort of reform that would strengthen the position of religion in the state; reform that would place secular power at Judaism's disposal. Persons who are lo-dati—though they may consider themselves to be observant of Reform or Conservative traditions—want the sort of reform that would separate, at least, the religious from the secular domains. Along with this they expect the recognition, without sectarianization, of Reform and Conservative Judaism. Many realize that religious reform in this direction is tied closely to political reform—to reducing the number of political parties and dismantling the list system. Only then, they argue, will the power of the datiim be diminished. In the meantime, they attempt to set up Reform and Conservative congregations throughout the country, establish schools based on these traditions, and found communal settlements affiliated formally with them.[5] They have met with resistance and even harassment in all these endeavors. Caterers who agree to host a wedding performed by a Conservative rabbi, for example, may learn, after a rabbinate inspection, that their *kashrut* certificate is endangered; landlords who agree to rent their buildings for a Conservative school may enjoy myriad visits from building inspectors, and so on. The "present situation," in the words of the letter-writer, is "reminiscent of the Ottoman period." The association having been made with a fair example of Oriental despotism, the Ottoman Empire, the implications of this sort of religious reform are clear: it demands Westernization of the religion; it demands "progress"; it entails a religious modernization.

Bureaucratic Reform. The range of problems Americans face in bureaucratic encounters was the subject of much of the previous chapter. The kind of reform they demand lies in the direction of increasing bureaucratic rationalization. The Association of Americans and Canadians in Israel is a constant critic of bureaucracy, and one AACI counselor told me that helping the new immigrant to negotiate or circumvent the bureaucracy is his "single most important task." From time to time, predominantly Anglo-Saxon volunteer counseling groups—often composed of younger bureaucrats—arise and offer their services to olim.[6] But it will be noted that such counseling aims at dealing with the bureaucracy on the bureaucracy's own terms: some olim spoke of the counseling groups as possessing proteksia. In general, though they desire it, few Americans believe that large-scale bureaucratic reform is possible in the near future. And, as I pointed out in Chapter 6, some young American bureaucrats themselves undergo a debureaucratic socialization, while other data indicate American clients learn eventually, among other things, that it "pays to ask for favors" and appeal to "altruism." Along with doing business, the problems of bureaucracy are seen to be central to the ills of Israeli Levantinism. Americans view the bureaucracy, not the problems of doing business, as especially resistant to change.

Reform of Business and Commerce. Perhaps the most visible and accessible roles for would-be reformers of doing business in Israel are those of consumer advocates—an almost direct importation from the United States. These are, however, not the most interesting roles. In my earlier discussion of doing business, I noted that the acquiescence with which olim accept traditionalizing demands in bureaucratic encounters is, for the most part, absent in their approaches to business. Bernard, a businessman, was willing to accept the rules of the bureaucratic game and to work with them. But, he said, "My business is a different thing. *It* is my own, and I try to run it like an American business, with service and efficiency and responsibility."

A minority of American olim are actively involved in doing business. Among those olim who are, however, the commitment to change (i.e., modernize) Israel, and the belief that they can effect this change, are very strong. These Americans base this belief on their perceptions of a potent force: a competitive free market.

Aaron: In business, Americans can have—and have had—great impact. Take the number-one ill in this country: the lack of business ethics. There are many ways to work on this ill. You can put pressure on those people through consumer groups, or you can come in yourself and set up a business in competition. And if a customer has a choice between an American business that's run ethically *and* with service, and the average Israeli concern, he'll choose the American. I believe this has been happening.

Channah: Americans have done things—in consumerism, in stores, in business. We see now products that look better, that *are* better, with better guarantees and so on. We see more efficiency in serving people. Maybe I should say that these are all areas Americans have potentially a very great impact on. Unfortunately so many become like Israelis: "Ah, this is the Middle East." We have a friend, an American, who just opened a pharmacy and who is making money hand over fist because customers are flocking to a drugstore run on American principles of courtesy and efficiency and honesty. I believe this sort of competition will provoke Israeli merchants to try and run their businesses on the same principles.

The belief that they can effect change is buttressed by their positive evaluation of another aspect of a reconstructed American identity: the "free-enterprising" American. In some cases this leads to a revaluation of the worth of certain occupations; and occasionally to a change of occupations in Israel. Denise was a schoolteacher in the United States; in Israel she founded and heads a public relations firm:

Denise: You know, in Israel I developed a tremendous respect for the businessman; in the U.S. I'd always looked down on business. But there are so many Americans here with professional degrees, in the academy. And I see that if some of them just brought their American enterprise to Israel, they could really make changes in this country. This is the problem

with Russian newcomers here. We were having a long discussion with some Russian new olim at a party, and they were
saying, "We don't know how to open a business." Because
they don't know what it is to put up capital, and reinvest capital, and make decisions without anyone telling them what to do.
This is really an American thing, being capitalists.

I was talking to a Russian woman who works for the Jewish
Agency, and I tried to convince her that if she went into business for herself, doing the same things she's doing for Russians
now at the Agency—consultation and placement—at a poor
salary, she'd have people *paying* her just to avoid the Agency
runaround. And she might even shame the Agency into getting
its act together. "Open up an employment agency!" I said to
her. And she said: "What's that?"

We have a friend who opened up a business in Tel Aviv,
selling kitchenware. He's making a fortune. And one of the
reasons he's making a fortune is that he deals with his customers in a way that nobody else does.

Lurking behind Denise's concern that the Russian woman get
paid for running an employment agency was another point:
perhaps by doing so she would shame the Jewish Agency into
self-reform. At this level the roles of the free-enterprising American and the reformer American tend to converge. It is to this
point that I now turn.

From among the olim there emerged two types of individuals
engaged in activities, playing roles, that are connected to change.
(The ideology of change, on the other hand, seems to be pervasive.) These types are the reformer and the entrepreneur.

It is possible, superficially at least, to distinguish these types by
reference to the major areas in which individuals involve themselves, or by the kinds of structures they use or build in their
pursuit of change. Thus, such areas as consumerism, ecology, the
quality of life, bureaucratic or electoral reform, are the concerns
of reformers; they work through quasi-formal, volunteeristic, or
semivolunteeristic organizations: committees in immigrants' associations, chambers of commerce, and so on. The entrepreneur,
classically, would be put in some area of business or commerce;
he works through organizations built for profit. The entrepreneur
differs from the average businessman or the "corporation man"
to the extent that he undertakes new things. This is the essence of
Barth's (1966) characterization of the entrepreneur: an individual

who bridges two previously incommensurate sets of goods, services, currencies, or values, making them commensurate and profiting because he has thus opened new markets. Further, to the extent that he does profit, is successful, in bridging values (or valuations) he has in effect created new ones; this is why we may link entrepreneurial activities with change.

Most of the Americans doing business in Israel are also entrepreneurs. They see themselves, as they are seen by other Americans, as engaged in the business of selling new things to Israel. Sometimes such new things are, literally, new goods, products, or services that the Americans introduce to Israeli markets: automatic, self-service laundromats, for example. But even when the products or services are not in themselves new, the Americans strive to sell them in new ways. To illustrate this point, let us take two businessmen: One, Sam, owns a television repair shop; the other, Fred, provides "sanitary services" and introduced automatic bathroom towel- and soap-dispensers to various public buildings (hotels, and so on), in Jerusalem. Sam described his business in these terms:

> My business is doing well now because I offer a service Israelis weren't getting before. When I fix a set it stays fixed, and if it doesn't I guarantee my work and come back and fix it again free of charge. Partly it's the American technical training I've had, but mostly it's the American values about honesty and dealing with customers on a fair, *business*like basis.
>
> I charge more than the other guys but now I've got an educated clientele—I mean *I* educated them—who are willing to pay more, because they know they're getting something they weren't getting before, that they can't get anywhere else.

Fred, who is more classically the entrepreneur, spoke of his success in the following terms, which are very close to Sam's:

> I provide a service, but the service is here because, in a sense, I invented the service, made the Israelis think it was necessary, educated them to use it. The Israelis didn't want it to begin with.
>
> I started when Jerusalem was like a little village, and I started with a motor-scooter and twelve towels. There were no public health laws—well, a few left over from the British—but no one gave a damn. You never used a public bathroom, even in the best hotels!

And what resistance I had! I went to see this big-shot in the
Ministry of Tourism—this was years ago—and I said: "I got
something here that you need for tourists!"
"What?"
"A clean-towel dispenser."
"Why do I need that?"
"So tourists can have clean towels!"
He said: "If a tourist wants a clean towel he can bring one
from home."
This is what the guy said! Or I went to the Jewish Agency and
talked to the guy in charge of supplies. I said: "Mr. B., I have
something for you that's fantastic!" I showed it to him. He
said: "I don't need it!"
"Why don't you need it?"
He said: "I'm from Poland, and in Poland I lived without this
so what do I need it here for?"
So I answered: "Mr. B., you're right. But you know in Po-
land you had a horse, what are you driving a car here for?"
He didn't know what to say. But that went on all the time.
Hygiene was unheard of—or at least *paying* for hygiene was.
Now, what business am I in?
I *sell* hygiene.

There is a sense in which a man who "started with a motor-
scooter and twelve towels," invented a product or service that
did not exist in Israel before, "educated" Israelis to need the
service,[7] and says things like "I sell hygiene," is unarguably our
image of the entrepreneur. (And, whether one takes the narrow,
aseptic view of facilities in public bathrooms or the grander one of
public hygiene, change has occurred.) But what of Sam? He
neither invented television nor opened the first repair shop in the
country. Yet he too provides a service—perhaps less tangible—
that was rare before, has educated a clientele to appreciate and
need the service, and "charges more for it"—he makes a profit.
To understand this service it is necessary to listen to olim, in
business or not, tell their stories:

There's an enormous difference between doing business here
and in the States. First of all, there is no such thing as business
ethics in Israel. A contract, a written agreement—much less a
handshake or someone's word—just doesn't mean anything
here.

What Sam intimates he is "selling" are American values—
"honesty," "fairness," and so on—and a particular conception
of the business relationship.

We have encountered this broad cultural entrepreneurship before, in a different setting. It was Dan, a lawyer, who looked at
"the state of published professional material" for attorneys, and
recalled his job interview: "I know where you're going," he'd
said. "I know the direction you're going but you're twenty-five
years behind . . . what we had in the States. In Israel I'm stepping
back in time twenty-five years, so I know how you're going
to . . . [you've] *got to* develop."

It may be said that Dan carries a model of development inside
his head. The model is validated by his perception that with aliya
he has "gone back twenty-five years" and therefore has a clear
view of the precise lines along which development should take
place. If we substitute, momentarily, the more neutral notion of
change for *development,* then we are faced with the essence of
entrepreneurial activity: the entrepreneur, too, carries a model of
change inside his head, a conception of how the new market will
look. He, however, is gambling on the model's validation. Change
is subsequent to successful entrepreneurial activity because it is
inherent in all entrepreneurial attempts. We may remember an
entrepreneur less for the amount he gambled than, ultimately, for
the covalidation of his model of change by others: his customers.
Barth has argued that, in general, successful entrepreneurship
means change, and I am saying that all entrepreneurship entails
the potentiality of change; and that as an entrepreneurial group,
American olim ought to be examined not only in terms of their
effectiveness as agents of change (their entrepreneurial suc-
cesses) but also for the particularities of the model of change
they, as a group, are drawing or gambling on.

In examining this model we see that it is the olim themselves
who substitute development for (mere) change. It is in this sub-
stitution, in fact, that the lines between entrepreneur and reformer grow unclear. Robert is an exporter, an entrepreneur "out
for profit." The last time we spoke he said he needed "close to a
million dollars" to launch an export business. He has had much
trouble raising the money and was living off his personal savings;
he also had turned down "lucrative offers" for positions in import
houses because he believes that

the Israeli economy desperately needs exporters, and not just more exporters in established markets like citrus or diamonds. More importers, we certainly don't need. So I guess I'm willing to stake my capital and take my chances on new markets and good deeds.

In the phrase "new markets and good deeds" we find the central metaphor of American entrepreneurs in Israel. There is the sense, too, in which they are sure that they need not even gamble. All entrepreneurs wager on models of change. American entrepreneurs in Israel believe they are wagering on a model of progress. Fred spoke in these words of a client he eventually lost:

> I worked with this factory for about four years, suddenly they decided to take out my towel machines because they're too expensive. Now look: They have two hundred workers; it comes out to ten *agurot* per worker per day. They're gonna hang up a cotton towel in the bathroom.
> I said to them: "Are you people crazy? You have to be important, you're making a finished product and all, for *export*. Your product has to at least *look* clean! How can you be so stupid? Your workers will clean their hands on your product!"
> You have to understand, this goes on all the time. There's no budget in this country for cleaning, for towels, stuff like that. This is the Middle East; still primitive; still dirty.
> It's a mentality, a conception—that's why we're still primitive. To save a few *agurot* those guys would wreck an export business that Israel needs.
> And me—I'm trying to change 'em and make a business from it.

Typically, change has been conceived as a function of successful entrepreneurial activities. It is clear, however, that we must also view American entrepreneurial activities as a function of their commitment to change. The American entrepreneur in Israel is one type of modernizer. He draws on a model of change which he believes to be also a model of progress and development. Development, especially if the alternative is seen to be Levantinism, is valued by the entrepreneur as—morally—a good thing. He is thus able to seek profits, like all entrepreneurs, and simultaneously fight the good fight—like all reformers. Indeed, those who view their aliya as a move backwards in time could hardly function as mere businessmen, brokers, or electronics repairmen; like Twain's Connecticut Yankee in King Arthur's court they may see themselves, even while seeking profits, becoming prophets.

The notion that Ephraim, Moshe, or Yehuda are Connecticut Yankees has another aspect. For as they advocate the certified good of honesty, efficiency, rationality, and progress, the American olim emerge as not only—with other English-speakers—the Anglo-Saxons of Israel; they are the Protestants of Israel, as well.

Modernizing and the Relegitimation of Modernity

In Chapter 5, when I introduced the ideas of traditionalization and traditionalizing social identities, I added in a note that these were particular responses to problems of modernity; traditionalization was itself a modern act. Central to the process of traditionalization was an image of American society the olim held to. It was an image of a society torn by conflict, anomie, and alienation, even in the face of affluence. It was a society where the individual was surplus and expendable, one wherein he could not attain a sense of belongingness. To a great degree, the critique of American society the olim articulated, grounded in such problems as crime, drugs, and so on, was also a critique of modernity.

In Israel, I argued, the olim saw a quite different image of society: society as gemeinschaft, society as a moral community. It was a particular image of tradition the olim held onto here. As all Jews were conceived to be "one *mishpaha*" ("family"), Israeli society was projected to be mishpaha writ large. By the time I followed these olim to Israel, a curious tension had developed. What I began to describe was how the olim who had traditionalized in making aliya soon learned that they had to traditionalize in other ways: in dealing with bureaucrats, businessmen, and other Israelis in a small-scale, multiplex, and Mediterranean social system. What they learned, perhaps, is that while it is true that there is no warmth like mishpaha-warmth, it is also true that one does things in one's own family, and to its members, that one would never dream of doing on the outside, to strangers. This tension I discussed as the difference between instrumental and expressive traditionalizing.

In the present chapter I have presented another American image of tradition. It is a revamped image; the Americans call this one by the name of Levantinism. Traditionalization which was not (in any case) made expressive was redefined to be Levantinization. It is a bad thing, a danger to the future of the Jewish state. In Israel, I argued, American identity is reconstructed. As it no longer presents direct danger to the identity Jew, the agent of progress/modernizer components of American identity are split from the goy, and the person is able to link up his Jewishness with that part of his Americanness that is good: that is, his modernity.

Alongside, and interdependent with, all of the identity transformations I have discussed there have been also transformations of the images of society—ideal, feared, and so on—that the olim hold onto; that they invest in and internalize. The olim become modernizers because that is how they are able to reconcile the dilemma of feeling themselves to be Americans when they had left America to be Jews (and perhaps also, to be Israelis). The oleh can face Israeli society as an American Jew only by selling the goods of his modernity and by proclaiming the Good of his modernity. In Israel, modernity has been relegitimated.

This, at least, is one route; there is another.

An Exception: The Religious Oleh and Gush Emunim

Briefly, I want to turn to one of the questions implicit in the discussion of entrepreneurs: Who are the American olim who engage in such activities?

During the course of my interviews, it appeared that nonobservant olim predominated as entrepreneurs. I formulated a hypothesis: Entrepreneurship varies inversely with religious observance. To the larger Jerusalem sample I presented two questions. Each dealt with an aspect of a person's propensity to go into business in Israel. This is not exactly the same as his propensity to be an entrepreneur, of course, but the close relationship between business and entrepreneurship, among American olim, led me to believe that such questions would tap some measure of an "entrepreneurial spirit." The first question aimed at finding out how likely it was that an individual would go into business in Israel; the second asked whether an individual would invest his own money to get a new product or idea "off the ground." The sample was stratified by (respondent self-categorized) religious observance. Tables 7.1 and 7.2 show the distribution of percentages by religious observance. It will be noted that the observant are, in general, less likely either to go into business or to invest their money in new products or ideas. Observant olim are less likely to engage in entrepreneurial activities. Why should this be so?

Table 7.1 "Likelihood" of Going into Business in Israel, by Religious Observance

	Likely (%)	Not Likely (%)
Observant	16.3	34.7
Nonobservant	25.5	23.5
		100.0

It was the economic historian Schumpeter who summarized the "entrepreneurial function" as consisting, essentially, "in getting things done." In this sense the entrepreneur is, above all, an activist. I have tried to indicate the dimensions of this activism by placing the entrepreneur in the framework of the Americans' ideology of change and, specifically, of progress. Entrepreneurial activism is of a special type. Among the olim it is directed towards implementing, in Israel and as if by example, efficiency, rationality, and a "Protestant" work ethic; a steady contractualization of presently status-based relationships. And the entrepreneurs feel themselves to be, as one put it, "fighting the Middle East." As a social or characterological type the entrepreneur is also special. He must be prepared to establish new relationships outside of existing structures, and it helps if he himself stands a little outside these structures. Socially or psychosocially, the entrepreneur is a marginal man (cf. Hoselitz 1955). In at least

Table 7.2 Willingness to Invest Money in "New Product" or or "Idea" in Israel, by Religious Observance

	Willing (%)	Unwilling (%)
Observant	19.8	31.3
Nonobservant	30.2	18.8
		100.1

these two senses, the direction of their activism and the nature of their marginality, the religious and nonreligious oleh differ.

In Chapter 5, when I presented my classification of immigrant types, I distinguished among three different involvements: religious, nationalist (Zionist), and culturalist. Typologies sometimes impose a sort of structural equivalence among things typologized, and sometimes this equivalence is misleading. The point is, religious involvement stands apart from the rest by its clarity; a clarity not only in the sense of a measurable social index but, for the individual, in the coherence such involvement lends to aliya.

If we think of aliya as a response to a felt need to maximize, to make more meaningful, one's Jewishness; of aliya as one solution to a complex equation of identities in motion, then the common remark by olim, "I felt more Jewish, more like a Jew, in the U.S. than I do in Israel," must strike one both by its irony and perplexity. But this remark is common only among the nonobservant: in the Jerusalem sample, only 4 percent of the observant agreed with such a statement, while more than a quarter of the nonobservant did. This remark is most often made by the nonobservant oleh, inveterate Zionist or culturalist that he may be.

In America, the nonobservant Jew (nonobservant in the Israeli sense of lo-dati) sets himself off from the majority by his attachment to symbols conceived to be "Jewish." These are, in one sense, the usual symbols of an ethnic identity: a language, a conception of culture-history (or myth), an ancestral and sacred home, a Great Tradition. For many there was also a political and cultural nationalism, Zionism; for many more the impact of the European Holocaust that will serve, forever, to set them apart. For these Jews religion (or religious observance) is, indeed, one more symbol of their Jewishness, and it may find its expression in the Reform, Conservative, or Reconstructionist movements.

In America, Jewishness was a bounded identity; it may be added that for those Jews who make aliya the maintenance of boundaries is an active, not a passive, concern. There is satisfaction and fulfillment in actively maintaining boundaries. Within boundaries there are worlds of meaning and integrity; beyond those boundaries there is a kind of chaos, a chaos that generates America's great threats—assimilation and intermarriage.

For these nonobservant olim, Israel is a boundary-destroying experience. In an environment where everything is Jewish by definition, the old symbols simply cannot carry the same potency they did in America. Moreover, the environment demands that one make an all-or-nothing commitment to religion: dati or lodati. In an equation of identities, the religious variable becomes a Boolean variable. "Absorption" is as much a forging of a new calculus as it is the finding of a new job.

The observant oleh encounters, and fashions for himself, a different reality. For him, the vagaries of defining an ethnic identity are never so troublesome. He is a Jew not merely by accident of birth or political history; nor is he a Jew by "culture." He is a Jew by the terms of a sacred covenant with God encoded in "the Torah given at Mount Sinai." Israel is not first the Jewish state, and only secondarily is it the Jewish society. It is, first *Eretz Yisrael,* the Land of Israel: the Land of the Children of Israel. His title deed dates back millennia. He has less need of a European-derived nationalism, though he may use its rhetoric. If his identity was bounded in America by his Jewishness, he finds that, in Israel, it is bounded by his religiousness. For though he is in a Jewish society it is still, largely, a secular society. Like the nonobservant oleh, he approaches Israel as a stranger, but there is a difference: his religiousness provides a cross-cutting tie, linking him to sabras or veteran settlers who share his *datiut* ("religiousness") and the boundedness this entails in Israel.

In this way the observant oleh can identify in Israel with a community. In many cases this is a community in the physical sense: the oleh chooses to live in a dati neighborhood, quarter, or settlement. Beyond the physical sense there is identification with other datiim, in Israel and abroad. The secular oleh lacks this immediate support. Both may be unable to identify with the "typical Israeli," and both may—through the imputation of Levantinism—turn this into a virtue, but the observant oleh has the edge. For the "typical Israeli" is not only secular but often antireligious. For this the observant are able to blame, among others, the Zionist founders of the state. Looking around them, they say, they see that the Zionist dream has not resulted in a truly *Jewish* state, where Torah and rabbinic law are the law of the land, but—in the words of several—in "nothing better than a Hebrew-speaking Portugal."

Olim, observant and nonobservant, are aware of these differences, and of some of their effects. Many of the secular olim with whom I spoke felt that the datiim had "an easier time of it" and "tend to stick it out." Ministry of Immigrant Absorption research supports this view. Of all olim who arrived in 1969–70, only 7 percent of those who considered themselves "completely observant" (literally: dati) had left Israel three years later. The percentage of out-migrants among those self-categorized "not at all observant" (lo-dati) was 17 percent. More interesting, perhaps, was the percentage of 1969–70 olim who stated they were "very active members" of Zionist organizations abroad: after three years, 20 percent of these olim had emigrated.[8]

As a measure of adjustment, or of acculturation or absorption, the statistic that differentiates those who stay from those who go has a tonic air of simplicity and finality about it. But while it is true that the observant and nonobservant oleh face the same sorts of problems—language, housing, schooling, employment—it may also be true that, ultimately, they are attempting to adjust to different versions of Israel. The above statistic convinces us that commitment to a religious world view is more efficacious for adjustment than is commitment to a political ideology (Zionism). But what is entailed in a commitment to a religious world view? If it is a personalistic, inner-directed commitment, in toto, then we are concerned with certain states of consciousness, essences, or excitations; with, perhaps, varieties of the religious experience. If, however, this commitment is effectively "socialistic," outer- and other-directed, then our concern, too, moves outward; we look to the effects of the commitment in societal terms.

Earlier I wrote that it is the adoption of a world view (and an image of society) at whose center is "family" and not "citizen" that is part of what I call traditionalization. The olim had adopted such a view. But the observant oleh has another version of tradition: the adoption of a world view (and an image of the ideal society) at whose center is religion and God, rather than (among other things) ideology or the state.

The link between the religious world view, tradition, and modernity has been postulated many times and in many ways. Usually, however, the link has been set up to work in a certain direction, because the emphasis was on modernization, not traditionalization. When Tawney followed Weber to write of capitalism and the "contrast between medieval and modern economic ideas," he spoke (1947:228) in these terms:

The elements which combined to produce that revolution are too numerous to be summarized in any neat formula. But, side by side with the expansion of trade and the rise of new classes to political power, there was a further cause, which, if not the most conspicuous, was not the least fundamental. *It was the contraction of the territory within which the spirit of religion was conceived to run.* (Emphasis added)

This tells us something about modernization: what does it have to say about traditionalization?

We know that the observant olim are less likely than the nonobservant to take on entrepreneurial roles, and that they are less likely to leave Israel. Recalling the connection between entrepreneurship and the Americans' ideology of change, perhaps we can relate the two in a simple manner. It might go like this: The observant olim fare differently in Israel. It may not be the case that the observant integrate into Israeli society, as a whole, any better than the nonobservant; but it may be the case that they are able to integrate into a small chunk of that society, the religious, more so than the nonobservant into a similar small chunk. The datiim face Israeli society from an encapsulated position within that society; the lo-datiim must, in a sense, face the whole society at once, with no such supportive encapsulation. In simple terms, he who is most uncomfortable agitates for change; he who has some comfort has some interest in maintaining the status quo.

This explanation would work very well if we could demonstrate that observant olim are not activists agitating for change; that they do not share with the nonobservant the American belief in individual citizen action; that they do not hold that individuals can act and effect unidirectional change. I can demonstrate none of these propositions; to the contrary, many of the observant olim do hold these beliefs, are advocates of change, and pursue activism towards these ends.

What ends? What kind of change? What sort of activism?

In the period following the Yom Kippur War (1973), a new movement has gained increasing popular support in Israel. Called *Gush Emunim* ("The Bloc of the Faithful"), the movement presents an irredentist stance vis-à-vis the West Bank (Judea and Samaria) and other administered territories (the Sinai, the Gaza Strip, the Golan Heights). The focus of Gush's activities has been the establishment of Jewish settlements in these territories, beyond the Green Line. The settlements were founded with volunteered labor and without the consent of the (then) Labour government.

The political opponents of Gush viewed these settlements as illegal, a blatant defiance of the government. Many critics demanded their removal, if necessary by force. Gush responded by rejecting the political arguments. In their view each settlement was a further move towards the integration of Eretz Yisrael into a Third Jewish Commonwealth. Thus the leaders and supporters of Gush saw themselves standing above party politics and, if necessary, above parliamentary process. They rejected the political arguments of their opponents by claiming for their movement a legitimacy based on religious (and not political) values. The ultimate value was that of messianic redemption. In this light the advent of the Jewish state was less the triumph of a particular movement of national liberation, that is, Zionism, than it was the beginnings of a divinely inspired and ordained redemptive process. This process depends on, among other things, the territorial integrity of Eretz Yisrael. Failure to settle the land or the withdrawal from presently occupied territories would be only secondarily a military-political "blunder." Such failure or withdrawal would constitute man's (or his government's) direct contravention of God's will: this would cause the interruption or, worse, the cessation of the redemptive process.[9]

Gush Emunim is an Israeli movement, with roots in Zionist and Israeli history. It is, however, a movement that has attracted the support of American observant olim in large numbers. Table 7.3 gives some idea of Gush's support among American olim (in Jerusalem), on the basis of religious observance.

Not all the American datiim support Gush; and among its support it counts a minority of secular American immigrants. But for the majority of observant who do support the movement, support

Table 7.3   Support of Gush Emunim, by Religious Observance

	Support (%)	Do Not Support (%)
Observant	41.7	12.5
Nonobservant	6.9	38.9
		100.0

entails a high degree of activism: they march with Gush; they work in the (Jerusalem) front office; they live on the settlements. One supporter spoke of his joining the movement both in terms of his religiousness and his Americanness.

> Why does the dati join? He has the element of faith in God. If you take this as a factor, you become, as they say, "a little less rational, a little less objective." But I say you become *ultimately realistic*. In the last analysis, if you want to be "objective" and "rational," you shouldn't even come to this country: this country shouldn't exist. Yet we're here; we came, we'll stay. We will make it because God is with us. Gush is today the expression in Israel of our belief in God: not anything called "Zionism." Gush is more than a settlement movement. It is a movement aimed at turning the State of Israel into the Land of Israel. Why did I join—why do so many Americans join? Because Americans have a sense of independence. And independence gives a person the courage to move, to act, that the person without independence lacks. So the American dati has both these factors—faith and his ability to act—that function within and for him. They move him along. With Gush, we'll move the country along.

Here, the American belief that individual action can bring about change ("movement") is still strong. But the belief in individual action has been wedded to a particular kind of change: the transformation of Medinat Yisrael, the State of Israel, into Eretz Yisrael, the Land of Israel. There is more involved in this transformation than a change of nomenclature:

> *Rabbi S:* I'm not sure we're ready for a truly Jewish Israel right now, but I'm sure we need an undergirding of religious direction. Gush provides that. The aim, of course, is to create a religiously Jewish State. Zionism was necessary for this—the establishment of Israel was the beginning of *ge'ula* ["redemption"]. But the people who built the state are showing that ideationally they are bankrupt. When young people raised on kibbutzim begin asking, "What is this all about, what right do we have to be here?"; when this happens, you find that the momentum that their parents brought with them to this country has expended itself. They came with a religious tradition; no matter how secular they were, none of the founders had

grandfathers who weren't religious. There was something sub-
consciously Jewish about them, a residue from their grandfathers. How long could this last? One generation? Two? Four?
By the fourth or fifth generation you never even heard of
"grandfather," so you ask the kinds of questions Israeli secular
youth ask today. With the result that people born in this country aren't sure why they're here, what they're fighting for.
There's no more residue, and the value of being a Jew and
being in Eretz Yisrael is not there. If we had an image of a
religious polity, even if we couldn't achieve one just yet, these
problems would be solved.

"An image of a religious polity"—an image of an ideal Jewish
society—is one that the observant supporters of Gush Emunim
can invest in. Gush Emunim provides the context for activism; the
image of a religiously Jewish Israel provides the direction for
change. We are facing here another vision of Israel's social future, one which Weingrod did not discuss. Dov, a supporter of
Gush with plans to move himself and his family to one of its
settlements, spoke of this version of the social future; it will be
noted that his main referents are in the historical past:

The future of the Jewish people at any time and in any
place—including Israel—is in the Jewish religion. You have to
understand that all the things that can occur to Jews in the
Diaspora can happen here in Israel, too. Assimilation can occur
here, maybe especially here. What was Hannukah about? It
wasn't just a revolt against the Syrian Greeks, a foreign power.
It happened when a Jew went and offered a pig to an idol. Isn't
that assimilation? We weren't fighting Syrian Greeks; we were
fighting assimilation: *hityavnut* [literally: "Hellenization"]. *This*
is where assimilation was, in Eretz Yisrael. And then, as now,
the only force that fought it was religious commitment. This is
what Hannukah is about—all the stuff about fighting for independence is secondary. Hannukah is about Hellenization, assimilation. Then, as now. Why do you think so many Israelis
are leaving? It is a manifestation of their weakening identification with being Jewish. Because if you identify strongly you'll
stick it out here under all costs.
So I'll tell you what the future of Israel is. The future of Israel
is the future of the Jewish people. And the future of the Jewish
people is the same as its past: Those Jews who have religious
commitment remain Jews; those who don't—or didn't—
assimilate.

Observant olim complain of Levantinization, to be sure. They share this complaint with the lo-dati. But among the dati supporters of Gush there is another, and more feared, sort of social change: *hityavnut,* Hellenization. With the secularist (and especially the secular Left) cast as Hellenizers, and Gush Emunim as the brave Maccabees, the battle ultimately becomes one against "the fear of the possibly unsettling or disintegrative effects of" nothing less than "Western culture" (O'Dea 1976:46).

Orthodoxy in religion and activism through Gush Emunim provide a potent hedge against the relegitimation of modernity: because the image of tradition that these individuals have invested in is not yet discredited. Their image of the ideal society is not only, as it was for the lo-datiim, a gemeinschaft with Levantinism lurking like a serpent in the grass. For these individuals the ideal society, a religiously Jewish society, is something yet to be striven for. And it can only be attained, to paraphrase Tawney, by activism in the service of one end: the expansion of the territory within which the spirit of the Jewish religion is conceived to run. I am speaking, once again, of traditionalization.

Perhaps it is clear, now, why the *oleh dati* is less likely to take on an entrepreneurial role, to act as an agent for modernity, and why he is less likely to make *yerida* (leave Israel). For the latter, I believe that the dichotomy I drew between instrumental and expressive traditionalizing holds for the datiim, but with less tension-producing effect. The *oleh dati* knows why he should not feel disappointment at being unable to play roles, expressively, like the "typical Israeli"; he has reasons other than amoral Levantinism to prevent him; he has, in addition, immoral Hellenism.

The American identity of the *oleh dati* probably differed in significant ways from that of the lo-dati *in* America; we should expect that reconstruction takes for him a different course. While the negative components of Israeli identity are very strongly accented, more so than in the case of the *oleh lo-dati,* I believe that there is less in the dati's American identity that is available for positive reconstruction: the attribute of citizen-action, perhaps, and perhaps also attributes of efficiency in the battle (a subsidiary one) against the Israeli Levant. But it is doubtful, in the case of the dati oleh, that "WASP" is ever effectively split from "goy."

One is tempted by the simplest explanations: the *oleh dati* (the Orthodox Jew) was probably less American to begin with; there is less of an American identity to reconstruct; the religious world view hampers seriously the emergence of a love affair with modernity. But all of these explanations lead only to further branchings in the lines of inquiry; for the analyst, to yet another starting point. Dov, who will move with his family to a Gush Emunim settlement, who believes that "the future of the Jewish people is the same as its past," ended his interview with me with these words:

I have thought a lot about what a truly "Jewish" state would look like. What about a democratic Jewish state? I've thought about it: I don't think you can have a "Jewish" state and a "democratic" state. Democracy is doing what the majority of the people want: the people don't want Judaism; it's too disciplinary, it's too hard.

There is a *midrash* [rabbinic homily] that the Jews in the desert were forced by God to accept the Torah: they didn't want it. He forced us. Sometimes I think about that midrash, and it bothers me.

Fieldwork among an Overly Complex People

It is interesting to note how the Nuer themselves figure a lineage system. When illustrating on the ground a number of related lineages they do not present them the way we figure them in this chapter as a series of bifurcations of descent, as a tree of descent, or as a series of triangles of ascent, but as a number of lines running at angles from a common point. . . . This representation and Nuer comments on it show several significant facts about the way in which Nuer see the system.
E. E. Evans-Pritchard, *The Nuer*

About halfway through my fieldwork I made an appointment to interview one evening an American immigrant named Benjamin. I arrived after he and his family had finished dinner. He told me that he had *mishmar ezrahi* ("civil guard") duty that night, and asked if I would mind if we held our talk while he patrolled. I said I wouldn't mind.

Benjamin changed his clothes and we drove the short distance from his home to the civil guard station in Ramat Eshkol, where he received his M-1 carbine and his guard partner for the night: an Israeli-born ("Orthodox") rabbi, a teacher in a local Yeshiva. The Rav looked to be a man in his early sixties; he seemed glad to have drawn Benjamin as a partner, for the American owned a car and that meant the team need not patrol on foot.

Benjamin introduced me to the Rav in Hebrew, as a "student of anthropology interested in the problems of the adjustment [*histaglut*] of new immigrants." The Rav told me that those were important problems to study, and then asked me what *antropologia* was. I explained. Very often I was asked to explain much more than this. My informants (and later, when I administered a questionnaire, my respondents) would ask a variety of questions of me—sometimes when we were on the phone and I was making initial contact with them. "I've always wondered," I would be asked, "what the difference was between anthropology—you don't dig for bones, do you?—and sociology." Or: "Now I know some of you guys call yourselves cultural anthropologists and some social anthropologists; which are you?" Or: "An anthropologist? I thought you people went to islands where tribes wore bones in their noses." The implication here, I fathomed, was that I'd gotten off the airplane at the wrong airport. I was challenged: What would an anthropologist want with American olim? "We're pretty modern types," I was told on one occasion; it was early on in the field and I failed to ask, "*Modern* types? What do you mean by that?" Sometimes the questions asked of me were strictly methodological in nature: "How are you collecting your sample?" "Is it random?" "Will you employ parametric or nonparametric statistics?"

I told the Rav what *antropologia* was, and we proceeded to patrol Ramat Eshkol and French Hill in Benjamin's car, making slow circles around the neighborhoods. Benjamin and the Rav sat in front, the carbines resting, butts down, on the floor. I sat in the back, holding the cassette tape-recorder high and forward, between the two front seats. As Benjamin drove, he told me of his early involvement with Zionism, of a previous aliya attempt in the early 1960s, of a small hardware store he opened in Jerusalem, since making aliya—for the second time—in 1971. The interview began in English, but since the Rav could not speak English Benjamin switched to answering questions in Hebrew or Yiddish, and I began to ask them in the same languages.

After an hour or so I asked Benjamin to tell me more about his hardware store. He had been a schoolteacher in the United States, and I was interested in why he had changed occupations; what drew him to business, in Israel; and what it was like "doing business" in Israel. He said he had been a schoolteacher for fifteen years and had wanted "to try something else." In a business such as his he could "be his own boss" and that appealed to him; and, he added—in what was already a fairly common refrain—he thought that "Americans had a lot to contribute to Israel, and a business was a good place to work from."

About doing business in Israel, Benjamin spoke of Levantinism and the shtetl mentality, about the necessity for proteksia and the impingements of *bureaucratia*. He turned to the Rav at this point and said: "I hope you don't think I'm talking *lashon hara* ["malicious gossip," a sin], Rav. It is important that this young man understand the problems of new olim." The Rav told him it wasn't lashon hara, and agreed it was important that I understood. Benjamin nodded, and continued:

"There is something else, something very basic. The attitudes of Israelis towards their jobs are different from those of the American. I know I'm generalizing, but basically the American worker wants a good life and he understands that he must *give* something: production. The Israeli attitude is: *Mage'a-lo* [he expects it; it's coming to him]. The fact that he lives here in Israel means *mage'a-lo*. Look, you want to say, you're making a living, all right, but you have to give something back, you've got to produce. But the Israeli says: *Ain devar—anahnu kvar mistadere* [Nothing of the sort—we're already managing, getting by]. Now, if you multiply this attitude by hundreds or thousands of people—I may sound to you like a conservative person, a reactionary, but I remember my father worked in a sweatshop in New York City. On piecework. You made two thousand pairs of pants, you got two cents times two thousand; you made a hundred pairs of pants, you got two cents times a hundred. Each person worked like this, and at the end of a day each person's wage was reckoned. A sweatshop was a terrible thing, but it was also what made America great."

The Rav nodded, and said in Yiddish: "Americans know how to work, that is true."

"More than that," said Benjamin in Yiddish, "When an American misses a day's work, it's like an *aveira* [sin]."

"Like a sin?" asked the Rav, perplexed. "To miss a day's work is like a *sin*?"

"Yes," said Benjamin. He was silent for a moment and then, half turning, he asked me in English: "Have you ever read Max Weber?"

"Max Weber?"

"Yes—wouldn't anthropologists read him?" Before I could reply he turned to the Rav and asked him in Yiddish: "Have you ever heard of Max Weber?"

"No," said the Rav. "Is he Jewish?"

"No. He was a German writer. He wrote about *di echtiga Protestantim*. Anyway, that's what Americans are: di echtiga Protestantim, when it comes to work. Weber wrote like this, Rav:

There was a Christian named Calvin...." And Benjamin proceeded to explain, to the Rav and myself, in Yiddish, Weber's argument in *The Protestant Ethic and the Spirit of Capitalism*. He explained to us how, for the Calvinists, that a man was successful in this world was a *simon* ["sign"] that he was chosen for *gan-eden* ["paradise"] in the world to come. To be a failure, or not to work hard for success, was likewise a sign that he was not among those chosen for paradise. Benjamin explained how these *Prot-estantim* "changed the world" with this ethic, and said that this ethic was brought to America by the Protestants who immigrated there. He said that now it is not only the American Protestants who have inherited similar ideas about work and success but, to a certain extent, all Americans, including Jewish Americans. And in part, he concluded, this is why American olim are "driven crazy" in Israel.

The Rav listened quietly but looked, at the end, a little confounded. He said: "They think it is an *aveira* to miss a day's work?"

The anthropologist had sat quietly in the back, tape-recorder held a little high and forward, between the seats, listening to a lecture in Yiddish on Max Weber and social theory while he rode through French Hill and Ramat Eshkol, staring occasionally at the two M-1s resting, butts down, on the floor of the Peugeot.

In some important ways, both the immigrant and the ethnographer set for themselves the same task. For both find themselves in the position of having to, wanting to, or needing to understand another culture. Both must learn its language, a language not only of linguistic but also of social and cultural discourse. For the immigrant, part of the very process of his absorption entails tasks of ethnographic dimensions, just as for the ethnographer certain problems of adjustment and integration must be faced. Nevertheless, immigrant and ethnographer differ in important ways, perhaps most crucially in the sort of commitment each brings to the attainment of cultural understanding; in the quality of things at stake should either one succeed or fail. The American immigrant has the need to understand American immigrants in Israel, for he is one of them; the ethnographer has the same need, for he is studying them. In both cases the immigrant is the object of study, of understanding; in the former case he is the *subject* of study, as well.

The distinction between object and subject, between analysand and analyst, is a familiar (and most would argue crucial) one in the enterprise of the social sciences. From this distinction we can make others, for example between "objective" understandings and ones that are "subjective."[1] For example, Dean MacCannell writes that the ethnographer "uses the explanations of social life volunteered by native respondents: as one part of the puzzle to be solved, not as one of its solutions" (1976:10). Now this sort of distinction makes a fine guide so long as the ethnographer can tell his "native respondents" from his own image in a mirror: so long as the native's explanation is patently distinguishable from the analyst's. But what happens, to put it simply, when the native explains social life by reference to *The Protestant Ethic and the Spirit of Capitalism?* What happens when part of the puzzle to be solved can be quite legitimately construed as one of the solutions? The native who recommends to you Max Weber is telling you something about himself; but what, if anything, is he telling you about Max Weber?

The American olim are individuals who, in the U.S., had made intense investments in their ethnic identity, Jewishness, to the point where their social identity was primordialized. At the same time, disengagement from American society was articulated in part as a defense against the anomie of American modernity, the insecurity and anxiety that mark the "modern condition." From the interaction between images of ideal (Jewish) self and feared (American) society, a particular picture of society in Israel is drawn. It is a Jewish society, to be sure; but it is more than this. It is a society wherein, the olim say, *Kol Yehudim mishpaha ahad:* All Jews constitute a single family. It is an ideal and idealized picture of the traditional society.

Once resident in Israel, the olim grapple with a society that is indeed more "traditional" than the one they left in the U.S.: and they begin to learn that tradition is not all gemütlichkeit. They object to particular features of Israeli society (like the conduct of business and bureaucracy) even as they must, in their absorption, learn to adapt to them. Those many aspects of tradition which they come to reject are redefined as Levantinism. As reformers or entrepreneurs they come to see themselves as agents of change in Israeli society. They define the sort of "change" very clearly: it is "development." It is movement towards increasing "efficiency" and "ra-

tionality." In their words, it is "progress." Although a minority
are able to retain an idealized image of tradition in the context of
Gush Emunim and messianic politics, the majority of American
immigrants attempt to introduce modernization to Israeli society.

With this precis of the book's argument it can be clearly seen
how I have used the notions of tradition/traditionalizing and
modernity/modernizing, to make sense of the immigrants' aliya
and absorption. The work can be seen, then, as a contribution to
the social psychology of modernity and tradition. For example,
Heilman (1976), in an ethnography of an American Orthodox
synagogue, focuses in some detail on the Orthodox Jew's dilemma regarding "traditionalism" vs. "modernity." In effect, I
have attempted to broaden the range of Jewish participants in this
dilemma to "nationalists" and "culturalists," as well as the religiously observant. More importantly, however, I have tried to
place the dilemma in the context of social identity dynamics and
their interdependence with images of society. These transcend
ethnographic locales like the synagogue, even as they transcend
the presence or absence of such attributes as Orthodoxy. They
involve conflicts engendered between dissonant images of self
and society.

But from the precis it ought to be equally clear that the olim
themselves use the notions tradition/traditionalizing and
modernity/modernizing. They express their alienation from
American society in terms of a values-critique of the modern
condition. They conceive of the ideal Israel as mishpaha writ
large; and as they come to battle Levantinism they do so in the
name of progress and development. Perhaps only a moment's
reflection is necessary to understand why "native" and
"analyst" have produced models explaining social life that are so
apparently similar. Neither is exotic to the other (both are Western); and the native is, in this case, sophisticated, educated, and
fiercely introspective on the subjects of his Jewishness, Israel,
and aliya. What is interesting here is not the *why* of similitude but
the brute fact of it. In some measure, these olim have invested in
the same images of "tradition" and "modernity" as has a body of
Western social science. What is more interesting still is that we
can see the olim using the tradition/modernity model to make
sense of and to give meaning to their worlds. And in this case, an
examination of the native's model is useful in revealing the weak-
nesses and deficiencies of the analyst's model.

For the olim—and for many social scientists who use the model analytically—tradition and modernity, whether evaluated in a given instance positively or negatively, are counterposed as structural opposites. They become dichotomous entities: states of being. They are disjunctive; and the contrast between them is invariably invidious (though not always in the same direction). Finally, they are used ideologically to evaluate, rationalize, criticize, praise, or condemn; and on this basis they become programs for action. Thus, the olim have construed and misconstrued the pair as ideal *images* of self and society, while Western social science has performed a similar calculus under the aegis of ideal *types*.

Reinhard Bendix has provided for us an intellectual history of the understandings and misunderstandings borne by the ideas "tradition" and "modernity," from the Scots Ferguson and Millar, through (among others) Goethe, Proudhon, and Marx, to such contemporary writers as Redfield and Lerner. Bendix underlines the invidious nature of the contrast, as he documents the ways in which the less euphoric aspects of traditional life often disappear, under ideological reconstruction, "in the roseate image of the community modeled on the familial pattern" (1967:282). Professor Bendix's phrase might serve aptly, if ironically, as a gloss for the olim's expressed vision of Israel as a community wherein *Kol Yehudim mishpaha ahad.* In a similar vein, while offering a critique of the concepts as "misplaced polarities" in studies of social change, Gusfield emphasizes the extent to which imputation of "traditional" or "modern" have served ideological functions in the public arenas of developing nations. Perceptively, he cautions,

> Tradition is not something waiting out there, always over one's shoulder. It is rather plucked, created and shaped to present needs and aspirations in a given historical situation. . . .
> . . . Just as "tradition" is renewed, created, and discovered, so too "modernity" as a goal toward which men aspire appears in some specific historical guise. (1967:358, 361)

In their portrayal of tradition *either* as moral gemeinschaft *or* the amoral Levant, in their portrayal of modernity *either* as unrooted normlessness *or* the salvation of efficiency, progress, and development, the olim model for us—indeed they act out—the analytic deficiencies of the concepts as they are pictured in structural dichotomy. At the same time, the immigrants' experience in aliya and absorption informs of alternatives to dichotomizing the pair as disjunctive states of being. For in the distinction between expressive and instrumental traditionalizing, in the fear of Levantinism and its use in the relegitimation of modernity, and even in the adherence to idealized tradition exemplified by support of Gush Emunim, we can see elements of the "traditional" and the "modern" coexisting and influencing one another; in the Rudolphs' phrase, they "infiltrate and transform each other" (1967:3). Neither tradition nor modernity are univocal entities but rather are multivocal goals. They are in a "contrapuntal interplay" (Smelser 1968:138), and in effect one should not speak of them as exclusive states but as processes: one should speak not of modernity but of modernizing; not of tradition but of traditionalizing.

This book was about a particular case of traditionalization, but I hope it has made clear a point noted earlier: traditionalization is an eminently modern act.[2] Bendix writes that "modernization in some sphere of life may occur without resulting in modernity" (1967:311). The olim traditionalize without "becoming traditional." A part of the epigraph for Chapter 7 is germane here: "For moderns, reality and authenticity are thought to be elsewhere: in other historical periods and other cultures, in purer, simpler life-styles." MacCannell uses this insight to understand moderns as tourists. It might also be applied towards the understanding of particular moderns as potential immigrants.

There is, after all, some distinction between object and subject, native and analyst, to be made. For the olim do not see their absorption (or their inability to become traditional even as they are becoming Israelis) as an "acting out" of inherent fallacies in the opposition of tradition to modernity. Most would find, for legitimate reasons, the comparison of oleh to tourist distasteful. The study should end, therefore, with a reflection on some of the issues of social identity transformations that have formed its core.

For the immigrants, images of Israel as ideal society were linked to images of the Jew as ideal self. These images were cathected. The immigrants' responses I have here described are responses to continuing states of cognitive and emotional dissonance, among images of selves and societies. Calling, for example, some of these traditionalizing olim "modernizers," in their roles of reformer or entrepreneur, will not reduce dissonance with the addition of irony. Nevertheless, in confronting aspects of Israel, these olim do come with the cultural baggage of models of progress and, ultimately, modernity that are based on the West and the United States. The irony, then, is supplied by the actors themselves. The Israeli may berate the American with some variant of, "You want to turn Israel into another United States of America." The oleh may answer, by word or deed, with some variant of, "Yes—but...." The "but" is important. For the person who left the United States for a life in Israel can be at best an ambiguous modernizer, an ambivalent Anglo-Saxon. He has come by choice to a Jewish state serving a Jewish society and, given *his* models of change, progress and modernity, there is a point at which his very success at modernizing endangers the ideals for which he made aliya in the first place.

Appendix
Immigration to Israel and Israeli Population

Table A1 The Waves of Immigration

First Aliya	1882–1903	20,000–30,000	Russia
Second Aliya	1904–14	35,000–40,000	Russia and Poland
Third Aliya	1919–23	35,000	Russia
Fourth Aliya	1924–31	82,000	Poland; some from America, the Middle East
Fifth Aliya	1932–38	201,000	Poland, Germany, Russia, Austria, Rumania
During and after WW II (Sixth Aliya)	1939–48	145,000	Poland, Germany, Rumania, Czechoslovakia, Russia, Bulgaria, Hungary, Italy, Austria, Yugoslavia

SOURCES: Adapted from data in Eisenstadt 1967:11 and Matras 1965:20–32.

Table A2   Sources of Population Increase in Israel (Population in 1,000s)

Years	1 At Beginning of Period	2 Natural Increase	3 Migration Balance	4 = 2 + 3 Total Increase	5 = 1 + 4 At End of Period	6 = 4:1 Yearly Increase	7 = 3:4 Migration Balance, Out of Total
1948–73*	649.6	886.7	1268.0	2160.8	2810.4	5.9%	58.7%
1948–51	649.6	88.4	666.4	754.8	1404.4	23.7	88.3
1952–54	1404.4	101.4	20.2	121.6	1526.0	2.8	16.6
1955–57	1526.0	100.7	136.1	236.8	1762.8	4.9	57.5
1958–60	1762.8	101.5	46.9	148.4	1911.2	2.8	31.6
1961–64	1911.2	134.2	193.8	328.0	2239.2	4.1	59.1
1965–71	2239.2	277.5	119.9	397.4	2636.6	2.3	30.2
1972–73	2636.6	89.1	84.7	173.8	2810.4	3.3	48.8
1969	2434.8	40.1	21.5	61.6	2496.4	2.5	34.8
1970	2496.4	43.0	22.0	65.0	2561.4	2.6	33.8
1971	2561.4	47.0	28.2	75.2	2636.6	2.9	37.5
1972	2636.6	44.8	42.2	87.0	2723.6	3.2	48.5
1973	2723.6	44.2	42.5	86.8	2810.4	3.2	49.0

SOURCE: *Statistical Abstract of Israel*, no. 25 (Jerusalem: Israel Central Bureau of Statistics, 1974), table II/2, p. 22.
*From May 15, 1948.

Table A3 World Jewish Population and Jewish Population in Israel

Year*	Total (in 1,000s)	Absolute Nos. (in Israel)	Jews in Israel as % of Total
1850	4,800	—	—
1882	7,700	24	0.3
1895	—	47	—
1900	10,700	50	0.5
1914	13,500	85	0.6
1916–18	—	57	—
Oct. 23, 1922	—	84	—
May 30, 1925	14,800	122	0.8
June 18, 1931	—	175	—
1935	—	355	—
1940	16,700	467	2.8
1945	11,000	564	5.1
1947	11,270	630	5.6
May 15, 1948	11,300	650	5.7
1951	11,533	1,404	12.2
1954	11,867	1,526	12.9
1957	12,035	1,763	14.6
May 22, 1961	12,866	1,932	15.0
1964	13,225	2,239	16.9
1965	13,411	2,299	17.1
1966	13,538	2,345	17.3
1967	13,628	2,384	17.5
1968	13,786	2,435	17.7
1972	14,371	2,724	19.0

SOURCE: *Statistical Abstract of Israel,* no. 25 (Jerusalem: Israel Central Bureau of Statistics, 1974), table III/3, p. 23.

*End of year unless otherwise stated.

Table A4   Immigrants and Tourists Settling, by Country of
                 Residence, 1950–72

Country of Residence	Number	Country of Residence	Number
Europe	430,106	*Africa*	348,309
USSR	60,933	Morocco	236,671
Poland	80,225	Algeria	17,175
Rumania	208,919	Tunisia	54,073
Yugoslavia	1,432	Libya	19,338
Bulgaria	4,409	Egypt-Sudan	30,855
Germany-Austria	4,850	South Africa	6,134
Czechoslovakia	2,962	Other	1,238
Hungary	14,469		
U.K.	11,750	*America & Oceania*	82,288
Netherlands	2,877	Canada	3,917
Belgium	2,689	U.S.	35,141
France	25,877	Mexico	1,344
Italy	2,705	Brazil	5,619
Other	6,009	Uruguay	4,164
		Argentina	22,482
Asia	253,627	Australia-	
Turkey	25,014	New Zealand	2,344
Syria-Lebanon	7,432	Other	7,287
Iraq	125,392	Continent not	
Yemen-Aden	11,953	known	7,257
Iran	57,047	Total (1950–72)	1,121,587
India	20,549		
Other	6,130		

SOURCE: *Immigration to Israel, 1948–1972,* special series no. 416, pt. 1 (Jerusalem: Israel Central Bureau of Statistics, 1973), table 4, pp. 20–21.

Notes

Chapter 2

1. "Orthodox" Judaism can be defined only in relation to "Reform" (and later, in the U.S., to "Conservative" or "Reconstructionist") Judaism. Orthodoxy is itself a response to modernity. Adherents of Orthodoxy will usually define "Orthodox Judaism" *as* Judaism. All other variants, in their eyes, are not legitimate; such, indeed, is the case in Israel today.

2. This scheme is idealized. In fact, there were at times religious labor-Zionists, and nonreligious right-wing Zionist factions.

3. Martin Buber said Herzl had "a countenance lit with the glance of the Messiah" (Urofsky 1975:23). Herzl was aware that the masses held this view of him, and it was, apparently, discomfiting. In his diary an entry in 1896 reads: "The people are sentimental; the masses do not see clearly, I believe that even now they no longer have a clear idea of me" (in Hertzberg 1959:231). On the issue of settlement in Eretz Yisrael or elsewhere, Herzl, in *The Jewish State,* included a section entitled "Palestine or Argentina?" He begged the question, preferring to leave the decision to a "duly constituted Society of Jews."

4. There were of course Jews (mostly Sephardic) resident in Palestine for centuries before the modern aliyot (i.e., those beginning in 1882). And even the First Aliya (1882–1903), predominantly Russian, contained some Jews from Yemen.

5. Some exceptions are made in the cases of potential immigrants with a "criminal past," or those likely to "endanger the public welfare," for example, due to disease or ill health.

6. The Law of Return and all its variants have embroiled Israeli courts in the knotty problem of defining "Who is a Jew?" for purposes of settlement, citizenship, and certain new-immigrant related subventions. At times this has become a major political issue between religious and nonreligious parties. For example, conversions to Judaism done by Reform or Conservative rabbis are not at present acceptable in Israel.

7. The Middle Eastern Jews were not, in the main, attracted to either the kibbutz life-style or its ideology. They preferred the more individualistic moshav setting.

8. Reform did not, however, attract formerly-settled Jews who were Sephardim. They continued to worship according to their own traditions.

9. In America, the problem of "emancipation" did eventually arise: over the American black. The strains of this emancipation have given shape to the unique "American dilemma."

213

Chapter 3

1. "Ein HaShofet" means "Spring of the Judge," so named in honor of Justice Brandeis.

2. Between 1961 and 1968, some 21,008 Americans entered Israel under the status "temporary resident." These were not tabulated in table 3.1 (cf. Goldscheider 1974:353).

3. The status "potential immigrant" also carries with it deferment of military responsibilities for the period in which it is in effect.

4. See Liebman 1973 for a fine discussion of the "religion of American Jews." On Conservative Judaism, in particular, see Sklare 1955.

5. Israeli data from *The Statistical Abstract of Israel*, no. 25, table II/9 (Israel Central Bureau of Statistics, Jerusalem 1974), p. 31.

6. Israeli data from ibid.

7. Israeli data from ibid., Table II/4, p. 25.

8. The estimate of 300,000 was cited in the *Jerusalem Post, International Edition*, December 27, 1977, p. 7. One telling example of relations between the Jewish community of Los Angeles and the approximately 50,000 Israelis who reside there is to be found in the fact that although the L.A. Jewish Federation Council has allocated $1 million towards helping some 500 Soviet Jewish immigrants in their adjustment to the U.S., the Council has no similar "budget line" for the Israelis. This information appeared in the *Los Angeles Times*, January 31, 1978, pt. 1, p. 13. The writer of this article added: "The (L.A.) Jewish establishment is given to the view that Israelis should not leave Israel, a position which annoys most Israelis here, who argue back that these same leaders should then be consistent and themselves embrace the harsher life found in Israel."

9. Canadian estimate from the *Jerusalem Post*, February 17, 1976, p. 3.

10. In several cases these individuals sought as spouses persons who would be willing to try with them another aliya.

Chapter 4

1. A description of one immigrant group's "self-absorption," their transformative goals and idealized society (a kibbutz, in this instance) may be found in Spiro 1970: chap. 3, esp. pp. 51–59.

2. There are other shlihim—those, for example, of the Youth and Hehalutz Department of the Jewish Agency—who are concerned with cultural, educational, and organizational work in the Diaspora and not, primarily, with aliya.

3. Jubas notes that 85 percent of his sample ($N = 1,178$) approached an Israel Aliya Center at least once (1974:291).

4. One example given me of such an organization is the Americans and Canadians for Aliya (AACA), a "sister organization" to the AACI.

5. Reported in the *Jerusalem Post, International Edition*, December 13, 1977, p. 5.

6. In this chapter, "potential immigrant" refers not to a technical visa status but to an individual in the period preceding his actual aliya.

7. The Agency is organized by "Desks," on the model of a Ministry of Foreign Affairs (or the U.S. State Department), dating from the days when it served diplomatic functions for the Yishuv.

8. I should note that it is in the area of loans that one encounters the greatest number of charges against shlihim of misinformation, duplicity, or "outright lying." Many olim complained they were "led to believe" their Agency loans would become grants if they remained in Israel more than three (or five) years. All the shlihim I interviewed denied these charges of misrepresentation—while admitting some olim are forced to repay loans that other olim avoid. The mechanics of this will be discussed in some detail when I turn to the issue of "proteksia" (Chapter 6).

9. According to the Ministry of Education, in 1975–76, enrollment in all forms of Israeli ulpanim totaled approximately 23,000.

10. For example, in 1977 a flat in Jerusalem that cost 210,000 IL, intended for four or five persons, was eligible for a mortgage of up to 110,000 IL. In contrast, a flat that cost 270,000 to 290,000 IL was eligible for a mortgage of only 40,000 IL. Flats that cost over 290,000 IL were not eligible for any size mortgage.

11. Quoted from the *Jerusalem Post*, May 26, 1976, p. 3.

12. Later in the same article cited in n.11, above, Mr. Rosen compared the views of one of his critics, a member of the Knesset from the then opposition Likud party, to those of the *Sovieteshe Heimland,* an anti-Zionist Yiddish magazine in the U.S.S.R.

Chapter 5

1. Even in these cases, assuming increasing anti-Jewish sentiments as a result of intensifying Arab nationalism, there must be pull components operating as well. The mass migration of Yemeni Jews in 1949–50 was motivated also by their messianic enthusiasm. On the other hand, while over 70,000 Moroccan Jews came to Israel between 1955 and 1957—presumably for predominantly push factors in Morocco—at Algeria's independence only some 8,000 (out of some 130,000) Algerian Jews immigrated to Israel. Most, although pushed from Algeria, were in fact pulled to France.

2. In order to protect the anonymity of informants I have used throughout pseudonyms. In addition, I have often changed certain nonessential details of their backgrounds: their American city of origin or—where it is not important to the discussion—their occupations in Israel. In some cases I use their initials (forename) only.

3. Cf. the distinction I drew in Chapter 3, on the basis of demographic data, between "observant Zionists" and "Orthodox Zionists."

4. In considering pulls I used Jubas's listing of "very important" motives for aliya. For the discussion of pushes here I use his listing of "combined importance"—i.e., at least "somewhat important." Because the pushes are less salient for olim than the pulls, the percentages of "very important" pushes are much smaller than those for "very important" pulls. Therefore, I used the combined importance ranking to give the reader a better feel for attitudes from Jubas's sample.

5. Some exceptions include Antonovsky (1968) and Antonovsky and Katz (1969). Pearl Katz's work (1974) also considers some rootedness issues but mainly in terms of social networks that the olim maintained in America.

6. The potent fear of assimilation implies a question of slightly different word-

ing: "Given who I am, can I remain that person—and guarantee that my children will become a similar sort of person—in America?"

7. "Early" and "late" investors may be correlated with our immigrant types, if not perfectly so. The great majority of religious olim were probably early investors. (An exception is the *ba'al tsuva*, literally "master of the return," a person who is converted to religious observance later in life. Indeed there is a minor academic industry in Jerusalem, where there are several yeshivot for *ba'alei tsuva*. Some were young tourists to Israel who were "grabbed" by recruiters; some are secular, young Israelis.) For the culturalists, if there was a strong Yiddishist referent, investment was probably early. Nationalists may be either early or late investors. I suspect that that proportion of olim who still cite objective Zionist reasons as primary motivations for aliya—like halutziut—are mostly early investors, while among the overtly subjective nationalists I would expect to find many late investors.

8. I use "potential immigrant" to refer here to an individual in the period before his aliya; it does not refer to a technical visa-status.

9. I use these two terms interchangeably; many do not (cf. Sherif 1968:151–52).

10. Persons may perceive accurately, or project, degrees of consensus. I should also mention that there is a third option in this situation, consisting of any number of defensive mechanisms, such as: "they are wrong, my hierarchy is superior" (grandiosity); "there is no conflict" (denial); "such conflict is part of the human condition" (rationalization); and so on. So long as these mechanisms are successfully employed, a decision about aliya may be avoided.

11. My work, however, is not meant to be an uncritical contribution to this literature. Some of the conceptual problems inherent in the tradition/modernity dichotomy are discussed in my final chapter.

12. Let me make clear that "traditionalization," as I have described it, I believe to be a particular response to problems of modernity. Traditionalization is itself, then, a modern act. Even in Israel, moreover, some of the contexts of traditionalizing are modern ones. For example, in Chapter 3, in the section on residential dispersion, I noted that American new immigrants are drawn in disproportionate numbers to settle, at least initially, on a kibbutz. Now the kibbutz ideology and structure are, in many ways, eminently modern. But I would argue that the Americans are drawn to the kibbutz for traditionalist reasons. They are drawn to it for they see it as a gemeinschaft par excellence, and as a "community" built on lines that are "moral." To point to the cooperative nature of kibbutz life, to its socialist ethic, is not to establish its modernity beyond doubt; for recall that some images of the most traditional of all societies—primitive ones—have at their center a vision of "primitive communalism." To be sure, communalism as it is found on kibbutzim is far from primitive; on the other hand, many olim learn that kibbutz society is not so much a gemeinschaft as they had thought it would be; nor, in many cases, does it satisfy their need for attachment to a moral community.

Chapter 6

1. The average family size is 4.7 in families originating in Africa and Asia, versus 2.8 in families originating in Europe and America.

2. One group, however, consisted of ex-inmates of camps for displaced persons; many of these were ex-inmates of concentration camps. They transcended positioning on the continuum.

3. Cf. my earlier discussion of this point with regard to Weingrod (1965) in the section on Zionism and the state in Chapter 2.

4. Cf. my earlier discussion of Americans' attraction to kibbutz life, n.12, Chapter 5.

5. This is true despite Israeli stereotypes of the "typical kibbutznik," "Jerusalemite," etc.

6. The other choices and the distribution of responses were as follows: bureaucrats not *efficient* (15 percent); they are not *courteous* (6 percent); they don't *know* as much as they ought to (11 percent); they don't *care* as much as they ought to (28 percent); they are *inflexible* about rules—they never make exceptions (0 percent); *nothing* in particular bothers me about the Israeli bureaucracy (1 percent). All the responses sum to 99 percent.

7. This appeared in the International Edition, May 30, 1978, p. 20.

8. There are many examples of this particular attitude in the Mediterranean literature; see, for example, Pitt-Rivers's (1961) chapter on "Friendship and Authority" in Andalusia. Given the Israeli sociological interest in traditional, Oriental Jews, however, many of whom came from Morocco, consider these several remarks by Lawrence Rosen (1972)—the subject of the paper is Moroccan Arab-Berber social relations: "The constant focus in Moroccan society is not . . . on corporate groups but on individuals . . . on arranging associations whenever they appear most advantageous" (p. 158); "Through ingratiation and role bargaining, manipulating intermediaries and performing 'favors,' each man plays on the expectation of some form of reciprocation to form a wide network of supporters and dependents whose potential aid will serve as a hedge against a host of natural and sociological uncertainties" (p. 160); "The emphasis is on personal networks of affiliation . . . and there are few people . . . who are willing to sacrifice long-term eventualities to the binding exigencies of a short-term alliance" (p. 163); "Indeed . . . the primary emphasis in this society seems to be placed on regularized ways in which two individuals can contract a personal bond of affiliation in order to secure the basis of their own well-being" (p. 172). It is clear, I think, that the description of "how to overcome bureaucracy" offered by the ministry article is closer to Rosen's Moroccan world than to Weber's rational ideal-typic one. Passages such as these make me wonder how much of modernity Israel represented to the Orientals, to begin with, or how effective their traditionalizing influences have been on Israeli society.

9. Cf. my earlier discussions of immigration and citizenship in Chapters 2 and 3. With regard to table 6.1, the low-medial position of France reflects the fact, I suspect, that many French Jewish citizens making aliya are North Africans, Algerians, and Moroccans, who might be more willing to accept the invitation on its status, not contract, basis.

Chapter 7

1. But cf. his earlier discussion, Weingrod 1965:12–14.

2. The "agent of progress" attribute of American identity has enduring histori-

cal roots: De Tocqueville wrote of the Americans' fervent belief in the idea of the "indefinite perfectibility of man."

3. In the elections of May 1977—after I had left the country—the DMC garnered about 12 percent of the vote and subsequently joined the ruling Likud party to form the government coalition. Yadin became deputy prime minister. It does not appear, however, that electoral reform has remained a major concern of the DMC.

4. The first two letters appeared in the edition of October 27, 1976; the third in the edition of October 11, 1976.

5. There are almost 6,000 (Orthodox) synagogues in Israel, compared to, in 1976, 23 Conservative ones, and even fewer Reform. The first Conservative congregation was established in 1937. In November of 1976, the first kibbutz to be formally affiliated with the Reform movement was established. The settlers were a mixed group of young Americans and (Ashkenazi) Israelis.

6. One, called "The Group," and operating out of an English-language Jerusalem bookstore, was active in 1976.

7. In part, Fred "educated" the Israelis by launching a letter-writing campaign to newspapers and the Ministry of Tourism. Each letter complained of the "terrible," "abysmal," or "medieval" public bathroom facilities in "the Holy Land." The letters were written by Fred and his friends, transported outside Israel, and mailed from "abroad." Fred told me that one particularly effective letter came from a "retired English vicar and his wife." The *Jerusalem Post* published it. A day later, Fred recounted, an Israeli friend of his—one unaware of the letter's source—met him on the street and said: "Did you see that letter yesterday about public bathrooms from the retired English vicar and his wife? As a Jerusalemite I must tell you I was ashamed to read it: something must be done."

8. Source: *Supplement to the Monthly Bulletin of Statistics,* no. 12 (Israel Central Bureau of Statistics, Jerusalem, 1975): 58–59.

9. Gush has roots in the Whole Land of Israel movement, begun after the Six-Day War (cf. Isaac 1976), and deeper roots in the history of the Zionist movement itself (see Avruch 1979).

Chapter 8

1. We can even, as Marvin Harris has done vigorously and repeatedly, turn the distinction into the false dichotomy of "etics" versus "emics." See Fisher and Werner (1978) for a natural history of this misunderstanding.

2. In large measure this is why I prefer the term to others, such as Dahrendorf's "refeudalization" or Isaacs's "retribalization" (cf. Chapter 1).

References

Antonovsky, Aaron
1960   "Identity, Anxiety, and the Jew." In *Identity and Anxiety,* ed.
            M. Stein, A. Vidick, and M. White. Glencoe: The Free Press.
1963   "Israeli Political-Social Attitudes." *Amot,* no. 6 (in Hebrew).
1968   *Americans and Canadians in Israel.* Report no. 1. Jerusalem:
            The Israel Institute of Applied Research.

Antonovsky, Aaron, and David Katz
1969   *Americans and Canadians in Israel.* Reports nos. 1–3.
            Jerusalem: The Israel Institute of Applied Research.
1970   "Factors in the Adjustment to Israeli Life of American and
            Canadian Immigrants." *Jewish Journal of Sociology* 12 (June):
            77–87.

Asch, Solomon E.
1952   *Social Psychology.* Englewood Cliffs, N.J.: Prentice-Hall.

Avruch, Kevin A.
1979   "Traditionalizing Israeli Nationalism: The Development of Gush
            Emunim." *Political Psychology* 1 (Spring): 47–57.

Bailey, F. G.
1969   *Strategems and Spoils: A Social Anthropology of Politics.* Ox-
            ford: Blackwell.
1971   "Gifts and Poison." In *Gifts and Poison,* ed. F. G. Bailey. Ox-
            ford: Blackwell.
1973   *Debate and Compromise.* Oxford: Blackwell.

Barnes, J.A.
1968   "Networks and Political Process." In *Local-Level Politics,* ed.
            M. Swartz. Chicago: Aldine, 1968.

Barth, Fredrik
1966   *Models of Social Organization.* Royal Anthropological Institute
            of Great Britain and Ireland, Occasional Papers, no. 23.

219

1969   Introduction. In *Ethnic Groups and Boundaries*, ed. F. Barth.
               Boston: Little, Brown.

Bell, Daniel
1975   "Ethnicity and Social Change." In *Ethnicity: Theory and Ex-
               perience*, ed. N. Glazer and D. P. Moynihan. Cambridge: Har-
               vard University Press, 1975.

Bendix, Reinhard
1967   "Tradition and Modernity Reconsidered," In *Essays in Com-
               parative Stratification*, ed. L. Plotnikov and A. Tuden. Pitts-
               burgh: University of Pittsburgh Press, 1970. Originally published
               in *Comparative Studies in Society and History* 9 (1967): 292–
               346.

Berman, Gerald S.
1977   *The Experience of Aliyah among Recently Arrived North Ameri-
               can Olim: The Role of the Shaliach*. Jerusalem: Hebrew Univer-
               sity, Work and Welfare Research Institute.

Black, C. E.
1967   *The Dynamics of Modernization: A Study of Comparative His-
               tory*. New York: Harper and Row.

Bruner, J., and R. Tagiuri
1954   "Person Perception." In *The Handbook of Social Psychology*,
               ed. G. Lindzey. Cambridge: Addison-Wesley, vol. 2.

Cohen, Abner
1974   "The Lesson of Ethnicity." In *Urban Ethnicity*, ed. A. Cohen.
               London: Tavistock, 1974.

Cooley, C. H.
1902   *Human Nature and the Social Order*. New York: Scribner's.

Danet, Brenda
1970   "Petitions and Persuasive Appeals: A Content Analysis of Let-
               ters to the Israeli Customs Authorities." Ph.D. Dissertation,
               University of Chicago.
1971   "The Language of Persuasion in Bureaucracy: Modern and
               Traditional Appeals to the Israel Customs Authorities." *Ameri-
               can Sociological Review* 36 (October): 847–59.
1973   "Giving the Underdog a Break: Latent Particularism among
               Custom Officials." In *Bureaucracy and the Public*, ed. E. Katz
               and B. Danet. New York: Basic Books, 1973.

Danet, Brenda, and Michael Gurevitch
1972   "Presentation of Self in Appeals to Bureaucracy: An Empirical

Study of Role Specificity." *American Journal of Sociology* 77 (May): 1165–90.

Danet, Brenda, and Harriet Hartman
1972a   "Coping with Bureaucracy: The Israeli Case." *Social Forces* 51 (September): 7–22.
1972b   "On Proteksia: Orientations towards the Use of Personal Influence in Israeli Bureaucracy." *Journal of Comparative Administration* 3 (February): 405–34.

David, Abraham
1972   "Sheluhei Eretz Yisrael" [Emissaries of The Land of Israel]. In *Encyclopaedia Judaica,* 14:1358–68. Jerusalem: Keter Publishing House.

De Vos, George
1975   "Ethnic Pluralism: Conflict and Accommodation." In *Ethnic Identity: Cultural Continuities and Change,* ed. G. De Vos and L. Romanucci-Ross. Palo Alto: Mayfield Publishing Company, 1975.

Deshen, Shlomo
1966   "Conflict and Social Change: The Case of an Israeli Village." *Sociologia Ruralis* 6:31–55.

Deshen, Shlomo, and Moshe Shokeid
1974   *The Predicament of Homecoming: Cultural and Social Life of North African Immigrants in Israel.* Ithaca: Cornell University Press.

Devereux, George
1975   "Ethnic Identity: Its Logical Foundations and Its Dysfunctions." In *Ethnic Identity,* ed. De Vos and Romanucci-Ross. Palo Alto: Mayfield Publishing Company, 1975.

Dinnerstein, Leonard
1977   "The Eastern European Jewish Migration." In *Uncertain Americans: Readings in Ethnic History,* ed. L. Dinnerstein and F. Jaher. New York: Oxford University Press, 1977.

Eisenstadt, S. N.
1952   "The Process of Absorption of New Immigrants in Israel." *Human Relations* 5:223–46.
1954   *The Absorption of Immigrants.* London: Routledge and Kegan Paul.
1967   *Israeli Society.* New York: Basic Books.
1970   "Bureaucracy, Bureaucratization, and Debureaucratization." In

A Sociological Reader on Complex Organizations, ed. A. Et-
zioni. New York: Holt, Rinehart and Winston, 1970.
1974   Preface. In S. Deshen and M. Shokeid. *The Predicament of
Homecoming.* Ithaca: Cornell University Press.

Elon, Amos
1977   Review of H. Halkin, *Letters to an American Friend. New York
Times Book Review,* August 28, p. 9.

Engel, Gerald
1970   "North American Settlers in Israel." In *The American Jewish
Yearbook.* Vol. 71:161–87.

Erikson, Erik
1959   "The Problem of Ego Identity." In *Psychological Issues,* ed.
D. Rappoport. 1:101–64.
1963   *Childhood and Society.* 2d ed. New York: W. W. Norton.
1968   "Psychosocial Identity." In *International Encyclopedia of the
Social Sciences,* ed. D. Sills. Vol. 7:61–65. New York: Macmillan and the Free Press.

Evans-Pritchard, E. E.
1940   *The Nuer.* New York: Oxford University Press.

Fairchild, Henry
1923   *Immigration: A World Movement and Its American Significance.*
Rev. ed. New York: Macmillan.

Fallers, Lloyd, ed.
1968   *Immigrants and Associations.* The Hague: Mouton.

Fisher, Lawrence E., and Oswald Werner
1978   "Explaining Explanation: Tension in American Anthropology."
Journal of Anthropological Research 34:194–218.

Foote, N. N.
1951   "Identification as the Basis for a Theory of Motivation." *American Sociological Review* 16:14–21.

Freud, Anna
1936   *The Ego and Mechanisms of Defense.* New York: International
Universities Press.

Friedmann, Georges
1967   *The End of the Jewish People?* New York: Doubleday.

Gartner, Lloyd
1969   "Immigration and the Formation of American Jewry, 1840–

1925." In *The Jew in American Society,* ed. M. Sklare. New York: Behrman House, 1974.

Geertz, Clifford
1963   "The Integrative Revolution." In *The Interpretation of Cultures.* New York: Basic Books, 1973.

George, Pierre
1959   "Types of Migration of the Population According to the Professional and Social Composition of Migrants." In *Readings on the Sociology of Migration,* ed. C. Jansen. London: Pergamon Press, 1970.

Gerth, Hans, and C. W. Mills
1958   *From Max Weber: Essays in Sociology.* New York: Oxford University Press.

Glazer, Nathan, and Daniel Moynihan
1963   *Beyond the Melting Pot.* Cambridge: Harvard University and MIT Presses.

Glazer, Nathan, and Daniel Moynihan, eds.
1975   *Ethnicity: Theory and Experience.* Cambridge: Harvard University Press.

Glazer, Nathan
1975   "The Universalization of Ethnicity," *Encounter* 44 (February): 8–17.

Goffman, Erving
1959   *The Presentation of Self in Everyday Life.* Garden City: Doubleday Anchor Books.
1963   *Stigma: Notes of the Management of Spoiled Identity.* Englewood Cliffs, N.J.: Prentice-Hall.

Goldberg, Harvey
1972   *Cave Dwellers and Citrus Growers: A Jewish Community in Libya and Israel.* Cambridge: Cambridge University Press.

Goldscheider, Calvin
1974   "American Aliya: Sociological and Demographic Perspectives." In *The Jew in American Society,* ed. M. Sklare. New York: Behrman House, 1974.

Goldstein, Sydney, and Calvin Goldscheider
1968   *Jewish Americans: Three Generations in a Jewish Community.* Englewood Cliffs: Prentice-Hall.

224   References

Goodenough, Ward
1965   "Rethinking Status and Role: Towards a General Model of the Cultural Organization of Social Relationships." In *Cognitive Anthropology*, ed. S. Tyler. New York: Holt, Rinehart and Winston, 1969.

Gordon, Milton M.
1964   *Assimilation in American Life: The Role of Race, Religion, and National Origins.* New York: Oxford University Press.

Gusfield, Joseph
1967   "Tradition and Modernity: Misplaced Polarities in the Study of Social Change." *American Journal of Sociology* 72 (January): 351–62.

Halpern, Ben
1961   *The Idea of the Jewish State.* Cambridge: Harvard University Press.

Hampson, Norman
1966   *A Social History of the French Revolution.* Toronto: University of Toronto Press.

Hartmann, H.
1939   *Ego Psychology and the Problem of Adaptation.* New York: International Universities Press.

Heilman, Samuel
1976   *Synagogue Life: A Study of Symbolic Interaction.* Chicago: University of Chicago Press.

Heller, Celia
1973   "The Emerging Consciousness of the Ethnic Problem among the Jews of Israel." In *Israel: Social Structure and Change*, ed. M. Curtis and M. Chertoff. New Brunswick: Transaction Books, 1973.
1975   "Ethnic Differentiation among the Jews of Israel." In *Migration and Development*, ed. H. Safa and B. Du Toit. The Hague: Mouton.

Herman, Simon
1970   *Israelis and Jews: A Study in the Continuity of an Identity.* New York: Random House.

Hertzberg, Arthur, ed.
1959   *The Zionist Idea.* Garden City: Doubleday and the Herzl Press.

Hoselitz, Bert
1955   "A Sociological Approach to Economic Development." In *Development and Society*, ed. D. Novack and R. Lekachman. New York: St. Martin's Press, 1964.

Inkeles, Alex, and David H. Smith
1974   *Becoming Modern: Individual Change in Six Developing Countries*. Cambridge: Harvard University Press.

Inkeles, Alex
1975   "Becoming Modern." In *Socialization as Cultural Communication*, ed. T. Schwartz. Berkeley: University of California Press, 1976.

Isaac, Rael
1976   *Israel Divided: Ideological Politics in the Jewish State*. Baltimore: The Johns Hopkins University Press.

Isaacs, Harold
1966   *American Jews in Israel*. New York: John Day.
1975   "Basic Group Identity: The Idols of the Tribe." In *Ethnicity: Theory and Experience*, ed. N. Glazer and D. Moynihan. Cambridge: Harvard University Press, 1975.

James, William
1890   *The Principles of Psychology*. Vol. 1. New York: Smith.

Jubas, Harry
1974   "The Adjustment Process of Americans and Canadians in Israel and Their Integration into Israel Society." Ph.D. Dissertation, Michigan State University.

Kahl, Joseph
1968   *The Measurement of Modernism*. Austin: University of Texas Press.

Katz, David and Aaron Antonovsky
1973   "Bureaucracy and Immigrant Adjustment." *International Migration Review* 7 (Fall): 247–56.

Katz, Elihu, and S. N. Eisenstadt
1960   "Some Sociological Observations on the Response of Israeli Organizations to New Immigrants." *Administrative Science Quarterly* 5 (June): 113–33.

Katz, Elihu, and Brenda Danet
1966   "Petitions and Persuasive Appeals: A Study of Official-Client

Relations.'' In *Bureaucracy and the Public,* ed. E. Katz and
B. Danet. New York: Basic Books, 1973. Originally published in
American Sociological Review 31 (December): 811–22.

1973   Introduction. In *Bureaucracy and the Public,* ed. E. Katz and
B. Danet. New York: Basic Books, 1973.

Katz, Elihu, and M. Gurevitch, B. Danet, and T. Peled
1969   "Petitions and Prayers: A Method for the Content Analysis of
Persuasive Appeals." *Social Forces* 47 (June): 447–63.

Katz, Jacob
1973   "Forerunners." In *Zionism.* Jerusalem: Keter Books, 1973.

Katz, Pearl
1974   "Acculturation and Social Networks of American Immigrants in
Israel." Ph.D. Dissertation, State University of New York at
Buffalo.

Kaufman, Yehezkel
1949   "Anti-Semitic Stereotypes in Zionism." *Commentary* 7:239–45.

Keesing, Roger
1970   "Toward a Model of Role Analysis." In *A Handbook of Methods
in Cultural Anthropology,* ed. R. Narrol and R. Cohen. Garden
City: Natural History Press, 1970.

Kushner, Gilbert
1973   *Immigrants from India in Israel: Planned Change in an Administered Community.* Tucson: University of Arizona Press.

Lapide, P.E.
1961   *A Century of U.S. Aliyah.* Jerusalem: The Association of Americans and Canadians in Israel.

Laqueur, Walter, ed.
1976   *The Israel-Arab Reader: A Documentary History of the Middle
East Conflict.* 3d ed. New York: Bantam Books.

Leon, Dan, and Yehuda Adin, eds.
1971   *The Voices of Jewish Emancipation.* Jerusalem: The Zionist Library.

Lerner, Daniel
1958   *The Passing of Traditional Society: Modernizing The Middle
East.* New York: The Free Press.

Liebman, Charles S.
1973   *The Ambivalent American Jew: Politics, Religion and Family in*

American Jewish Life. Philadelphia: The Jewish Publication Society of America.

Linton, Ralph
1936   *The Study of Man*. New York: Appleton-Century.

Lipset, Seymour Martin
1970   "The American Jewish Community in a Comparative Perspective." In *Revolution and Counter-Revolution*. Rev. ed. New York: Doubleday.

Lissak, Moshe
1969   *Social Mobility in Israel*. Jerusalem: Israel University Press.

MacCannell, Dean
1976   *The Tourist: A New Theory of the Leisure Class*. New York: Schocken Books.

Matras, Judah
1965   *Social Change in Israel*. Chicago: Aldine.

Mead, G. H.
1934   *Mind, Self, and Society*. Chicago: University of Chicago Press.

Merton, Robert
1957   "The Role-Set: Problems in Sociological Theory." *British Journal of Sociology* 8:106–20.

Miller, Daniel
1961   "Personality and Social Interaction." In *Studying Personality Cross-Culturally*, ed. B. Kaplan. New York: Harper and Row.
Morris, Ya'akov
1953   *Pioneers from the West*. Jerusalem: Youth and Hechalutz Department, The World Zionist Organization.

Nadel, Elizabeth, J. Fishman, and R. Cooper
1977   "English in Israel: A Sociolinguistic Study." *Anthropological Linguistics* 19 (January): 26–53.

Nadel, S. F.
1957   *The Theory of Social Structure*. New York: The Free Press.

O'Dea, Janet
1976   "Gush Emunim: Roots and Ambiguities." *Forum* (Jerusalem) 2 (25): 39–50.

Parsons, Talcott
1951   *The Social System*. New York: The Free Press.

Peacock, James, and A. T. Kirsch
1970   *The Human Direction*. New York: Appleton-Century-Crofts.

Petersen, W.
1958   "A General Typology of Migration." *American Sociological Review* 23:256–66.

Pitt-Rivers, Julian
1961   *The People of the Sierra*. Chicago: University of Chicago Press.

Riesman, David, N. Glazer, and R. Denney
1953   *The Lonely Crowd: A Study of the Changing American Character*. Abridged ed. New York: Doubleday.

Rosen, Lawrence
1972   "The Social and Conceptual Framework of Arab-Berber Relations in Central Morocco." In *Arabs and Berbers: From Tribe to Nation in North Africa*, ed. E. Gellner and C. Micaud. Lexington, Mass.: Lexington Books, 1972.

Rudolph, Lloyd, and Suzanne Rudolph
1967   *The Modernity of Tradition: Political Development in India*. Chicago: University of Chicago Press.

Safa, Helen
1975   Introduction. In *Migration and Development*, ed. H. Safa and B. du Toit. The Hague: Mouton.

Sarbin, Theodore
1954   "Role Theory." In *Handbook of Social Psychology*, ed. G. Lindzey. Vol. 1. Cambridge, Mass.: Addison-Wesley.

Shaw, R. Paul
1975   *Migration Theory and Fact*. Philadelphia: Regional Science Research Institute, Bibliography Series No. 5.

Sherif, Muzafer
1968   "The Self-Concept." In *International Encyclopedia of the Social Sciences*, ed. D. Sills. New York: Macmillan and the Free Press, pp. 150–59.

Shibutani, Tamotsu
1961   *Society and Personality: An Interactionist Approach to Social Psychology*. Englewood Cliffs: Prentice-Hall.

Shils, Edward
1957   "Primordial, Personal, Sacred and Civil Ties." In *Center and Periphery: Essays in Macrosociology*. Chicago: University of

Chicago Press, 1975. Originally published in the *British Journal of Sociology* 8 (1957): 130–45.

Shokeid, Moshe (Minkovitz)
1971   *The Dual Heritage: Immigrants from the Atlas Mountains in an Israeli Village*. Manchester: Manchester University Press.

Shuval, Judith T.
1963   *Immigrants on the Threshold*. New York: Atherton Press.

Silverstone, Meir
1973   "The Law of Return." In *Immigration and Settlement*. Jerusalem: Keter Books.

Sklare, Marshall
1955   *Conservative Judaism*. New York: The Free Press.

Sklare, Marshall, ed.
1974   *The Jew in American Society*. New York: Behrman House.

Smelser, Neil
1968   *Essays in Sociological Explanation*. Englewood Cliffs: Prentice-Hall.

Smooha, Sammy
1972   "Black Panthers: The Ethnic Dilemma." *Society* (Transactions) (May), pp. 31–36.

Spiro, Melford E.
1957   "The Sabras and Zionism: A Study in Personality and Ideology." *Social Problems* 5 (Fall): 100–110.
1961   "Social Systems, Personality, and Functional Analysis." In *Studying Personality Cross-Culturally*, ed. B. Kaplan. New York: Harper and Row.
1970   *Kibbutz: Venture in Utopia*. Augmented ed. New York: Schocken Books.

Swartz, Marc J.
1968   Introduction. In *Local-Level Politics*, ed. M. Swartz. Chicago: Aldine.

Taft, D. R., and R. Robbing
1955   *International Migrations: The Immigrant in the Modern World*. New York: The Ronald Press.

Tawney, R. H.
1947   *Religion and Rise of Capitalism*. New York: Mentor Books.

Turner, Ralph
1968   "Role: Sociological Aspects." In *International Encyclopedia of the Social Sciences,* ed. D. Sills. Vol. 13:552–57, New York: Macmillan and The Free Press.

Urofsky, Melvin I.
1975   *American Zionism from Herzl to the Holocaust.* Garden City: Doubleday and Anchor Press.

Wallace, A. F. C., and Raymond D. Fogelson
1965   "The Identity Struggle." In *Intensive Family Therapy: Theoretical and Practical Aspects,* ed. I. Boszomenyi-Nagy and J. L. Framo. New York: Harper and Row.

Weinberg, Abraham A.
1961   *Migration and Belonging: A Study of Mental Health and Personal Adjustment in Israel.* The Hague: Martinus Nijhoff.

Weingrod, Alex
1965   *Israel: Group Relations in a New Society.* London: Pall Mall Press.
1966   *Reluctant Pioneers: Village Development in Israel.* Ithaca: Cornell University Press.
1971   "Israel." In *The Central Middle East: A Handbook of Anthropology and Published Research,* ed. L. Sweet. New Haven: HRAF Press.

Weller, Leonard
1974   *Sociology in Israel.* Westport, Conn.: Greenwood Press.

Willner, Dorothy
1969   *Nation-Building and Community in Israel.* Princeton: Princeton University Press.

Wolpert, J.
1965   "Behavioral Aspects of the Decision to Migrate." Regional Science Association Papers 15:159–169.

Zald, Mayer N., and Roberta Ash
1966   "Social Movements Organizations: Growth, Decay and Change." *Social Forces* 44:327–40.

Zavalloni, Marisa
1973   "Social Identity: Perspectives and Prospects." *Social Science Information* 12 (3):65–91.

Zborowski, Mark, and Elizabeth Herzog
1962   *Life Is with People: The Culture of the Shtetl.* New York: Schocken Books.

Zinger, Zvi (Yaron)
1973   "Immigration and Settlement, The State of Israel, 1948–1972."
               In *Immigration and Settlement*, Jerusalem: Keter Books, 1973.

Zwergbaum, Aharon
1973   "Zionist Organization." In *Zionism*, n.e. Jerusalem: Keter
               Books, 1973.

Israel Government Publications

Israel Central Bureau of Statistics
1973   *Supplement to the Monthly Bulletin of Statistics*, no. 1.
               Jerusalem.
1974   *Statistical Abstract of Israel*, no. 25.
1975   *Supplement to the Monthly Bulletin of Statistics*, no. 12.
               Jerusalem.
1975   *Immigration Statistics*, vol. 6, no. 12 (December).

Israel Central Bureau of Statistics and Ministry of Immigrant Absorption
1973   *Immigration to Israel, 1948–1972*, special series no. 416. Part I,
               Annual Data.
1974   *Immigration to Israel, 1973*, special series no. 457.
1975   *Immigration to Israel, 1948–1972*, special series no. 489. Part II,
               Composition by Period of Immigration.

Ministry of Immigrant Absorption
1975   *Annual Report, 1974*. Jerusalem.
1976   *Annual Report, 1975*. Jerusalem.

Index

AACI. *See* Association of Americans and Canadians in Israel

Absorption: Americans' efforts towards, 164; and assimilation, 160; and the dati/lo-dati split, 190–93; dynamics of, 123–28; Eisenstadt on, 7, 60, 81; and ethnography, 202–3; the Horev Report on, 82; institutional support of, 60–82 passim; and modernization, 134–37; and multiplexity, 133; and naturalization, 157; and Oriental Jews, 124–28; strategies of, 22, 143–44; and traditionalization, 152–54. *See also* Klita

Absorption center, 68, 71–76, 80, 142

Acculturation, 23, 60, 79, 133, 153, 192. *See also* Absorption; Klita

Activism, 175, 189, 193, 195, 197

Aden, 22, 212

Adin, Yehuda, 24

Algeria, 212, 215n, 217n

Alienation, in America, 115, 187

Aliya: age and sex of American, 41–43; American-Jewish attitudes towards, 32–34; American motivation for, 90–106; compared to *hagira*, 56, 85; economic explanations of, 87–91, 101, 106; education and occupation of American, 43–48, 181–82; as "free," 86; generational status of American, 40–1; group, 76; as international migration, 3–4, 85–90; meaning of, in Bible, 20, 56; meaning of, to olim, 159; mediating

Zionist history, 20–21, 23–25; "push" and "pull," 93–94, 114; religious aspect of American, 45–53; regional distribution of American, 39–40; and the shaliah, 68–69; volume of American, 35–37; waves of, 21–23, 86, 213n

Alkalai, Yehuda, 15

Altruism, 136, 180

Ambivalence, 171, 207

America: compared to Israel, 128–30, 187–88; criticism of, 100, 104–5, 114–22; as *di goldenah medinah*, 26, 29; Erikson on, 85, 122; as gesellschaft/gemeinschaft, 158–59

Americans and Canadians for Aliya (AACA), 214n

"Anglo-Saxon," as immigrant category, 172, 174–76, 177, 180, 187, 207

Anomie, in America, 115, 187

Anthropologists, in Israel, 120, 199–200

Anti-Semitism: and the Dreyfus affair, 14; in Eastern Europe, 14–15; and the Enlightenment, 13; felt by American olim, 93; in Israel, 167; as motivating aliya, 105, 115

Antonovsky, Aaron, 41, 45, 49, 51, 53, 60, 91–92, 107, 137–38, 215n

Arabs, 21, 23, 142–43, 215n, 217n

Architects, as olim, 45–46

Argentina, immigrants from, 158, 212

Army, Israeli, 78, 131, 141, 154, 158, 172

Asch, Solomon E., 108

Hula Valley, the, 23
Hygiene, 184
Hypercathexis: and aliya, 120; in total identity, 112–13. *See also* Investments, differential

Identity: American, 5, 107, 166–72, 187–88, 195; American and Israeli, 167; American and Jewish, 168; as Anglo-Saxon, 172, 207; clusters, 110–11; dati and lo-dati, 190–91, 197–98; Devereux on, 110–11; Erikson on, 85, 109–10; as a hierarchy, 109–10, 113, 118; personal, 108, 110; polarized, 112; reconstruction of, 166–72, 188; splitting of, 165, 167, 188. *See also* Investments, differential; Hypercathexis; Self
Identity, ethnic, 4–5, 91; expressively viewed, 4, 96; and hypercathexis, 117–22; instrumentally viewed, 4; and Jewishness, 190; and social identity, 106–7. *See also* Ethnicity; Expressive traditionalizing; Identity; Instrumental traditionalizing
Identity, social: compartmentalized, 96; instrumental and expressive, 154–58; and Jewishness, 113–14, 190; primordialized, 117–20, 203; reevaluated by Americans, 165–75; and role-playing, 155; and society, 105–6; the study of, 107–13; and traditionalization, 6, 120–22; usage of, 110. *See also* Ethnicity; Expressive traditionalizing; Identity; Ethnic; Images, of society; Instrumental traditionalizing; Self
Images, of society, 119, 121, 128, 152, 158–59, 165, 187–88, 196–97, 203, 205–6
Immigrants, types of: culturalists, 99–101, 190, 204, 216; nationalist (Zionist), 96–99, 190, 204, 216; religiously observant, 95–96, 190, 204, 216. *See also* Oleh; Zionism; Dati
Immigrant absorption, 8, 36, 49; ministry of, 64–66, 71–72, 74–76, 79, 82, 144–46, 174, 192

Inkeles, Alex, 121
Instrumental traditionalizing, 154–58, 164, 197. *See also* Traditionalizing
Interior, Ministry of, 36, 70–71, 158
Intermarriage, fear of by olim, 190
Interviews. *See* Fieldwork, methods of
Investments, differential: in identity, 111–12, 117, 152, 165–67, 203. *See also* Hypercathexis
Iran, immigrants from, 158, 212
Iraq, immigrants from, 22, 212
Isaac, Rael, 218
Isaacs, Harold, 6, 45, 77, 79, 172, 218n
Israel Aliya Center, 66–67, 214n
Israel, Michael Boaz. *See* Cresson, Ward
Israel, State of: attitude towards aliya, 21–25, 157–58; compared to United States, 20; emigration from (*see* Yerida); and the Jewish Agency-WZO, 62–66; as a Jewish state, 195–98; vs. Land of Israel, 191, 193–97; as a modern nation-state, 127; and Zionism, 11, 20, 191, 213n. *See also* Israeli society
Israeli society: as a colonizing society, 20; compared to American society, 20, 124, 152; and ethnic groups, 127–28; as gemeinschaft, 158–59; as Levantine, 159, 160–66, 217n; as the Middle East, 69, 140–41, 181–87; as a modern society, 20, 124, 152; as a moral community, 98–99, 114, 152, 187; as a small-scale society, 130–33. *See also* Israel, state of; Images of society; Tradition

James, William, 108
Jerusalem: American olim in, 53–55, 77, 131, 149–50, 168, 183, 194–95, 200, 216n, 218n; Conservative Judaism in, 70; destruction of, 11, 67; as holy city, 11–12, 35; housing in, 215n; Jewish Agency and WZO based in, 34; residential segregation in, 177; survey in, 9. *See also* French Hill; Ramat Eshkol; Rehavia

strumental, 152–59, 170, 187, 197, 206; and Levantinism, 165–66; of olim, in Israel, 129, 137, 146, 216n; skills of businessmen, 148, 151; of social identity, 6, 120–22; and world view, 192, 196–98. *See also* Society, traditional; Tradition
Tsuva, 70
Turner, Ralph, 108
Types, ideal, 205, 217n

Uganda affair, the (1903), 18, 19, 31
Ulpan, 9–10, 63–64, 68, 71, 73–75, 80, 215n
Ulpan Etzion (Jerusalem), 73
Underdevelopment, of Israel, 128
United Synagogue of America, 70
Universalism, 119, 129, 135, 138, 145–46, 153
Urban areas, Americans in, 53–55
Urofsky, Melvin I., 28, 30, 32, 213n

Va'ad Le'umi, the, 62
Vietnam, 97, 105, 115, 152
Visas, 36, 78, 145, 158, 177
Volunteers, American (in Israel), 38, 58, 78

Wallace, A. F. C., 110, 120, 158
War: of Israel's Independence, 36; in Sinai, 22, 132; Six-Day, 8, 36–39, 103–4, 158, 218n; Yom Kippur, 38, 104, 193
WASP, the, 105, 149, 152, 162, 169, 171, 197. *See also* Gentile
Weber, Max, 24, 122, 142, 192, 201–3, 217n
Weinberg, Abraham A., 123
Weingrod, Alex, 22–23, 123, 125, 127, 160–61, 196, 217n
Weizmann, Chaim, 31
Weller, Leonard, 57, 126–27, 137–38
Werner, Oswald, 218n
West Bank, the, 177, 193
Whole Land of Israel movement, the, 218n
Widowhood, and aliya, 101

Willner, Dorothy, 125
Wilson, Woodrow, 30
Wolpert, J., 90
World War II, 21, 116
World Zionist Organization, 34, 62–66, 77, 81–82. *See also* Jewish Agency, the

Yadin, Yigael, 176, 218n
Yahudim, 28, 31
Yemen, immigrants, from, 22, 23, 127, 134, 152, 212, 213n, 215n
Yerida (emigration from Israel), 35, 56–59, 76, 159, 192, 197, 214n
Yiddin, 28–29, 31
Yiddish: in America, 26–27, 34, 52, 97, 99–101; in Israel, 143, 150, 200–202
Yiddishkeit, 31–32, 100–101
Yishuv, the, 21, 60–61, 123–24, 125, 214n
Yom Kippur War. *See* War, Yom Kippur
Yugoslavia, immigrants from, 22, 212

Zald, Mayer N., 24
Zangwill, Israel, 18
Zavalloni, Marisa, 109–12, 120
Zborowski, Mark, 34
Zinger, Zvi (Yaron), 38, 61
Zionism: and aliya, 10, 20, 25, 102, 154; in America, 26, 29–34, 122, 215n; among American olim, 50–52, 92–93; crisis of, 24–25; critical of Judaism, 167; and the Hegelian dialectic, 16–17, 19; Marxist critique of, 17; and messianism, 12, 194, 215n; as a nationalist movement, 16–17, 190; Orthodox critique of, 17–18, 191; threatened by Levantinism, 161, 171; and tradition, modernity, 10, 20, 122; and yerida, 192. *See also* Herzl, Theodor; Zionist movement, the
Zionist movement, the: in America, 30–40; during British mandate, 62; structure of, 17, 213n, 218n. *See also* Brandeis, Louis D.; Herzl,